oving the Needle With Lean OKRs

oving the Needle With Lean OKRs

Setting Objectives and Key Results to Reach Your Most Ambitious Goal

Bart den Haak

BEP

BUSINESS EXPERT PRESS

Leader in applied, concise business books

Moving the Needle With Lean OKRs:
Setting Objectives and Key Results to Reach Your Most Ambitious Goal

Cover design by Albert-Jan Massenberg

Interior design by Exeter Premedia Services Private Ltd., Chennai, India

First published in 2021 by
Business Expert Press, LLC
222 East 46th Street, New York, NY 10017
www.businessexpertpress.com

ISBN-13: 978-1-63742-363-9
ISBN-13: 978-1-63742-116-1 (e-book)

Business Expert Press Portfolio and Project Management Collection

Collection ISSN: 2156-8189 (print)
Collection ISSN: 2156-8200 (electronic)

First edition: 2021

10 9 8 7 6 5 4 3 2 1

To Melody and Kyte

Description

This book introduces a thorough but lightweight goal setting system for achieving breakthrough corporate results. OKR is shorthand for "Objective and Key Results"—a goal-setting tool for both individuals and teams that involves setting ambitious goals that have measurable results. Lean OKRs are the evolved version of the OKR strategy execution tool that has powered the transformational journeys of giants like Google and Facebook. Den Haak's expansive experience in corporate coaching, solid theoretical background, and fresh voice make this insightful publication an asset for business students and leaders who are starting-up or expanding their enterprise. The tested, easy-to-use method the book presents is rooted in applied behavioral science and management techniques, building on Toyota Kata, Cynefin, 4DX, and even game design. Thus, it is perfectly fitted to meet the needs of contemporary companies who want to achieve "big hairy audacious goals" in a world of increasing uncertainty.

The book presents insightful anecdotes, creative exercises, clear figures, and step-by-step models to make the reader familiar with the Lean OKRs systematic method. Designed to be a comprehensive guide, it covers everything from theoretical roots to the practical execution of OKR workshops, from implementation procedures to integrating metrics on dashboards, and from company-wide strategy alignment to emotional management. Applicable to small companies as well as large organizations, *Lean OKRs* drives innovation through behavioral changes, empowering and motivating teams, and bringing the soul back to OKRs. Practical and to the point throughout, the book convincingly integrates a unique combination of structural and leadership strategies, resulting in a new approach to OKRs that conquers the hurdles experienced by most companies today.

Keywords

growth; innovation; objectives and key results; OKR; OKRs; lean; goal setting; strategy execution; stretched goals; empowered teams; agile; check-ins; moving the needle; behavior change; key performance indicators/KPIs; performance management; metrics; experiments; culture change; workshops; dashboard; quality; project; project management

Contents

Testimonials

"I've had the privilege of collaborating with Bart den Haak in a community of practice (Agile Fluency® Project). There I've appreciated his straightforward approach and willingness to share his insights about OKR's. Now he has produced this excellent guide to everything you need to know and do for success with OKR's in your organization. Notice how often he cautions against a superficial implementation. His thoughtful attention to the fundamentals of agile approaches shine through. The many stories of his experiences across industries shows his depth and breadth of knowledge about success and failure patterns. If you're curious about OKR's, read this book. Follow den Haak's guidance. Find your path to directed success."—**Diana Larsen. Co-Author of** *Agile Retrospectives and Lift off.* **Co-Founder of the Agile Fluency® Project**

"If there is one book to recommend to move your organisation forward with OKRs, it is this book. Many books overcomplicate and make the reader puzzled where and how to start with OKRs.

This book is unique in providing you a comprehensive overview and use of OKRs while guiding you with refreshing use cases, tips and practical steps to make change with OKRs happen in your organization.

Last not least, this book is enjoyable to read and will make you energized making things happen."—**Arran McLean, Senior Product Manager at Aptic AB**

"I worry that many potential readers, who would benefit greatly from this book, may be put off just by the mere mention of an 'OKR', due to past experiences where OKRs have failed to live up to expectations.

I have been fortunate enough to have worked alongside Bart earlier in my career and have also shared such an experience with him. While I became indifferent, or even skeptical, of OKRs – an opinion compounded, in turn, my meeting others with the same view as the years went on – Bart was different.

Bart saw past OKRs as something pioneered by the mighty Google, but out of reach in reality to the rest of us. Or an over-hyped management silver bullet *touted by hungry consultants. He saw the real value in OKRs, as an evolution of established theory and practice in goal setting, which could be further strengthened by the proven principles of Lean Thinking.*

By combining his unique insight, decades of collated research and his hands-on experience of knowing how and why OKRs fail, Bart has created Moving the Needle with Lean OKRs; essential and motivating reading for anyone wanting to do just that: move the needle, in their organization.

Moving the Needle with Lean OKRs explains why mission, vision and strategy are paramount to forward-thinking organizations and how setting ambitious, measurable goals, enriched with Lean concepts, can be transformational in realizing them.

The book moves from the theoretical to the more pragmatic side of working with OKRs. This also serves as great reference material to revisit when brushing up on, for example, OKR check-ins or best practices for measuring objectives. It then goes on from the getting started to more advanced topics such as how OKRs relate to team empowerment and cultural and behavioral transformations.

One criticism may be that it reads a little academically at times, but conversely this style serves as a goldmine of references for those wanting to continue exploring the subject in more depth.

In summary, Moving the Needle with Lean OKRs is an incredibly comprehensive and essential addition to the bookshelves of those wanting tangible concepts and practices for realizing their, and of their organization's ambitions; even stretching those ambitions to something you may not have thought possible."—**Phil Mander, VP of Technology at Harver**

"The topic of OKRs has been on my radar since 2014 when I observed its failure first hand. Since then I was both fascinated by its simplicity and all the success stories as much as anxious to start implementing it, as I know doing it wrong inevitably leads to more harm than value.

I knew Bart long before he started to write the book and I have trusted him to come and help us implement OKRs the "right way" and one of the reasons I've trusted him is his pragmatic Lean approach that he describes in this book in great detail. Although we are still in the middle of our journey, this approach was instrumental in getting us to where we are right now. None of the methods or practices is a silver bullet and will not give you an answer about your own strategy or objectives. Bart guided us towards figuring out exactly that by asking the right questions and bringing us back to the reason why we are doing OKRs in the first place.

In his book, Bart has managed to combine the broad wisdom of the industry knowledge and project it into the simple yet difficult to get it done right topic of OKRs. There are many books on OKRs today, but very little of them go one step further and describe the opinionated way to implement OKRs to actually leverage the full potential, going from fundamentals of how to define the impactful objectives and outcome-driven Key Results to review cycles and alignment workshops. "**—Ben Goldin, CTO of Mambu, The Cloud Banking Platform**

"*Implementing OKR is hard. Writing a book about it should be harder than imagined, but Burt makes it very easy going with real life experiences.*

And when you think that you already know everything about OKR, it is when you read only the first chapter of this book and you understand that there is still much to discover and learn.

As an OKR fan and ambassador, this book reconnected me to the very essence of the system: simplicity to achieve great things."**—Tomás Pando, Co-Founder Master Me Up, Partner at Sunamers and Angel Investor at Aivo**

"*Moving the Needle with Lean OKRs*" *will be a great companion to any effort to implement OKRs. The book will not convince anyone to the method, this job is already done by books from Doerr and Wodtke. But it may serve as a field book, an inspiration and reference guide which shows approaches and points to various sources about "all things OKRs". There are many of them and Bart's knowledge here is impressive. His experience with OKRs is among the longest in the world, it would be a mistake not to learn from him.*"
—Tomasz Bienias. OKRy.pl

"Bart has put great effort in sharing all his knowledge and experience on OKR's in a comprehensive do-it-yourself guide. It explains everything from the OKR concepts to defining your own KPI's and putting them in practice to improve your results. This has resulted in a standard work for everyone interested in achieving great results."—**Maurits Cieremans, Tribe Lead, Mortgages, ING The Netherlands**

Foreword

When I read forewords I wonder, who is this person and why should I listen to them? So, here it goes: My name is Christina Wodtke and I wrote the first book on OKRs called "Radical Focus: Achieving Your Most Important Goals with Objectives and Key Results." Along with Rick Klau, John Doerr, and a handful of others, I'm responsible for OKRs popularity. In fact, OKRs have become so popular, we are beginning to see a backlash against using them, just as Agile and Lean Startup have seen their own backlashes. I'm writing this foreword because I think "Moving the Needle with Lean OKRs" can explain and redeem OKRs, so you can use them to accomplish your most difficult goals.

But wait, you say, what are OKRs? Well, they are a little like SMART goals, in the sense that they are a way to phrase a goal in an optimal way. O is for Objective: an inspiring phrase describing a strategically important goal. The Key Results are the metrics you will see in the world if you reach your goal. They are often things such as new users, revenue, or lifetime value.

The thing that makes OKRs work: the cadence. SMART goals don't tell you how to accomplish your goals. But OKRs do. Each Monday we commit to some activities that we hope will get us the results we seek. Each Friday we celebrate the progress. The constant checking in—that Monday realization of "Oh yeah, we were going to do something about these goals, weren't we?," making sure we spend time on the strategic goals during the week and then on Fridays, we reflect and think "Hey, look at all the cool stuff we did"—it all offsets the pain of being uncertain you'll make the stretch goals you've set. The cadence is where the magic happens. It's where all the brilliant people you've hired put their minds to work on how to make the company's critical goals happen; the Head of Quality Assurance might suddenly come up with a great product idea, the Head of Product might get an insight into a better way to market.

Simple, right? Here is where it gets tricky: In recent years, after all of the books and videos came out, a ton of people jumped on the OKR bandwagon, and fearful of upsetting their boss or clients, they started getting sloppy. People ignored best practices and started putting metrics in the Objective, or worse, they made the Key Results into milestones. Suddenly we saw OKR sets like "Objective: 50 million in revenue. Key Result: Launch our new CRM." (If you think this is fine, you definitely need this book!) OKRs became a project management tool rather than the strategic goal-setting tool it was invented to be. Further, people in toxic organizations created and committed to aspirational goals because they were too scared of a performance review based on failing to make ambitious goals. Pretty soon organizations were setting goals that were vague, complex, and demotivating.

Adding to that, many people hate meetings so much they refuse to participate, even if it's one that could make or break a company. So again, the OKR process was watered down; some meetings were skipped, others shortened to the point where they lost their impact. We now see dozens of watered-down OKR processes drifting around and they aren't going to do anything for you anymore. You need a better approach if you are going to win your market.

This is where Bart's book comes in. OKRs were born from a mature product process that includes Agile's iterative approach and Lean's constant hypothesis and testing approach. Bart's experience with Lean and Agile has given him the tools to put the bloated OKR process on a diet. He explains how to effectively use OKRs to accomplish your strategy. He provides the examples and details you need to get your head around the hardest management problems there are: How does strategy become execution? How do we make a real impact in the marketplace? How do we get diverse groups of people aligned so we can accomplish great things?

The book you are holding in your hands is what you need to be able to realize the promise of Objectives and Key Results. Bart does this with approachable prose and rigorous research—both from scientific literature and his own boots-on-the-ground learnings. So get a pen and a notebook, because you are going to want to take notes. This book will guide you in your own attempts to achieve audacious goals. Whether you are just starting out with OKRs or desperately trying to figure out how to fix the ones you've got, you are in good hands.

Christina Wodtke

Author of *Radical Focus*, *The Team that Managed Itself* and *Pencil Me In*
Lecturer at Stanford University in the HCI program in Computer Science

Preface

In this book, I've combined my two favorite management techniques, Lean and OKRs. OKRs stands for Objectives and Key Results, and it forms a collaborative goal setting tool that can be used by teams and individuals alike to set challenging, ambitious goals that have measurable results. The approach I have developed in this book is an answer to the persistent requests from clients, teams, and leaders to have a guide on how to successfully apply OKRs in practice.

Many have read the success stories of OKRs in the landmark book *Measure What Matters* (2017) by John Doerr. In this book, he describes how Intel and Google became tech giants fueled by this seemingly simple goal setting technique. YouTube reached its, now classic, Objective of "one billion hours of daily watch time" within four years. The team behind the Google Chrome browser achieved their Objective of "100 million seven-day active users" in just a few years. However, OKRs are not only for commercial companies but are also used by non-profit organizations that fight for better healthcare, clean energy, accessible water, or combat poverty, malaria, HIV/AIDS, and Covid-19. These "big hairy audacious goals" and the underlaying system to achieving them have caught the attention of many leaders around the world, and the interest is rapidly growing.

Unfortunately, the number of failed implementations is rising simultaneously. As a coach specialized in improving SaaS performance, growth, and innovation, many leaders have approached me to help them get their OKRs back on track. Despite setbacks and failures, deep down they still feel that OKRs have huge potential to bring their company to the next level, growing and innovating faster than their competitors. This spurred me to investigate why so many companies fail to implement this world-famous goal-setting system, and to develop and test processes to guide founders and managers of companies and organizations toward greater success.

The first time I was "told" to start using OKRs professionally, I was the Technical Head of a research and software development company. Like others, I immediately noticed their huge potential. However, without any books or guidance, everybody in the organization was just setting mundane goals, written as OKRs. We only had access to a few blog articles and a YouTube video from Rick Klau (2013). Looking back, novices as we were, we did everything just plain wrong. As a result, we had an excess of goals under the guise of "Objectives," the OKR process was cumbersome and complex, and our generic goals had no soul. We even needed software to "manage" all these goals. People got demotivated and OKRs became reduced to just the necessary paperwork and filling in timesheets. Any significant results eluded us. It's a classic story for those that tried implementing OKRs back in those days. Why was it that only a few seemed to be successful with them?

Luckily, today there are some great books written about OKRs. Not only can we learn about the success stories (Doerr 2017), but also about how to write good OKRs, how to use them in a start-up setting (Wodtke 2016) or enterprise setting (Niven and Lamorte 2016, 76–79) and even how to employ them to build great tech products (Cagan 2018). Leaders have access to all these great resources, so why do organizations still fail to implement OKRs successfully? Even if they are implemented, why do people still struggle to move the needle and achieve any significant results? These questions became the central part of my research over the years.

I've coached hundreds of executives and operational teams all around the world on how they can craft, improve and achieve their OKRs. At some point, I started to discover patterns in the causes for OKRs failures. These patterns are universal, regardless of the company culture, people, and industry. Furthermore, they are not explained well in the OKR literature that currently exists. The book you are holding in your hands now is unique because it will not only clearly describe these underlying patterns and their root causes, but also provide you with pragmatic tools and techniques that you can start using today to help you move the needle of your ambitious growth plans.

My approach is rooted in the theory of constraints (Goldratt 1984), Lean Thinking (Womack 2003), and Agile software development. I picked up on these ideas during my early days as a software engineer and manager, and they have become fundamental throughout my work: To me, these aren't just improvement techniques that optimize processes, rather, they represent a mindset, a way of thinking. Lean Thinking has always fascinated me most. Through it, I've learnt to think critically, to understand the bigger picture, to understand (customer) value, how to take small steps toward an ambitious goal, and how to systematically (and significantly) improve processes using concepts from scientific thinking. Lean Thinking originates from the Toyota Production System (TPS), created in the 1950s and 60s to optimize Toyota's car production plants. This management philosophy and practice not only transformed business in Japan, but has had a worldwide impact. When it got traction outside the manufacturing floor as well, it changed and revolutionized entire industries.

When people think about Lean, they often believe Lean is only applicable in a manufacturing context. However, that the Lean mindset can also be successfully applied to other domains has been proven in a variety of realms, as described in books like *Lean Startup* (Ries 2011), *Running Lean* (Maurya 2012), *Lean Analytics* (Croll and Yoskovitz 2013) and *Lean Software Development* (Poppendieck and Poppendieck 2003). The worldwide adoption of Agile and Lean Thinking in business school curriculums has resulted in the fact that Lean is known to many leaders today, but as Ballé et al. (2017) argue, I believe it is truly understood by only few. Truly Lean companies optimize their organization as a whole (compared to local optimization), remove non-value adding activities, make their customers and suppliers happy, but above all, respect and empower their own people.

A Lean concept that is not well known is called *Kaikaku*, which means "radical improvement" (Womack 2003, 23). In my eyes, this expresses what OKRs are all about: creating breakthrough results that move the most important needle of your business. Another less known Lean concept is *Hoshin Kanri*, the strategic planning process used by Toyota (Dennis 2006). In this book, I've applied these and other Lean Thinking concepts to OKRs and to the process of achieving them. The result is a lightweight and easy to use strategy execution and goal-setting system, geared to achieving breakthroughs. Perhaps most importantly, it brings the soul back to OKRs.

It's my pragmatic intention to be more than explicit in applying Lean philosophy to the context of practical OKR practice. Thus, you don't need to be familiar with Lean to read this book. However, if you are, you will recognize similarities with tools and techniques you already know which will only be beneficial to your OKR success. No matter your background, if you follow the described practices, I'm convinced they will help you and everybody in your organization to succeed with OKRs, achieve sustainable growth and unleash innovation.

Acknowledgments

My greatest thanks go to my loving partner Melody and, of course, my son Kyte. Melody, for each and every moment that you have supported me, even before the idea that I should maybe write a book. Your acts of love and support have not gone unnoticed. You have encouraged me, been my sounding board on our coffee breaks, helped me with my drawings, and even taken on extra bath and bed time duties so I could burn the midnight oil. Thank you, deeply and sincerely. Kyte, thanks for your jokes over breakfast, demonstrating your magic tricks to reset my mind, your eagerness to win every board game, and reminding me to get some fresh air once in a while. You're the best project manager I could ever have the privilege of working with.

I couldn't have written this book without the help of my editor, Amanda Dercks. I want to thank her for her patience and for helping me to avoid all my English-Dutch grammar mistakes. During the course of editing of this book, she gave birth to her wonderful daughter, Josephine. The book has seen quite a few major changes over the past few months, but you always jumped back in with an open mind and fresh eyes.

To Dr. Vanessa Wijngaarden for her input and helping me make the final version a reality. Your thoughtful insights, inquisitiveness and genuine critiques have been truly welcome and have made the book a pleasure to read.

To my friend and colleague Alvaro de Salvo for keeping me motivated, accountable and refusing to let me give up. His charming manner of coaching me to get off the bench and back in the game, his desire to see a friend fulfill his dream, and comical text messages that offered little sanity checks now and then were so needed and welcome. To Melanie Wessels and Ewout Meijer for our early conversations on OKRs and the introduction to the OKR Meetup Group in Amsterdam. The Amsterdam meetup group really got the ball moving for me.

I want to thank my early proof-readers Aaron Gaff, Mik de Hertog, Arran McClean, Dr. Kam Jugdev, and Tim Kloppenborg for their input in finalizing this book. To adapt an old adage: It takes a village to write a book and you each have helped immeasurably in the creation of this book from a blank page to what it is now.

My family and friends who have supported me, their patience and understanding. Thank you for checking in on me every so often to make sure I was still alive.

Finally, thank you to all of the great minds who contributed directly and indirectly to this book, like the leaders of the companies I have worked with and my great sources for inspiration like John Doerr, Christina Wodtke, Marty Cagan, Paul Niven, Chris McChesney, James Womack, Jez Humble, and many more.

Introduction

To achieve a goal you have never achieved before, you must start
doing things you have never done before.

—Jim Stuart

So, you have recently heard about this new management goal-setting methodology called OKRs and you are really eager to implement it within your organization. If Google and all of the other big tech giants are using it, then it must be good, right? So, what do you do next? As with any other management technique, you pore over all of the books, TED talks, podcasts, and blog articles you can get your hands on. How hard can it be to implement such a simple tool?

What is often not explained, is that to work with OKRs successfully you need to think deeply about your business: How is your company or organization unique in the market? What kind of customers do you serve? What key capabilities do you need to pursue? And, equally important, what are you *not* going to do? To answer these questions, leaders should develop a sound company strategy. A plan that will bring the organization closer to its vision and mission, the achievement of its ultimate goals, and reason for existence.

In business school, leaders can learn how to develop sound business strategies to beat their competitors, to build sustainable businesses, and to take the company to the next level. However, many of the classic teachings used do not suffice anymore. In the past, the pace of change wasn't as fast and strategic initiatives could last for many years. Within today's digital era, companies innovate almost at the speed of light. As the pace has picked up exponentially, it also has become increasingly difficult to make predictions. Leaders need to break open new markets, disrupt exiting ones, learn, innovate, change, and pivot faster, and with more precision than ever before to keep up with their competitors. To grow sustainably, to innovate more quickly, to learn faster, and to rapidly experiment with ideas and technology, you need to have a system in place that can help you execute these very ambitious strategies under circumstances that are highly uncertain.

Objectives and Key Result (OKRs for short) is an open source goal setting system with broad applications which was originally designed to create faster learning within an organization and achieve extraordinary results. When implemented correctly, OKRs drive growth and innovation. They were invented by and for technology companies. They should be used when you want to achieve things you couldn't easily achieve at a normal rate of operation. OKRs are transformative, challenge the status quo and help companies to actualize significant change in performance to get a step closer to their vision. OKRs are therefore not applicable in every context. Not all companies can, should or need to implement significant change, something people new to OKRs not always realize. In this book we will explore why and when OKRs are a good fit for your organization.

With OKRs, leaders first define a 90-day (or shorter) challenge for their whole company to get one step closer to their longer term company-wide strategic or audacious goal. OKRs are set both top-down (by the executive team) and bottom-up (by operational department and teams) and are linked together throughout the whole company. This bi-directional linking of Objectives is a key characteristic of this powerful framework. In this book, I describe how leaders can implement structures and a culture that make this feature reach its full potential. Furthermore, I make a strong case that OKRs in the workplace are a team sport, and you will be provided with concrete practices and strategies to motivate your teams toward success. Thus, this book uniquely combines structural and leadership approaches in a detailed systematic implementation strategy, which informs a way of working with OKRs that overcomes the hurdles experienced by most companies.

OKRs have much in common with other popular strategy execution frameworks like Hoshin Kanri, Balanced Scorecard (BSC), and Management by Objectives (MBO). Leaders should always examine if OKRs are the right tool for them. Often leaders that say they "need" OKRs but are actually better off using an adjusted version of one of the alternative frameworks above. However, if you need to grow and innovate faster than your competitors, OKRs may be right for you because they are the most sophisticated tool in situations that call for a boost in company and team performance.

In terms of agility and simplicity, OKRs are clearly distinct from other strategies, and equip you better to reach your greatest goals. Their effects extend widely and deeply. Besides powerfully spurring innovation, OKRs simultaneously help you to critically reflect your current business ideas and strategy—something most leaders and managers only wish they had the time to do. Critical thinking and reflection are embedded in the OKR process, greatly enhancing its potential to help leaders improve their business. Interweaving OKRs with the right leadership strategies, produces the most powerful tool for reaching goals that I know of.

Why OKRs Fail

In his noteworthy TED Talk, John Doerr started with these words: "We're at a critical moment. Our leaders, some of our great institutions are failing us. Why? In some cases, it's because they're bad or unethical, but often, they've taken us to the wrong Objectives. And this is unacceptable. This has to stop" (Doerr 2018). Most companies are setting the wrong goals, and these companies could make a big impact in the world if only their leaders understood and better implemented goal-setting strategies. However, simply converting all of your goals into OKRs will not help you magically become the next Google or Facebook, nor will it automatically help your company grow faster and make a significant impact in the world.

Most books on OKRs focus on explaining the basic OKR concepts and sharing of success stories, but what I hear from clients, teams and leaders time and again, is that they would love to have a guide on how to apply them in practice. Too often, the great transformative potential of OKRs is not translated into extraordinary results, merely because they are not used correctly. The majority of organizations I've encountered are "doing OKRs" without reaping their benefits, and an actually great tool is diminished to being a superfluous layer of administration and a burden for employees. As you will learn in this book, there is a common root cause. The solutions I have developed address these difficulties at their foundation, so the leverage OKRs potentially offer can be set free and enjoyed fully.

I've devoted years of research and run hundreds of OKR sessions and implementations to understand why leaders have difficulty setting and achieving the right goals. I've discovered patterns that explain why strategy execution and goal setting programs fail. In this book, I share these discoveries with you. I will also provide you with a proven method that I have developed to help organizations and teams create sustainable growth and innovations. This method is based on tested ideas from the fields of Applied Behavioral Science such as ABC analysis, and it includes observations and behavioral experiments and management techniques such as Systems Thinking. It employs the sense-making framework Cynefin, as well as ideas from Toyota Kata, which are new in the context of achieving OKRs, and potentially ground-breaking for many organizations. It further includes insights from the Four Disciplines of Execution, performance management, game design, Lean and Agile thinking, which have been specifically tailored to meet the needs and requirements of companies applying OKRs.

A Novel Strategy Towards OKRs

Although the original intent of OKRs was to execute part of a growth strategy, there is a global trend towards adoption of OKRs for all sorts of goals. This development worries me, because it will reduce this goal-setting tool's transformational power. The OKR community can be divided into two camps. One that says that it is fine to use OKRs broadly and widely within your company. The other camp suggests to radically focus on only one company Objective per OKRs Cycle (Wodtke 2016). In this book I will explain why the latter is the preferred strategy when you want to achieve great results, and how you can implement this approach in your organization.

Novel in my approach is how I direct OKRs by focusing them on changing underlying patterns of behavior. New results require new behavior, sustainability as well as leverage, and are greatly improved when targeting human habits and attitudes. It isn't a coincidence that Andy Grove, father of OKRs, studied behavior science and cognitive psychology. My years of experience have shown me that most leaders don't realize their strategy execution toolset should also contain behavior change strategies. The reason why the OKR approach described in this book works so well, is because it is focused on *changing the human behavior* that drives business results. I do not focus on helping you to address outcomes, but provide a method that enables you to produce changes at the sources of those outcomes.

Secondly, I pose that OKRs should be used as a team-based goal setting methodology (see also Gothelf 2020), thus omitting the level of individual OKRs. I have never seen individual OKRs work well, because they are almost always related to personal development goals, which may not be in the best interest of the team or company. So, although individuals may benefit from using OKRs in their personal life, in companies, OKRs should be used on a team level. Significant change in companies cannot be achieved alone, and sustainable behavioral changes are more easily committed to in team contexts. Furthermore, structurally, OKRs are meant to be connected throughout the entire organization and to the company's overarching mission and vision. The team focus facilitates their use as a tool that helps everybody in the company see the big picture, and tune in to the role they play in it. As you will learn in this book, this sense of purpose can motivate your entire workforce. With OKRs, everybody starts to understand the greater goal and see the system as a whole, thus transforming not only your company's results, but also its culture.

Furthermore, I suggest that an ideal working culture is one where each employee feels their influence on the bottom line. In such a culture where risk taking is not only accepted but encouraged, what is referred to as a "generative" culture, teams and individuals alike have a stake in bringing the company to the next level. Stanford professor Robert Burgelman researched Intel for 12 years and worked alongside Andy Grove, the founding father of OKRs. He is quoted as saying that "successful firms are characterized by maintaining bottom-up internal experimentation and selection processes while simultaneously maintaining top-driven strategic intent" (Burgelman 2012). Simply put, everyone should have something at stake, should feel that their work is meaningful and purpose-driven in order for OKRs to work. When we talk about OKRs cascading, we often mean from the top-down, but the most effective method is to incorporate bottom-up initiatives that support the company's overall strategy and are set by empowered teams. These initiatives take the form of experiments and we will look deeper into this in *Chapter 12*.

Finally, I have developed unique tools about how to move the needle for your OKRs, through techniques and step-by-step guides that I have developed over the years. For one, your OKRs will be closely tracked and monitored during weekly check-ins and made visual on dashboards. How to visualize and track performance is an important aspect of OKRs, but has been absent from other OKR resources.

Lean OKRs in a Nutshell

With its root in Lean Thinking, the OKR approach in this book helps you to do more with less by defining single OKRs that (ideally) focus on customer value. As you will learn in Part 1 of this book, this revolutionary idea is not only for small start-ups, but also for large and established enterprises. Lean considers inventory as a form of waste. In my unique application of Lean to OKRs, I reduce the excess inventory of goals by using just a single set of OKRs (that consist of *one* Objective and accompanying key results). Thus, your whole organization will finally be focused on achieving the breakthrough goal that it so desperately needs to innovate and grow.

Central to the Lean OKR approach is to install a lightweight process, based on Lean's Plan-Do-Check-Act (PDCA) Cycle to set, align, communicate, execute and reflect on your behavior change strategy. This Cycle will be discussed throughout the book and form the foundation of the practical and detailed OKR Cycle in Part 2, as well as the OKR experiment loop outlined in Part 3.

Finally, the approach to leadership that is embedded in my approach is inspired by Lean Thinking. In Lean, respect for people is one of the most important pillars, and the strategy I propose is importantly devoted to empowering teams to achieve their OKRs.

How To Use This Book

This book is meant as a comprehensive guide, which provides all information you need to successfully implement Lean OKRs in a company. I will first explain the basic OKR concepts, to enable anyone, also those completely new to OKRs, to access all material provided. If you are more experienced with OKRs, you can jump to any of the chapters at any time, but I suggest you do read Chapters 1 to 6 to refresh your general understanding of the concepts, learn why most organizations fail with OKRs and get get familiar with the rationale of the Lean approach that I propose. Parts 2 and 3 consist of detailed step-by-step guides and advanced strategies for Lean OKR implementation.

Every chapter contains practical exercises which help you to start using OKRs straight away.

At the end of each chapter, you will find a recap and list of the references used, so you will have all resources for further study in one place.

Part 1—The Foundation and Beyond

Once you have great, inspirational goals in place, you need to have a system to achieve them. If you are using OKRs as a tool for attaining your most ambitious goals, this comes with a critical prerequisite: You need a solid strategy in place. In Part 1, I will outline the details of why so many organizations struggle and fail when implementing OKRs, and provide strategies to address this.

The main subjects are:

- Defining OKRs (despite what you think you already know) and a little bit of history.
- Overcoming organizational challenges, why most organizations fail and how to execute behavior change strategies with OKRs.
- Designing OKRs that will inspire people.
- Measures and metrics: elements of the Key Results.
- A single OKR "to rule them all" and to stay focused on a goal despite the daily whirlwind of business as usual.

- Scaling and cascading OKRs.
- How to succeed with OKRs by empowering people.

Part 2—Running Successful OKR Workshops

This part of the book is about how to run a lightweight process of setting, aligning, achieving and reflecting on your OKRs, called the OKR cycle. In this practical set of chapters, we explore how to run successful OKR workshops when practically applying the OKR cycle, including functional schedules and powerful questions to ask. How exactly are you going to get closer to your OKRs? To do that, you need to develop powerful habits.

The main subjects are as follows:

- A system of structured workshops for setting, aligning and reviewing OKRs.
- OKR Timelines.
- Frequent check-ins to fight against the daily grind; keeping people engaged while going for your biggest challenge yet.
- Reflections and reviews of your OKRs.

Part 3—How to Move the Needle

This part focuses on how to employ your OKRs to achieve extraordinary results. From my experience, achieving breakthrough goals works best if you work with empowered teams of professionals all equipped with a growth mindset and the necessary skills to explore and experiment, but I also realize this might be science fiction for many established organizations. This part of the book is designed to help you transform science fiction into science fact.

The main subjects are as follows:

- A step-by-step model to select the right approach to move the needle based on the sense-making framework called Cynefin.
- Understanding how scientific thinking can help you move the needle by affecting daily behavior patterns through Toyota Kata inspired techniques.

- Running experiments.
- Measuring performance of your critical metrics and understanding signals from your data.
- The OKR dashboard as an integrative tool, where teams and companies track their results and visualize their endgame.
- How techniques from game design can help to build engaging dashboards.

Implementing Lean OKRs is simple, but not simplistic. It requires a big shift in thinking from everybody in your organization, including you. With this book, you have the opportunity to achieve something big. Let it be your guide toward implementing OKRs that really work, moving the needle on your most important challenges and goals by overcoming hurdles others stumble over, and increase the likelihood of realizing your most ambitious strategy, your moonshot.

PART I

The Foundation and Beyond

CHAPTER 1

Power Your Mission With OKRs

All successful people have a goal. No one can get anywhere unless he knows where he wants to go and what he wants to be or do.

—Norman Vincent Peale

Chapter Highlights

- Goal setting and a formula for motivation
- Alternative goal-setting strategies and the birth of Objectives and Key Results (OKRs)
- Main advantages of OKRs
- The three core concepts of OKRs
- In pursuit of something bigger
- Getting started with OKRs

Goals have always been an important part of my life. Like most kids, I had a dream. I was fascinated by outer space, the planets, the universe, but for some reason, I didn't want to become an astronaut. My dream was to work on robots that drove on Mars and satellites flying around Jupiter's moons. That was my big hairy audacious goal.

My choices in my studies were always focused on that one goal, and I decided to go for information technology, software, and electrical engineering. In 2007, I graduated and my career had kicked off, when I found myself walking into the lunch area of the European Space Agency (ESA). I was to have lunch with the program lead at a Dutch test facility of the European Space Research and Technology Centre (ESTEC), playing the role of a lead engineer in a team of software engineers. Without even realizing, I had come to live the goal I set myself up to achieve as a young boy.

But something was off ...

It felt like any other lunch area in a big corporation. We were discussing plans regarding some innovation projects for self-driving cars, highway lane detection, and virtual toll ports, all made possible because of the extremely high accuracy of the new European navigation satellites called GALILEO, a constellation of 25 active satellites orbiting earth's lower orbit. When you think about space programs, you think about state-of-the-art technologies, such as robots and rockets. However, in my day-to-day work over the years, I had to work with a lot of low tech that needed to reach "proven" technology status before it could be launched into space. This was far from the exciting stuff I wanted to work on, but still, there I was, being part of a multibillion European space program with an expected lead time of about 10 years, if all things went well. I realized goals are moving targets because when our achievements grow, our dreams do too.

At the time of writing (2021), the program is still not complete. I achieved my personal goal, but I got frustrated by the lack of trackable progress of the overall program. One of the reasons I left ESA was the lack of accountability and the total disconnection between our daily work and the final goal. Looking back, I now realize that the final Objective was to become independent from the United States, but that was nowhere reflected in our daily motivation.

I vividly remember my first encounter with OKRs. The video from Rick Klau from 2013 had just been released on YouTube and we, the leadership team of the product department at a (now) successful Dutch Fintech company, were asked to view the video before the off-site OKR workshop next week.

One week later, all department leads were there off-site. After the initial kick-off by the chief executive officer (CEO), we were tasked to create OKRs for our department in less than two hours. We had no experience with them, we only had seen the video from Rick Klau.

It was a complete mess. We did everything wrong that we could possibly do wrong, almost a textbook example of how not to do OKRs. At the corporate level, we had too many, and on top of that, each leader had five OKRs, and each department had five OKRs as well. They were all milestone based, in fact wrapping our backlogs list into OKRs. We then put them all in the OKR software system that the organization bought. Luckily, we stopped at the department level with setting OKRs. At the end of each quarter, we scored the OKRs. Just one week before the next kick-off, we put some arbitrary numbers in the system to make them "look good." This went on and on for several quarters. No retrospectives, no check-ins. I don't need to tell you the OKR implementation was a disaster.

Somehow the company managed to achieve significant growth. I believe this is the result of highly motivated and inspiring leaders, not because of the OKRs. However, I remained fascinated with the beauty of the system and all its potential. This led me to an insatiable quest to master them. And looking back, if I could apply my current knowledge about OKRs back then, the company could have achieved much more significant and sustainable growth.

OKRs will never replace solid, strong, and inspirational leadership, but it does help to replicate the essence of the views of such leaders into the tranches of your organization. OKRs help you to create mini versions of you, as a leader, throughout the company with the same visionary perspective.

Every now and then, I cannot help but imagine how much more successful the ESA would be if they ran their projects using a solid method like the one you are about to learn in this book. Not only would their performance improve, but the motivation of their teams would most likely skyrocket, as everyone involved could see their work in relation to and support of the ultimate goal.

Be aware, the knowledge you are about to take in is powerful and transformational. Handle it with care.

Goals, Purpose, and Motivation

Early ideas about setting goals can be found in ancient Greek philosophy. Aristotle believed that having a specific purpose, a goal, drives action forward. That goals are inextricably linked and, in a sense, form the basis for our "reason of being". Setting goals is something humans love to do, but even more, we love achieving these goals. These days, neuroscientists have shown that we get a shot of dopamine (Berridge and Robinson 2003) from achieving our Objectives. We get that kick partly because successfully achieving challenging goals is difficult. The harder the challenge, the greater the reward, and research indicates that in some situations, people therefore perceive higher goals as easier to attain than lower ones—and even when that's not the case, they still can find those more challenging goals more appealing (Chattopadhyay, et al. 2018). So, before we dive deeper into how all of this applies to OKRs, let's have a quick look at some of the principles of the most prominent theories of goal setting.

In 1968, the psychologist Edwin A. Locke and Gary P. Latham published their book *Toward a Theory of Task Motivation and Incentives*, containing the ground breaking Goal-Setting Theory (GST) to explain human behavior in specific work situations. A few years later, Locke and Latham started studying the theory in practice and confirmed that the link between goal setting and performance was both real and crucial. The two key findings of this theory are that setting specific goals (e.g., reduce calorie intake from 2,500 to 1,700 per day) leads to higher performance than setting nonspecific, general goals (e.g., reduce calories), and that goal difficulty is linearly and positively related to performance. This means that the harder the goal is, the greater the effort, focus, and persistence, which results in higher performance.

In his 2009 book *Drive: The Surprising Truth About What Motivates Us*, Daniel H. Pink describes what truly motivates people to come to work. In his research, he found out that people don't get motivated because of monetary rewards. Instead, he discovered that motivation comes from three things: autonomy—the desire to direct our own lives; mastery—the urge to get better and better at something that matters; and purpose—the yearning to do what we do in the service of something larger than ourselves.

Combining insights from ancient Greek philosophers, modern psychologists, neuroscientists, and praxis-based research as done by Pink and myself, I argue for a specific use of OKRs. Following Pink, the formula for motivation is: Motivation = Purpose + Mastery + Autonomy. Thus, OKRs should be used to help people understand (1) their purpose in their work; (2) that they have the competencies and skills to do their job; and (3) that you as a leader provide them autonomy to do so. This use of OKRs will result in a highly motivated workforce. OKRs are especially fit to define purpose, and as a leader, you can provide the other two through your OKR implementation process (Part 2) and by teaching people the necessary skills and techniques to continuously improve (Part 3).

Why Set Goals?

Setting goals helps us achieve something ambitious and challenging, like Olympic gold. However, the main focus of OKRs, which are designed to help businesses achieve ambitious goals, should be centered around two things: innovation and growth.

Here are some of the more important reasons why leaders set goals. The list isn't complete, of course, so why not see if you can think of some of your own?

- Help decision making: Goals provide direction and help us focus on what matters.
- Help with the company's, team's, or one's personal growth.
- Stimulate innovation: Setting ambitious goals forces people to think out of the box and be more visionary.
- Provide guidelines to help everybody execute on strategy.
- Help people stay motivated.
- Provide clarity and direction.
- Give your work and that of others meaning (this is my personal favorite—I enjoy seeing my impact on business goals).
- Help set priorities: Helping organizations that struggle with prioritizing to be bold and make difficult choices. Which projects are important and related to the goal?
- Help stay productive: Do note that productivity isn't the same as efficiency.
- Improve efficiency: To achieve challenging business goals, you sometimes need to be inefficient (e.g., by simultaneously pursuing multiple options to see which one delivers).
- Reduce uncertainty: If you track progress toward the goals on a weekly basis and when people see positive progress toward a goal, it can reassure and make people happy.

Over to You

Exercise: Your Why (15 min)

We've just looked at some of the reasons why you might want to set goals. What's your main reason for working with goals?

Take 15 minutes to try to identify your main reason for working with goal setting. First, take five to ten minutes to dream up scenarios to move beyond preconceived boundaries. You can use free writing or mind mapping. Even meditation to clear up your mind and then focus to receive inspiration can also help. Feel free to refer to the previous list or ignore it! Then complete this sentence:

I want to set goals in order to: _____

Goal-Setting Strategies

OKRs were preceded by the development of several concrete goal-setting strategies. In the classic book *The Practice of Management*, Drucker (1954) introduced the concept of Management by Objectives (MBO). In this legendary publication, he described a framework for executing an organization's strategic plan that aims to improve the performance of the organization by defining Objectives that are created and agreed to mutually between management and the employees. He assumes that when mutually agreeing on a goal, employees feel more committed, aligned to organizational objectives, and encouraged to participate. One of the early adapters of MBO was Hewlett Packard. The success with MBO showed off, but eventually, its users ran into some problems with this way of goal setting. Specifically, Hewlett Packard as well as other companies had challenges in tracking the Objectives and keeping people motivated and engaged.

SMART Objectives

Another common problem with MBO was that leaders found it difficult to write meaningful Objectives. In the November 1981 issue of

Management Review, George T. Doran suggested five criteria to help leaders think critically about their Objectives. Doran defined them as SMART: specific, measurable, assignable, realistic, and timely. These criteria formed a very powerful thinking framework, and for many leaders using MBOs in combination with the right SMART Objectives, this was (and still is today) a good way to define corporate goals.

However, for some companies, especially in the upcoming digital era, this was not good enough. Some need to break open new markets, disrupt markets, learn faster, innovate faster, change faster, and pivot faster to keep up with their competitors. Something else was needed.

Birth of OKRs

OKR as a goal-setting technique was invented at Intel by Andy Grove, who was executive vice president (VP) of Intel in the late 1970s and was later popularized by Google and other giants in Silicon Valley.

Grove observed that the existing way of goal setting with MBO was insufficient. To set an Objective at the beginning of the year only to find out at year's end that nothing has been achieved, simply didn't work. So, in looking for alternatives, he studied budding fields of behavior science and cognitive psychology and took the existing MBO technique, added key results to the Objectives, and shortened the feedback cycle from yearly to quarterly. These key results were the measurable outputs that showed progress toward the Objective. He called this new framework Intel's MBO or iMBO, which he later referred to as OKRs. The resulting method had some very positive effects on the company, and OKRs were born. Recent studies (Amabile and Kramer 2011) revealed that Grove was ahead of his time; tracking and seeing progress later became known as the *progress principle* which is key to boost inner work life.

John Doerr, who started out as an electrical engineer at Intel, learned about OKRs from Grove in the 1970s (Figure 1.1). He became a venture capitalist, and in the early years of the OKRs framework back in 1999, showed them to Larry Page and Sergey Brin at Google. Many argue that without OKRs, Google would never have enjoyed the hyper-growth it

The Progress Principle

Through exhaustive analysis of diaries kept by knowledge workers, it appears that Professor Teresa M. Amabile and researcher Steven J. Kramer stumbled upon a remarkable phenomenon which they called the *progress principle*. In their *Harvard Business Review* (HBR) article "The Power of Small Wins" (2011, 70–80), they wrote: "Of all the things that can boost emotions, motivation, and perceptions during a workday, the single most important is making progress in meaningful work. And the more frequently people experience that sense of progress, the more likely they are to be creatively productive in the long run. Whether they are trying to solve a major scientific mystery or simply produce a high-quality product or service, everyday progress—even a small win—can make all the difference in how they feel and perform."

did. Later on, other Silicon Valley companies such as Oracle, Facebook, Zynga, and LinkedIn all started to use OKRs as well. It was at Zynga in 2011 where Christina Wodtke first encountered OKRs and started to publically write about them. It was after Rick Klau published his video on YouTube (Klau 2013) that Wodtke published her legendary article *The Art of the OKR* on her blog (Wodtke 2014), and subsequently then did OKRs really start to gain traction.

The first official print publication of OKRs was made by Christina Wodtke, in her milestone book *Radical Focus* (Wodtke 2016) where she explained how OKRs work in the form of a business novel. In the same year, Paul Niven and Ben Lamorte wrote their book *Objectives and Key Results* (Niven and Lamorte 2016). OKRs became incredibly popular after Doerr (2018) wrote the book *Measure What Matters*, which sparked this unique management technique to go mainstream.

Let's look at the main advantages of OKRs.

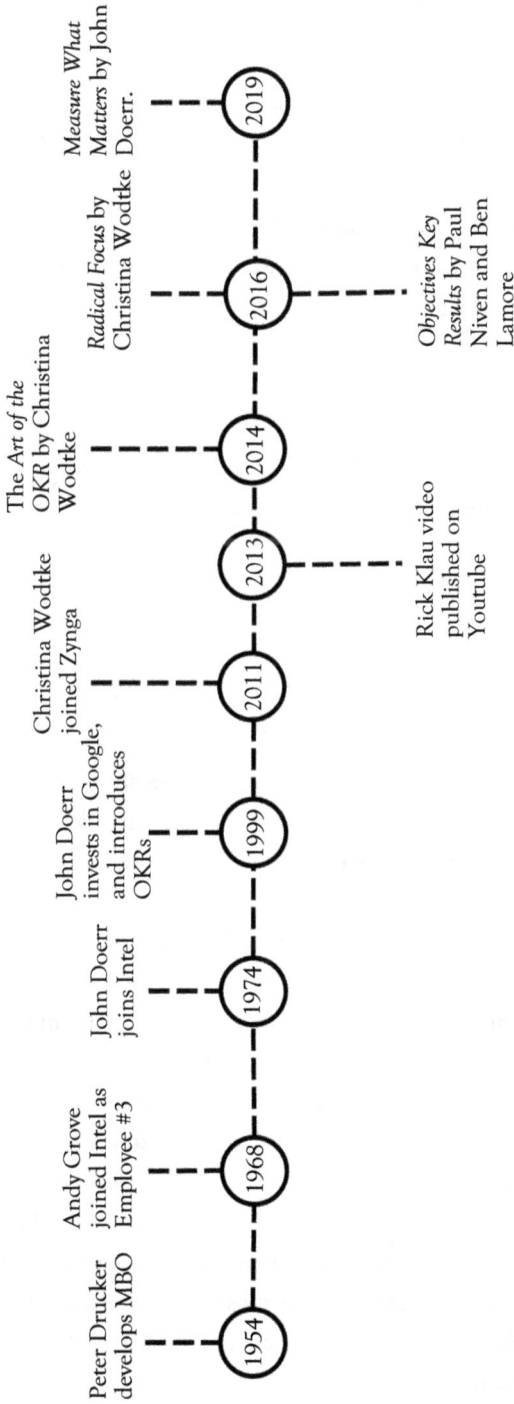

Figure 1.1 History of OKRs since 1954

Advantages of OKRs

In a conversation with Massachusetts Institute of Technology (MIT)'s Donald Sull, John Doerr explains the five advantages of OKRs. He uses the acronym FACTS as a memory aid to describe the advantages of OKRs: Focus, Alignment, Commitment, Tracking, and Stretching.

Because of these (really) hard to achieve goals, these moonshots, OKRs drive a learning and experimental culture. OKRs must *never* be tied to compensation and bonuses, as they can only function when providing people the safety to *stretch* themselves outside of their comfort zone where they can experiment and learn new things. Stretching also happens when companies are threatened with disruption and must innovate to gain competitive advantage. By using the OKR cycles, an organization can acquire the necessary agility. Furthermore, OKRs encourage visionary thinking. When getting out of your comfort zone, you are learning faster than your competitors, which obviously gives you a competitive advantage.

Here is a transcript of John Doerr's conversation with Donald Sull:

"You get exceptional **Focus**, and because OKRs are transparent, you get a high degree of **Alignment**. Then an uncommon degree of **Commitment**. These goals end up being your social contract between everyone in the organization as they declare: I'm going for these Key Results that relate to this Objective. And then you can **Track** the progress through the course of days and weeks and months in the life of an organization. Finally, like at Intel, at Google, this kind of transparent goal system is not tied to compensation; you don't pay bonuses and people aren't promoted based on them. That allows you to really build a risk-taking culture, where it is okay to **Stretch** for something almost impossible to do and not quite make it, but still have a considerable accomplishment. Indeed, at Google, if you are achieving all your goals, you are getting all greens as grades, you probably weren't stretching far or hard enough. But those five payoffs, the focus, the alignment, the commitment, the tracking and the stretching are powerful. They don't come with most other goal setting systems."

Innovation With a Capital I

Five percent improvement on a critical business metric will probably require people to run the extra mile or perform small improvement projects. In an HBR article from 2007, George Day wrote: "Minor innovations make up 85% to 90% of companies' development portfolios, on average, but they rarely generate the growth companies seek" (Day 2007, 110–120). These small incremental innovations (Day called them "small i" innovations) might be great for companies that want to squeeze some more juice out of their already great cash cow, but this isn't the realm of OKRs. If you continue with OKRs, you are probably ending up with a lot of minor innovations and miss the chance of achieving greatness.

Achieving greatness means being bold. Larry Page, for example, lives by the "gospel of 10×," that is setting a target that is tenfold of your current target. You want 100 more customers next year, instead, why not set 1,000 more customers as a target. In a 2013 interview with *WIRED* magazine, he said "incremental improvement is guaranteed to be obsolete over time. Especially in technology, where you know there's going to be non-incremental change" (Page 2013). The way Page sees it, a 10 percent improvement means that you're basically doing the same thing as everybody else.

Innovation with a capital "I" (Day called it "big I") will require senior executives to take on risky innovation projects that push companies into new markets or toward novel technologies and can generate the profits needed to close the gap between revenue forecasts and growth goals. A saying that is often attributed to Albert Einstein applies here: The definition of insanity is doing the same things, the same way, and expecting a different result. If you want to achieve extraordinary results, you need to do things you have never done before. You cannot continue the way you've always operated. That means you need to implement a process toward fundamental change.

No Silver Bullet

OKRs are not a silver bullet. They don't work in every organization or every culture. If in an organization where there is low cooperation, responsibilities are shirked or failure leads to scapegoating, then OKRs won't help to fix that. In Chapter 2, we will explore different types of organizational cultures and understand in which OKRs thrive best.

Use OKRs incorrectly and they can do an organization more harm than good, as the famous HBR article "Goals Gone Wild" all too clearly explains. The authors warned against aggressive goal setting, explaining that it is "a prescription-strength medication that requires careful dosing … and close supervision" (Ordóñez et al. 2009, 19). The price paid for having too narrow focus, placing stretch goals and sales quotas above ethics and the law can be colossal. Scandals at Volkswagen (Hakim et al. 2015), Wells Fargo (Cowley and Flitter 2018), and more recently at Boeing (Gelles and Kitroeff 2019) are direct evidence of this. Without strong leadership and a healthy organizational culture, OKRs can be dangerous. You need to have leaders that encourage and embrace aggressive goal setting, while putting measures in place to avoid unethical behavior.

On the other hand, if you merely sprinkle OKRs over your all of your existing mediocre goals, you won't reap their benefits either. Like any other management framework or methodology, you should try to adapt OKRs to your particular needs and only use them where appropriate. To adapt OKRs to your needs, I've included guidelines and alternatives in every chapter for you to consider. I see them work best at organizations that need to grow, want to enter a new market, or try to find a product market fit. If the organization is risk averse and doesn't have the right company culture, OKRs will probably do more harm than good.

OKRs: The Core Concepts

The three key ingredients of OKRs are Objectives, Key Results, and the OKR Cycle. This last one isn't as obvious, but without it, OKRs are a worthless tool, as you need to systematically reflect on the Objectives and key results you set.

Objectives

An Objective is a memorable, short, qualitative, and inspirational description of *what* you want to achieve. An Objective should make a significant impact on your most critical business metric. Ideally, you want just one

Objective per quarter. We'll dive deeper into what makes a good Objective in Chapter 3. Objectives should not describe activities you were planning to do anyway. They should be a challenge for you and your teams. Originally, an Objective is expected to be achieved within 90 days or one quarter, or as I like to call it the "90-day challenge." Framing Objectives as "challenges" brings a positive vibe to the team. People love a good challenge. It engages a bit of friendly competition in a game-like manner. However, there are also different durations possible, which we will explore in Chapter 5.

Key Results

If the Objective is what you want to achieve, then the key results (KRs from now on) are the measurables that indicate whether you've achieved them. KRs are a set of metrics that show your progress toward the Objective. They describe how you're going to achieve that Objective, not by saying what you need to do, but by describing an aspirational *result*.

In an interview with OKRs expert Felipe Castro, Itamar Gilad, former lead product manager and head of growth at Gmail, pointed out that in the early days at Google, the KRs were still more output focused. That has evolved over the years toward the outcome-based KRs we know today. The difference between the two is explained in the book *Outcomes over Output* by Joshua Seiden (2019). An output is an amount of something produced by a person, team, machine, factory, country, and so on. For example, the number of product features delivered or the launch of an e-mail campaign. He defined an outcome as *a change in human behavior that drives business results.* For example, customers that promote your product to others because you have automated their boring manual tasks. Another example would be higher product quality because your software engineers started to use automated tests to prevent product defects.

It, therefore, has to be realized that good KRs are not only about an amount of something but also about changing human behavior. That behavior change is targeted not only among your customers but also your stakeholders, governments, suppliers, board members, managers, and your employees. To change human behavior, you need to observe and measure people's current habits and behavior. Then, you need to make decisions on how to modify that behavior with techniques that will be explained in more detail in Chapter 11. To eventually move the needle, it is required that you run small, targeted experiments. We will look how you can create experiments in Chapter 12.

KRs should be challenging but not impossible. When you define your OKRs at the beginning of each cycle, you should have about a 50 percent chance of achieving them. If you end with a final score of 70 to 80 percent of achievement, your OKR is considered a stretch goal. Stretch goals thus reflect the level of difficulty of achievement. If the score is 100 percent at the end, then it wasn't that much of a stretch. If you achieve all of your KRs and the end of the 90 days, you will have achieved your Objective, but it probably wasn't ambitious enough. We'll look more closely at what makes a good KR in Chapter 3.

OKRs are written in a simple format:
Objective: [What you want to achieve]
KRs:

- Key result 1
- Key result 2

An example of a good OKR:
Objective: Customers choose us over [competitor]
KRs:

- Increase the percentage of customers that prefer our product to the competitor's in a blind test from 30 to 75 percent.
- Increase the average order rating from 3.1 to 5.0.

Hypotheses and Bets

Some might refer to OKRs as organizational hypotheses or bets, because in the end that is what they are: a series of strategic and daring pledges to impact growth and innovation. Since OKRs are stretch goals, every time you create an Objective and corresponding KRs, you take a risk; you don't know if you are actually going to realize them. Given their uncertainty of achievement, you need to expand into unknown territory to fulfill your commitment to the OKRs. That is why you don't want to set OKRs for a long period of time. A reason why many executives abandon OKRs is because, as leaders, they are risk averse. However, taking too little risk is also counterproductive for a company's growth. To reduce risk, it helps to receive fast feedback, so you are able to evaluate and correct your course before it is too late. That is where the OKR cycle comes in, which is 90 days or one quarter by default. Taking a bet for 90 days is not too much of a risk.

Over to You

Now that you've learnt the basics, why not create your own. Try to fill in the following template:

Objective: _____ [What do you want to achieve?]

KRs:
- Key result 1: __ [How to measure that you've achieved the Objective?]
- Key result 2: __ [How to measure that you've achieved the Objective?]

OKR Cycle

Companies that do goal setting quarterly are 3.5× more likely to be top performers in their industry.
—Stacia S. Garr, High-Impact Performance Management, Bersin
by Deloitte, December 2014

The OKR cycle (Figure 1.2) is the system for achieving your OKRs, and there are many variants available. In its basic form, it looks like Deming's circle: the Plan–Do–Check–Adjust (PDCA) cycle (Tague 2005). The PDCA cycle (sometimes with additions) is a form of scientific problem solving and an important tool in Lean Thinking which is often used to implement change or improvement initiatives.

In this book, I'll discuss the version of the cycle I've found the most useful for organizations to start out with. If you've already implemented the OKR cycle in your organization and some phases are missing, then I urge you to implement them to improve the success of OKRs. If you have

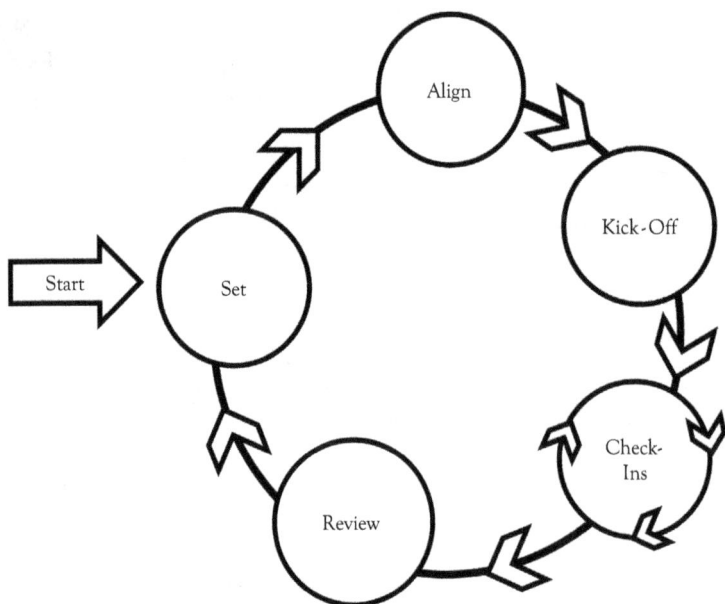

Figure 1.2 The OKR cycle

more than five phases, then you might want to simplify them to keep the process as lightweight as possible.

The OKR cycle is the starting point for many organizations, and it's vital to ensure your organization adjusts the cycle to its needs and culture. The cycle has five phases that repeat every 90 days:

1. Setting phase: where you develop new OKRs during the OKR setting workshop.
2. Alignment phase: during the alignment workshops, you align OKRs with other teams, managers, and leadership.
3. Kick-off phase: where you announce and make OKRs transparent to the rest of the organization.
4. Execution phase: by performing weekly OKR check-ins, people track status on their KRs and make commitments. It is in this phase that leaders and teams continuously discover, learn, and experiment on how to move the needle. More on this is provided in Part 3.
5. Review phase: where you reflect back at both your OKRs and the process and define actions for improvement.

There are also different rhythms possible (e.g., monthly, trimesterly, or semesterly). Which rhythm is best depends on the size of your organization, your culture, and your business domain. My advice is to start with 90 days and adjust if necessary. We'll get into the OKR cycle in more detail in Part 2.

Over to You

Exercise: Food for Thought (15 min)

Watch John Doerr's TED Talk titled "Why the Secret to Success Is Setting the Right Goals."

It is one of the most inspirational OKR videos I have come across. Click on the link or find the TED talk online.

LINK:
www.ted.com/talks/john_doerr_why_the_secret_to_success_is_setting_the_right_goals

---

In Pursuit of Something Bigger

Originally, OKRs were created for tactical goal setting on a quarterly basis. On company level, senior executives set quarterly OKRs, then departments and operational teams connect to the quarterly company OKRs (Figure 1.3). That was also the model Google used until 2011. As more companies adopted OKRs, they were missing a longer-term, strategic, and planning aspect in the OKR process. That is why most companies also adopted annual or longer-term OKRs. As you will learn in Chapter 5, setting long-term goals with OKRs is optional, but strongly recommended. To create effective OKRs, you need to understand the context you are in. Merely setting OKRs in isolation (e.g., only setting them for a department or team) will result in local optimization. OKRs need to be connected to the big picture. To understand the bigger picture, you need to need to start to see the system as a whole. That understanding starts by asking "why?" thus relating OKRs to the mission, vision, and strategy of your company.

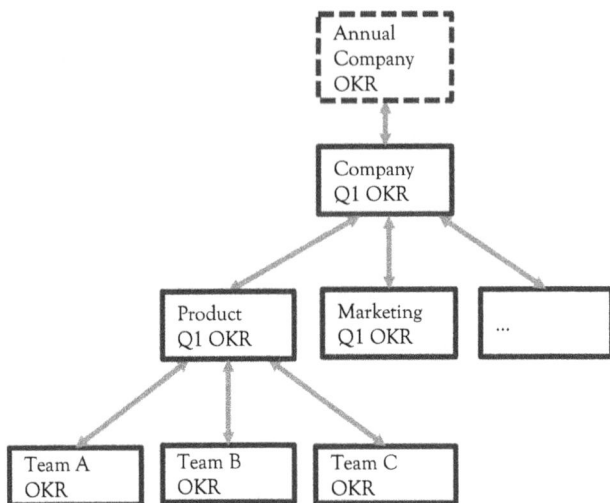

Figure 1.3 *Hierarchy of company, department, and team OKRs, sometimes connected to annual company OKRs*

It All Starts With a Mission

Hopefully, all leaders understand the reason why their company exists in the first place. Younger companies have this often fresh in their minds. Sometimes, scaled-up companies lose track of what their "raison d'être" is and how they are still relevant. It is often effective to dedicate a few days off-site to reflect on why the company was started in the first place. The reason why a company exists is often called your *mission* or *purpose* (Figure 1.4). It will never change and may need more than a lifetime to achieve. To quote an old Greek proverb: "Society grows great when old men plant trees whose shade they know they shall never sit in."

Simon Sinek teaches us about the Golden Circle in his book *Start With Why: How Great Leaders Inspire Everyone to Take Action* (2011). The "why" is the core belief of the business and the reason the business exists. The "how" is the actions taken by the business to fulfill that core belief. The "what" is the company's means and methods to fulfil that core belief. Sinek found out that most companies execute their strategy backwards, they start with what they do. He illustrates this point by how Apple would put out a marketing message: "We make great computers. They're user friendly,

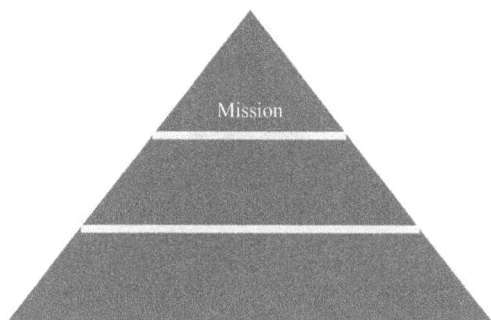

Figure 1.4 It all starts with a mission

beautifully designed, and easy to use. Want to buy one?" The real marketing message from Apple is: "With everything we do, we aim to challenge the status quo. We aim to think differently. Our products are user-friendly, beautifully designed, and easy to use. We just happen to make great computers. Want to buy one?" Mission-driven companies don't deliver "stuff" to their customers; they are making an impact in the world.

Examples of mission statements:

- Apple: To bring the best user experience to its customers through its innovative hardware, software, and services.
- Tesla: To accelerate the world's transition to sustainable energy.
- Amazon: To be Earth's most customer-centric company, where customers can find and discover anything they might want to buy online, and endeavors to offer its customers the lowest possible prices.
- Disney: To create happiness by providing the finest in entertainment for people of all ages, everywhere.
- Google: To organize the world's information and make it universally accessible and useful.
- Alibaba: To make it easy to do business anywhere.

The prior examples provide inspiration and focus to everyone in the organization. Defining a good mission statement is hard. It should be inspirational, yet specific. If it is too vague, it cannot help people to focus.

Take a look at these: "To refresh the world in mind, body, and spirit" and "To inspire moments of happiness." Do these statements provide you with any clarity and focus?

It isn't just companies that can have a mission. Teams can too, as they should also have a reason for existing. If you want to use OKRs to achieve something big, then it is very important that your teams can also answer their "why."

Vision

If you have a why, then you probably also have a vision: a dream of the future that won't remain a dream forever because you have a plan to achieve it (Figure 1.5). If you have a vision, then in principle you have a baseline for measuring success, be it a North Star Metric (NSM), a Big Hairy Audacious Goal (BHAG), or any measurable long-term goal that helps you to focus on the upcoming years. This metric will be the main long-term priority for you and everybody in your company. Alternatively, some companies prefer to use long-term OKR (called ultimate OKRs) to describe their visionary goal. You will learn more about ultimate OKRs in Chapter 5. Having a clear (ideally customer-centric) metric defined inspires, motivates, and helps people to understand the big game you are playing.

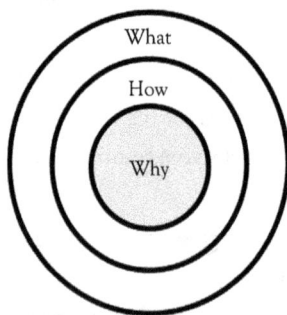

Figure 1.5 Simon Sinek's Golden Circle

Core Values

Core values are the personality of your company. They shouldn't be a list of feel-good values you would like everybody to pursue, but rather a small set of phrases. Values can sometimes be formulated in an abstract or vague way. However, when you explicitly define your core values in terms of concrete norms and behaviors, you can help people to understand how to live up to them. For example, a core value could be "Everyone is an entrepreneur." When I'm reading this core value, I don't know how to act or behave accordingly. If you then attach a behavioral norm like "you should always get feedback from customers," you make it very concrete how teams may act on and live up to the value. Defining your core values as phrases and attaching them to a clear set of norms and behaviors also helps to measure and evaluate them during continuous performance reviews. This will be discussed in more detail in Chapter 6 (Figure 1.6).

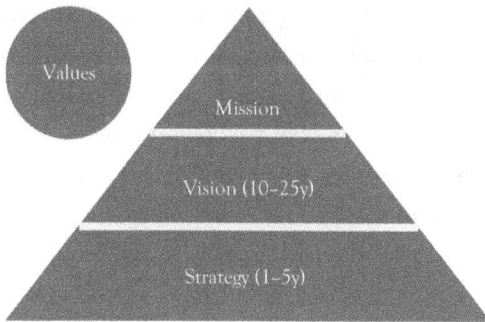

Figure 1.6 Mission, vision, strategy, and company values

Strategy and Execution

Once you have defined a clear purpose, vision, and core values, it's time to develop a high-level plan on how to get closer to your vision under conditions of uncertainty. That plan is called a *strategy*. How are you unique in the market? What kind of customers do you serve? What key capabilities do you need to pursue? More importantly, what are you *not* going to do? It's the plan that will get you closer to long-term visionary goal.

OKRs can never replace a complete strategic plan! An extensive amount of literature and a number of tools have been developed in recent decades on how to create a good strategic plan for your business. Developing a sound strategy is beyond the focus of this book, but I can make some suggestions. Personally, I favor visual techniques such as Strategy Maps

(Kaplan and Norton 2004), Result Maps (Barr 2017, 111), and Wardley Maps (Wardley 2017). Other lightweight techniques such as the One-Page-Strategic-Plan (Harnish 2014, 93), Lean Canvas (Maurya 2012, 5), Business Model Canvas (Osterwalder et al. 2010), or the Where-To-Play Canvas (Gruber and Tal 2017) are also interesting to explore and will help you to define a sound strategy. At the end of this chapter, you will find references to these methods.

Once you have developed a corporate strategy, it is time to execute it. Formulating a strategic plan is what most executives are good at. Most of them learn this during their MBA education. It's the execution part of their strategy that is considered challenging, and what most organizations struggle with. Studies have found that two-thirds to three-quarters of large organizations struggle to implement their strategies (Sull, et al. 2015, 58–66). In 2016, it was estimated that 67 percent of well-formulated strategies failed due to poor execution (Carucci 2017). Less optimistic reports even show only a 10 percent success rate. By improving the quality of strategy execution with 35 percent, firms can expect a 30 percent increase in shareholder value. But why is strategy execution hard? Because most ambitious strategies require people to *change their behavior*. Most leaders don't realize the need for a behavior change strategy as part of their strategy execution toolset. OKRs can be exceptionally well used to *change human behavior*, the outcomes. It is in the next chapter that you will learn how OKRs can help you execute a behavior change strategy.

It bears repeating: The reason you need a strategy is that it provides you with context. You simply cannot set OKRs (or goals in general) in isolation; what would be the point of that? For example, "improving customer satisfaction" seems like a reasonable Objective for any business, but why is it important now? If your strategy is to gain competitive advantage by providing best in class customer support, then the Objective to increase customer satisfaction for your service desk will be better understood by everyone. Without this strategic context, people cannot set OKRs.

Once your strategy is in place, the company's executive team can develop company OKRs that can bring your company closer to its strategic goals. Then leaders, in close collaboration with their teams, can develop OKRs that will *influence* the company KRs (see Figure 1.3). Developing

OKRs both top-down *and* bottom-up is a powerful technique to create alignment throughout the company and can be considered a core feature of the OKR system. How to connect company, department, and team OKRs will be discussed in more detail in Chapter 5.

Operational Framework

In her great book *Escaping the Build Trap* (2019, 72), Melissa Perri wrote: "A good company strategy is made up of two parts: the operational framework, [...] and the strategic framework [...]. Many companies confuse these two frameworks and treat them as one and the same." I argue that OKRs can form a great strategic framework. However, you also need to have an operational framework in place.

You can monitor and track performance of your operations with Key Performance Indicators (KPIs) or *health metrics* as Christina Wodtke like to call them (Wodtke 2016, 121). They measure the performance of your company (and therefore the success of your strategy) or team over time on an ongoing basis. These, for example, may contain the Net Promoter Score (NPS) of your core product, the number of customers, your Annual or Monthly Recurring Revenue (ARR or MRR), your profit/loss ratio, your Earnings Before Interest and Taxes (EBIT), and/or your Customer Lifetime Value (CLTV). These are all KPIs that could measure the success of your business strategy, but they are not inspirational.

When you use OKRs, it is critical to also use health metrics to avoid people becoming blinded to important issues that appear unrelated to their goal. In fact, I recommend you to first invest in having appropriate health metrics in place before you even start with OKRs (Figure 1.7).

Some companies use health metrics during a monthly or quarterly business review (QBR) to make sure the current operation is running smoothly and to determine actions for improvement. You can even set targets or goals for them which are different than OKRs. For example, to sustain your profit margins, improve production lead times, improve profits, and keep your employees happy and engaged. This list of essential goals is called your life support goals (Table 1.1).

Avoid mixing these two frameworks at all costs, even if this is not always easy. In an article on Google's ReWork blog, author Rick Klau

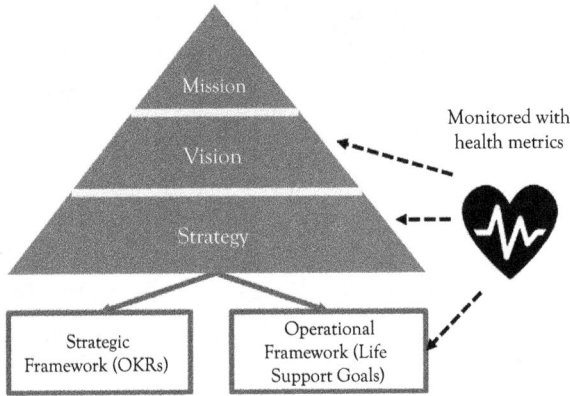

Figure 1.7 Strategy is made up of two parts: the strategy and operational framework

Table 1.1 Examples of OKRs, life support goals, and health metrics

Strategic framework		Operational framework	
Objective	Key results	Life support goals	Health metrics
O: Change the game	KR 1: Increase [game-changer measure] from X to Y	Increase profit by 10% Improve gross margins by 5% Sustain customer base Sustain employee engagement Increase product quality by 5%	Market capture NPS Profit Costs EBIT(DA) MRR/ARR Process lead time

wrote: "Their quarterly goals were an overwrought laundry list of everything the CEO wanted accomplished to demonstrate progress. And the pile of annual priorities mixed moonshots and the mundane, confusing the scope of the company's ambitions" (Klau 2018). So how can you avoid mixing mundane goals with OKRs? Check if you are in the realm of the operational framework and life support, or if you are dealing with strategic game-changing stretch goals that are best achieved through OKRs. In Chapter 13, you will learn how to manage health metrics and OKRs separately while using one dashboard so that you can keep an eye on all important elements.

> **Origins of Performance Management**
>
> Performance measurement and appraisals can be traced back to the Han Dynasty Wright (2002). The precise origin of performance appraisals is not known, but the practice dates back to the third century when the emperors of the Wei Dynasty (221–265 AD) rated the performance of the official family members (Banner and Cooke 1984; Coens and Jenkins 2000).

Getting Started With OKRs

What is the difference between high-performing companies and low-performing companies, you might wonder? It's their ability to execute their goals and learn faster than their competitors.

Their success is not simply because they have implemented a goal-setting framework like OKRs, but also because they have aligned them across departments, and the transparency of their goals makes everybody understand the direction the company is moving in. Finally, goals are prerequisites for exceptional growth only through targeted, calculated action.

In his book *Atomic Habits*, James Clear says: "Forget about goals, focus on systems instead" (Clear 2018, 23). What he means is that you can use goals to describe the result that you want to achieve, but only describing your OKRs doesn't bring you very far. Systems are the processes that lead to those results. Implementing OKRs means you are overhauling your system.

As with any other big-change initiative, it can be extremely challenging to implement any new changes within an organization, and OKRs are no different. If you've heard of OKRs, then it's likely that you have also heard of change management. OKRs require a significant cultural shift. Remember the last time your organization tried to adopt Scrum, DevOps, or method XYZ? OKRs could be even more of a challenge. Sure, if you are a five-person start-up, things can go fast and smooth with everyone on the same page from the very beginning. If, on the other hand, you are a scale-up company or you want to introduce OKRs within a large enterprise, prepare yourself for facing some severe push-back.

My Favorite Question

When companies ask me to help them with OKRs, my favorite first question to the executive team is: Why do you want to use OKRs and what specific business problem do you think they're going to solve? "Because Google is doing it" is not a sufficient answer.

This is also my question to you, of course. A handy rule of thumb here is that while it's fine to start your answer with "Because … ," you should also always be able to replace "Because … " with "In order to … ." Thus "In order to replicate what Google is doing" doesn't make sense (as "Google is doing it" isn't an Objective), but "In order to be voted the company's #1 franchise" does make sense, and is a legitimate Objective.

Answers such as "achieve alignment, focus or engagement" are also not very good answers. These are nice side effects of goal setting, but simply aren't goals in and of themselves. I mean, could you achieve your current business goals with unaligned teams? My guess is sure, you probably could. Most business goals are risk averse, mostly follow business as usual, and are careful with setting goals as managers' bonuses are attached to them. They are not as aggressive in their pursuit of progress as businesses that work with OKRs. The OKR approach turns things around: First you define really aggressive, stretched goals, then following that, you will see that team alignment becomes essential.

Clearly formulating the reason why you want to start using OKRs is just as important as good preparation, even if during phase one, you are repeating it mainly for yourself. It is essential to chew over this before ushering in change within your organization. When you start with OKRs, people within your organization will ask "Why OKRs? Why now? Don't we have enough on our plate?" You can't blame them. These are very legitimate questions. Do you have an answer? You should!

Be clear with yourself: Do you know what you want to solve with OKRs? What significant and sustainable impact on your organizational and team performance you want to make? Steer clear of ambiguous "goals" such as increasing alignment, transparency, and focus. Indeed, they are nice added benefits of a successful OKR implementation, but it is your role to paint the picture of how OKRs will help solve real, tangible problems that affect everyone. Remember that OKRs cannot work without a well-defined mission, vision, and strategy. In fact, OKRs need to connect to them. If there is nothing to connect with, the whole exercise will be futile.

OKRs are first and foremost a tool and, when utilized properly, can solve specific problems, position you as a market leader within your industry, and set you up for accomplishing ambitious Objectives. To use an everyday metaphor: if your organizational problems could be materialized as a DIY assembly kitchen from IKEA, OKRs would *not* be a hammer designed for smashing the problems to bits, but rather the multipurpose Allen key paired with a clear instruction manual, and everyone is clear on their specific role of the construction process.

> **Over to You**
>
> Sit down with a pen and paper and define the Objectives, the scope, and the advantages (and if you want to be extra prepared, then have solid, honest answers for the naysayers, too, when it comes to what prospective challenges or risks there could be).

To master setting OKRs that really move the needle, you need to (deliberately) practice it on the job throughout many OKR cycles. This is the reason why a typical OKR implementation takes, on average, about 1.5 years. In the next chapter, we will explore why so many organizations fail to achieve their goals and what to do about it.

Chapter Recap

In this chapter, we've established the origins of OKRs, including how they allow for faster innovation than other goal-setting techniques, the importance of changing human behavior, and the relationship between motivation or purpose to the mission and vision of a company. We have identified the many advantages and benefits they can offer your organization in terms of focus, alignment, commitment, tracking, and stretching—if they are used correctly. Importantly, we've developed a clear understanding of the commitment required to successfully implement OKRs as a vehicle for tangible change.

We've talked about the three key ingredients of OKRs—Objectives, key results, and the OKR cycle—and defined how they should be used for maximum impact. We've also taken our first look at the OKR cycle and established the importance of the 90-day (quarterly) structure.

At this point, you should have a clearer vision of your company's "why"—the overriding purpose that influences the goals you want to achieve. You should now be considering how OKRs might fit that vision as a goal-setting technique and how you can align OKRs with your company's bigger picture to ensure everybody buys in and understands the direction the company is moving in.

Preface, Introduction and Chapter References

Amabile, T.M., and S.J. Kramer. 2011. *The Power of Small Wins*, 70–80. Boston: Harvard Business Review.

Ballé, M., D. Jones, J. Chaize, and O. Fiume. 2017. *The Lean Strategy: Using Lean to Create Competitive Advantage, Unleash Innovation, and Deliver Sustainable Growth.* 1st ed. New York, NY: McGraw-Hill Education.

Berkman, E.T. March 2018. "The Neuroscience of Goals and Behavior Change." *Consulting Psychology Journal: Practice and Research* 70, no. 1, pp. 28–44.

Berridge, K.C., and T.E. Robinson. 2003. "Parsing Reward." *Trends in Neurosciences* 26, no. 9, 507–13. doi:10.1016/S0166-2236(03)00233-9 *Erratum in: Trends Neurosciences* 26, no. 11, 581. PMID: 12948663

Cagan, M. 2018. *Inspired: How to Create Tech Products Customers Love*, 2nd ed. New Jersey, NJ: Wiley.

Carucci, R. 2017. *Executives Fail to Execute Strategy Because They're Too Internally Focused.* Boston: Harvard Business Review.

Chattopadhyay, A., A. Stamatogiannakis, and D. Chakravarti. November 2018. *Why You Should Stop Setting Easy Goals.* Boston: Harvard Business Review.

Clear, J. 2018. *Atomic Habits*, 1st ed. New York, NY: Avery.

Cowley, S., and E. Flitter. 2018. *Wells Fargo Agrees to Pay $575 Million to Resolve State Investigations.* New York, NY: New York Times.

Day, G. 2007. *Is It Real? Can We Win? Is It Worth Doing?: Managing Risk and Reward in an Innovation Portfolio.* Boston: Harvard Business Review.

Doerr, J. 2018. *Measure What Matters.* London: Portfolio Penguin.

Doerr, J. April 2018. *Why the Secret to Success is Setting the Right Goals.* Vancouver: TED Conference. www.ted.com/talks/john_doerr_why_the_secret_to_success_is_setting_the_right_goals/transcript?language=en

Doerr, J. June 27, 2018. "Conversation with John Doerr and Donald Sull." *MIT Sloan Management Review*, YouTube https://youtu.be/HiQ3Ofcmo50

Drucker, P.F. 2006. *The Practice of Management*. Reissue ed. Harper Business.

Gelles, D., and N. Kitroeff. December 11, 2019. *Boeing Hearing Puts Heat on F.A.A. Chief Over Max Crisis*. New York, NY: New York Times.

Gilad, I. n.d. "How OKR Helped Gmail Reach 1 Billion Users: an Interview with Itamar Gilad." Interview by Felipe Castro. Blog: https://felipecastro.com/en/blog/okr-gmail-itamar-gilad/

Gothelf, J. 2020. *Use OKRs to Set Goals for Teams, Not Individuals*. Boston: Harvard Business Review.

Hakim, D., A.M. Kessler, J. Ewing. September 26, 2015. *As Volkswagen Pushed to Be No. 1, Ambitions Fuelled a Scandal*. New York, NY: New York Times.

Klau, R. May 14, 2013. *Startup Lab Workshop: How Google Sets goals: OKRs*. YouTube. Recorded at Google Ventures Startup Lab.

Wodtke, C. Feb 01, 2014. *The Art of the OKR*. https://eleganthack.com/the-art-of-the-okr/. eleganthack.com. (accessed July 19, 2021).

Wodtke, C. September 02, 2016. "One Objective to Rule them All." http://eleganthack.com/one-objective-to-rule-them-all/ (accessed February 10, 2021).

Locke, E.A., and G.P. Latham. 2002. "Building a Practically Useful Theory of goal Setting and Task Motivation: A 35-Year Odyssey." *American Psychologist* 57, no. 9, pp. 705–717.

Niven, P.R., and B. Lamorte. 2016. *Objectives and Key Results: Driving Focus, Alignment, and Engagement with OKRs*, 1st ed. New Jersey: Wiley.

Ordóñez, L.D., M.E. Schweitzer, A.D. Galinsky, and M.H. Bazerman. January 2009. *Goals Gone Wild: The Systematic Side Effects of Over-Prescribing Goal Setting*. Boston: Harvard Business School. Working Paper.

Page, L. 2013. "Google's Larry Page on Why Moon Shots Matter." Interview by Steven Levy. Wired www.wired.com/2013/01/ff-qa-larry-page/

Pink, D.H. 2011. *Drive: The Surprising Truth About What Motivates Us*. New York, NY: Riverhead Books.

Ries, E. 2011. *The Lean Startup: How Today's Entrepreneurs Use Continuous Innovation to Create Radically Successful Businesses*. New York, NY: Currency.

Robert, S.K., and D.P. Norton. January–February 1992. *The Balanced Scorecard—Measures that Drive Performance*. Boston: Harvard Business Review.

Seiden, J. April 8, 2019. *Outcomes Over Output: Why Customer Behavior is the Key Metric for Business Success*. Independently Published.

Sinek, S. 2011. *Start with Why: How Great Leaders Inspire Everyone to Take Action*. London: Portfolio.

Sull, D., R. Homkes, and S. Charles. March 2015. *Why Strategy Execution Unravels—and What to Do About It*, 58–66. Boston: Harvard Business Review.

Tague, N.R. 2005. *Plan–Do–Study–Act Cycle*. *The Quality Toolbox*, 2nd ed, 390–392. Milwaukee: ASQ Quality Press.

Vermeulen, F. November 08, 2017. *Many Strategies Fail Because They're Not Actually Strategies*. Boston: Harvard Business Review.

Wodtke, C. 2016. *Radical Focus: Achieving Your Most Important Goals with Objectives and Key Results*. Palo Alto: Cucina Media LLC.

Tool for Creating and Visualizing Strategy

Barr, S. 2017. *How to Create a High-Performance Culture and Measurable Success, Prove It!*, 1st ed, 111. New Jersey, NJ: Wiley.

Gruber, M., and S. Tal. 2017. *Where to Play: 3 Steps for Discovering your Most Valuable Market Opportunities*. Upper Saddle River, New Jersey, NJ: FT Press.

Harnish, V. 2014. *Scaling Up: How a Few Companies Make It...and Why the Rest Don't (Rockefeller Habits 2.0)*. USA: Gazelles, Inc.

Kaplan, R.S., and D.P Norton. February 2, 2004. *Strategy Maps: Converting Intangible Assets into Tangible Outcomes*, 1st ed. Boston: Harvard Business School Press.

Maurya, A. 2012. *Running Lean: Iterate from Plan A to a Plan That Works*, 2nd ed. Sebastopol: O'Reilly Media Inc.

Osterwalder, A., Y. Pigneur, and T. Clark. 2010. *Business Model Generation: A Handbook For Visionaries, Game Changers, and Challengers*. Strategyzer Series. Hoboken, NJ: John Wiley and Sons.

Wardley, S. 2017. "Wardley Maps: Topographical Intelligence in Business." Chapter 2. Published on Medium. https://medium.com/wardleymaps/finding-a-path-cdb1249078c0 (accessed February 26, 2021).

CHAPTER 2

Overcoming Organizational Challenges

I am just a child who has never grown up. I still keep asking these "how" and "why" questions. Occasionally, I find an answer.

—Stephen Hawking

Chapter Highlights

- Top five reasons why most organizations fail with OKRs
- Interactions between OKRs and cultures of safety
- The approach to achieving big results
- Challenges with strategy execution
- How not to use OKRs
- Scope of change—how to introduce OKRs

Not so long ago, a large Fintech company approached me to help them grow their customer base by 300 percent over the next two years. This was part of their core strategy to gain more market share and attract investors.

They decided to use OKRs to execute their ambitious strategy. The executive team did an amazing job by defining a handful of company OKRs. But after some months, their OKRs didn't make the expected impact on their customer numbers. The expected growth results remained elusive. They considered about abandoning OKRs altogether.

Fortunately, they decided to collaborate with me to give OKRs a second chance. They still believed in the potential power of them.

My strategy consisted of helping them to reduce their initial set of company OKRs to just one, explaining to them the concepts of behavior change strategies and how Lean OKRs can play a big role in this. These eye-opening concepts, which I'll explain in this chapter, really resonated with them. By focusing on a single OKR per cycle, they were given another chance to achieve their growth numbers. To keep everybody engaged and committed, we installed the OKR cycle for all of their teams.

After only one OKR cycle (90 days), their most critical needle already started to move and customer numbers went up. They had overcome the number one enemy of OKRs: "business as usual."

Why Most Organizations Fail With OKRs

I've been lucky to meet many company CEOs who have been open enough to share their OKRs and their systems with me. As good as OKRs sound on paper, a lot of companies struggle to implement them. Applying OKRs takes time, discipline, and hard work. There is no magic formula that helps you implement them.

What I noticed after almost a decade of working with OKRs in all kinds of companies around the world is that there are some common patterns in all failing OKR implementations. There are five main reasons why OKR implementations fail 95 percent of the time:

1. The organization is based on a command-and-control model and doesn't have empowered (product) teams.
2. Leaders fail to communicate why they want to use OKRs.
3. The OKRs are poorly written and set the wrong goals.
4. Lack of focus, because there are too many OKRs.
5. People get discouraged and disengage due to a lack of visible results.

There are also secondary challenges that organizations might experience and reasons why OKR implementations fail:

- People quit before they see any benefits (OKRs take time and patience).
- People set and forget the OKRs.
- OKRs start as an initiative in a department without support from the executive team (often initiated by HR).
- People don't know how to move the needle on the KRs.

- People don't know how to scale OKRs.
- Fear of experimentation (see Chapter 12 experiments).
- Lack of leadership support.
- Companies don't have true cross-functional or product teams.
- OKRs linked to compensation and bonuses cause sandbagging and anxiety.
- Low psychological safety (we don't trust people to set the right OKRs).

Most of these challenges are related to the aforementioned five main reasons, so let's look at them and discover why OKRs might fail in your organization.

Reason 1: Command-and-Control Model

By far the biggest reason why OKRs fail is due to a command-and-control organizational model (often associated with Taylorism), rather than a mission-command model. In a command-and-control model, leaders dictate the rules by providing teams with solutions to implement, rather than inspiring teams to work towards certain outcomes by allowing them to solve problems. Some typical signs that you work in a command-and-control environment are as follows:

- Publicity or vanity-driven metrics influence business decisions (Willis 2012).
- Yearly employee ranking systems (Willis 2012).
- Measurement systems ignore variation and process control (Willis 2012).
- Strategic information is hidden for most employees. Financial numbers such as ARR/MMR, EBIT, and customer churn rate are not made transparent.
- The primary measure of success is delivered features, not achieved outcomes. When product features are not used, they don't get removed. Labor investments are rarely discarded in light of data and learning. Often, the team lacks the prerequisite safety to admit misfires (Cutler 2016).

- A culture of handoffs. There is a front-loaded process in place to "get ahead of the work" so that items are "ready for engineering." The team is not directly involved in research, problem exploration, or experimentation and validation. Once the product is shipped, the team has little contact with support, customer success, and sales (Cutler 2016).
- The presence of "project" or "feature" teams.
- The roadmaps consist of a list of features which are shipped without measuring their impact. For example, feature or project teams work on tasks assigned by their managers, giving them little room to use their skills and creativity.
- Engineers are afraid to run rapid experimentation loops on production systems. Software products are not instrumented with tools to measure business results.
- Direct contact with customers is discouraged. There is a "proxy" person who often can only transmit part of the information that teams need to make good decisions.
- You are still struggling to get Scrum to work or try to "scale" Agile with frameworks such as LeSS and SAFe.

For OKRs to work well, instead you need a mission-command organization, where leaders share information transparently and bring Objectives (problems to solve or "jobs to be done") to empowered, stable long-term teams. This is a model that entices strong leaders to hire great people and then *coach* them to help them solve complex problems. Leaders should *trust* and *empower* their teams to achieve results. These empowered teams are then able to solve problems and can be held accountable for their results (Cagan and Jones 2020, 4). This number one reason why OKRs fail will be addressed more deeply in the second part of this chapter and will be dealt with in relation to different aspects throughout the book. Especially important is Chapter 6, where I discuss how you, as a leader, can empower and trust your teams. Although most leaders would agree with these ideas, many (especially in top management) still find it hard to see how this can work in practice. OKRs work only in an environment where you have true cross-functional and empowered teams. If you haven't created these conditions in your organization, then OKRs are likely to fail. However, OKRs can also be the catalyst to set such an organizational culture in motion, and this will be explained later in this chapter.

Reason 2: Why, Why, Why?

What specific business problem do you want to solve with OKRs? As we saw in Chapter 1, alignment and focus aren't the right answers here. You want to take on OKRs to achieve something. Can you articulate and communicate this to your entire workforce? You should. Why OKRs? Why now? Why not? What pain does it solve for you and your employees? What big, hairy, audacious goal does it work toward? Have you looked at any alternatives? As with any change initiative within your organization, you must have answers to these questions. If you fail at this, OKRs are doomed to begin with. In this chapter, I provide you with information to determine where and when OKRs are the right choice.

Reason 3: Perfect Is the Enemy of Good

The best is the enemy of the good.

—Voltaire

When people start with OKRs, it can sometimes be confusing. What makes a good Objective? What do we look at in a KR? People can become really religious about this. Here, the general advice of "perfect is the enemy of good" applies. OKRs are a learning experience that encourages you to stretch what you think is achievable or possible. That means you will constantly improve the OKR system to suit your needs. You will discover how to do this in detail through the OKR Cycle in Part 2. However, there are some important guidelines you probably want to use. For example, an Objective needs to inspire people. How are you going to do this with just words?

Secondly, OKRs are about measuring and tracking progress toward your Objective. Measuring progress and performance can be very hard. How do we define good metrics? How do we collect data? What strategies should be used to interpret the data? How do we measure intangible things like behavior? How do we check in on our OKRs on a weekly basis and see progress? In Chapter 3, you will learn how to create (not perfect but good) OKRs. Good OKRs are a strong prerequisite to achieve big goals.

Over to You

In Chapter 1, you took a shot at writing some Objectives. Be honest, do they sound inspiring to you? Can you adjust or change them so that they could ignite that spark in your team?

Reason 4: A Lack of Focus

Peter Drucker wrote that innovation requires knowledge, ingenuity, and above all else, focus. OKRs help with focus, but only if you have the discipline to focus on one, or a maximum of two OKRs, at a time. Leaders and their teams easily get distracted by their business as usual (BAU) and (urgent) work, thus failing to work on important strategic goals. As they fight a constant battle between keeping the lights on and trying to move forward with their strategy, the BAU work will almost always gain prominence, stealing the focus away from stategic initiatives. With Lean OKRs, you will have the tools in place to win this battle.

Many organizations that make the decision to start with OKRs make the same mistake: They create too many OKRs at the executive level. Often, this is because they try to capture all the work (strategic and operational) into OKRs, which then cascade throughout the organization. When you follow this approach, you will end up with hundreds of OKRs throughout the organization. There is a well-known management consulting firm (I won't name names) that is still sending out junior consultants who advise that you should execute all your initiatives by only using OKRs. In my view, this is very disadvantageous, and in this chapter, I will outline in detail where and when OKRs should not be used. Lean OKRs are about creating less goals, the minimal amount of goals that are necessary to make the biggest impact for your organization. In Chapter 5, I'll dive deeper into the essence of the concept of Lean OKRs, the idea behind selecting a single OKR to rule them all.

Reason 5: Lack of Visible Results

Companies start with OKRs with good intentions and motivations. At the beginning of the year, OKRs for the year and quarter are formulated. For each Objective, perhaps there will be three or four KRs. Then, at the end of the first quarter, management or teams begin to notice that very little or nothing has yet been accomplished. They are left scratching their heads and wondering what went wrong. They might continue along this path for another quarter, but most probably, they will abandon OKRs and switch back to the status quo, all before reviewing the KRs and analyzing if they consisted of strong, appropriate indicators to measure the needle moving. It takes at least five quarters to start getting the hang of OKRs and their Cycle.

I can't blame management teams if they decide to no longer use OKRs. It is a logical response to the well-meant implementation of a system designed to keep us on track and accountable, but (similar to the gym) without discipline and seeing some motivating results, the desire to continue diminishes among the firefighting of BAU and instead is seen as just a waste of time. So, how can we get back on track? To keep people engaged, you need the data, measures, and a dashboard that are worth looking at, something we will look into in more detail in Chapter 13.

When and Where Are OKRs the Right Choice?

In recent years, OKRs have also gotten traction in other fields like personal development and product management. They are thus widely applicable. In this book, I focus on outlining the contexts in which using OKRs makes sense when you are in business.

OKRs evolved from MBOs, which are a tool to execute strategy. Therefore, OKR's primary purpose is too to *execute your strategy*, also known as *strategy deployment*. If your strategy is about how to achieve 10× growth, you need to think out of the box, innovate, take bold steps, and learn as fast as possible from your customers. By growth, I don't necessarily mean monetary growth. It can be growth of customers, intellectual property, human capital, and so on.

OKRs help execute your strategy to achieve this huge growth surge and help to simultaneously communicate your goals throughout the organization by making them transparent. They enable everyone close to your customers to make decisions based on what best aligns with the organization's strategic goals. So, OKRs can be applied when you want to execute an ambitious strategy, and as you will see below, they are especially suitable to drive innovation through behavior changes.

Culture Change

Human capital, your resources, or "people" as I like to call them, are the most valuable asset of your company. They've also created your "company culture," which is a set of behaviors typical for your company. Some attribute Peter Drucker to have said: "Culture eats strategy for breakfast." In fact, research has proven that there is a link between culture and outcomes: "When aligned with strategy and leadership, a strong culture drives positive organizational outcomes" (Groysberg, et al. 2018, 44–52). I can only confirm that having the right company culture is critical for achieving OKRs (outcomes). As I explained, the first reason why OKRs fail is because of the command-and-control model, which, unfortunately, is still used by many organizations today.

However, OKRs can also be used as a vehicle to drive the right culture change. When brave leaders of an organization that is leaning toward a command-and-control model start implementing OKRs, they are not entirely doomed. There are a few examples of companies that completely transformed their way of working in just a few years, effectively changing company culture, through the use of OKRs. One is the ING Bank in the Netherlands, which managed to transform its entire company to an Agile organization by successfully employing OKRs to overcome its main challenges, successfully shifting power from the top, getting buy-in from stakeholders, and changing employees' views about professional development (Birkinshaw 2017). This success was due to strong and visionary leaders at the top and caused a revolution in the enterprise world, both in organization modeling and ideas about company culture. I joined ING Bank after their transformation, and the result was remarkable: True cross-functional teams worked on complex customer problems. Of course, the transformation is never finished, but I was happy to see their efforts paying off. OKRs can thus be used to change the company culture, even when they are implemented with care in a command-and-control model. The organization will then change toward that of a mission-command model with the accompanying more generative culture, in which risk taking is encouraged and all have a stake in bringing the company to the next level.

There are several interrelated cultural factors that enhance the successful implementation of OKRs, and when OKRs are used, these cultural factors are further strengthened. Firstly, OKRs require transparency. OKRs require leaders and teams to be transparent about their goals by announcing them publicly, in turn fostering a more transparent way of working throughout the organization.

Secondly, OKRs are associated with a culture of transformation, because they require as well new ways of working, and to achieve this, people need to change their habits and behaviors. These behavior changes start with the executive team. Can these leaders let go of their control and shift their power to teams? Do they trust their teams, and if not, can they free up their precious time to actively coach their teams so trust can be established?

Thirdly, OKRs require and produce alignment. To move the needle of the company OKRs, leaders and their teams need to work collaboratively with other teams. Without alignment of your OKRs, you will keep organization silos intact and achieve only modest cooperation. My Lean approach to OKRs aligns all leaders, departments, and teams around one common goal, one company OKR, or one product OKR, which will set up teams for cross-department collaboration, giving them broad access to information. As a result, they will be encouraged to experiment and take risks in a physiologically safe environment and will be inclined to share their experiences openly because they are now all "in it together." In Chapter 8, we look at which different alignment strategies can be used in more detail and how the OKR alignment workshop facilitates and strengthens collaborative processes.

Finally, experimentation is required and failed experiments are inevitable (Kohavi and Thomke 2017). Experimentation is thus embedded within the process of OKRs and therefore will thrive if leaders provide teams the autonomy and safety to do so, fostering a culture where failure leads not to condemnation but to inquiry.

The fact that you enroll OKRs and the OKR cycle can thus help to change the mindsets of many, catalyzing changes toward a generative culture. As part of this culture change, OKRs can simultaneously be used strategically to build new empowered team topologies, although this requires careful timing and active involvement of senior management. One caveat with culture change is that you need to pay attention to emotional management too, which we touch upon later in this chapter.

Team Effectiveness

OKRs help to focus on structure and clarity, provide meaning and purpose, and let you see your impact on the bigger picture. They contribute to what Google found to be the five pillars of high-performance teams (Duhigg 2016). Psychological safety is by far the most important pillar and prerequisite. OKRs also play an important role to support the other pillars, like dependability, structure and clarity, meaning, and seeing impact.

For me, the striking similarity between these found five pillars of highly successful teams and the philosophy, and practice of OKRs was a great eye opener, and kindled my motivation to fully adopt them. When used properly, OKRs can make a *significant* change in how teams perform. For many companies, this can lead them to achieve the breakthrough goal they need to get closer to their vision and mission. In Chapter 6, we will explore how OKRs can help to charter effective teams.

Innovation

Peter Drucker is famously quoted as saying: "Because the purpose of business is to create a customer, the business enterprise has two—and only two—basic functions: *marketing* and *innovation*. Marketing and innovation produce results; all the rest are costs" (Drucker 1977, 90).

Keeping that in mind, how many of you have sat through C-level meetings where their priorities are finances, sales, production, legal issues, and (finally) people. Typically missing from their list of concerns is marketing and innovation. Exactly the two areas that Drucker argues are the only two that matter. Take a moment to close your eyes and imagine companies that focus on constant innovation and then the marketing of their products (and their story). Compare that against companies that you know are floundering. It's not a stretch to see that if they would be able to shift their focus to those two key areas, there could be light at the end of the tunnel for them.

Innovation brings more customers (or as Seth Godin likes to put it: better customers) and better results (Godin 2018). Sounds easy right? Just set very ambitious goals: "Travel to Mars within 20 seconds" and innovation will happen. I wish it was that easy. Innovation requires trust, agility, the ability to try and fail, and to learn from failures.

Innovation is not about technology nor about implementing the latest organizational models. I always giggle a bit when companies adopt an organization model from a completely different type of business (e.g., banks that adopted the "Spotify organization model"). Unfortunately, many leaders still believe they can take shortcuts to innovation: by starting accelerators, business incubators, research and development hubs, hiring innovation consultants, acquiring start-ups, or blindly adopting the latest digital technologies. I propose a strategy toward innovation that hinges on bringing complex problems to cross-functional (product) teams that will find unique and creative solutions to these problems. That requires teams to generate insights and then to run considerable numbers of experiments to find the right solution for the problem. As Marty Cagan said: "Innovation is the function of the number of experiments we can run" (Cagan 2019). As a great measure for innovation, I very much like the idea to "measure the percentage of revenue that was coming from products and services introduced in the past few years" (Cagan 2011). This metric will almost always force leaders to completely rethink their revenue models every couple of years and help them to come up with great innovative products.

Is your organization ready to experiment, cannibalize stale business practices, or suspend today's distribution model? What can you achieve within your constraints (time, costs, and scope)? The higher the goal temperature, the more innovation it requires to reach those goals. This leads to demands on both people and processes:

- People: Innovation requires you to have diverse people with a growth mindset in your organization, willing to solve complex problems. For example, MIT's Mediated Matter research group, headed by Professor Neri Oxman, is using a diverse group of artists, biochemists, and engineers to solve climate problems (Green 2018).

- Process: How fast can we learn from our market, customers, and other stakeholders. If you cannot experiment and learn faster than your competitors, you will be out of business soon. Hence, the "disrupters," small technology companies that learn and experiment at high speed.

Finally, behavior is where people and processes come together. If you want to generate significant positive cash flow, what kind of human (customer or employee) behavior is required to achieve that goal? Can you measure that? If you want to reduce customer churn, the desired behavior might be that your employees will greet customers in a different way. Or maybe, it's that you need to offer them better products or services or limit choices to increase quality. Depending on your goal, you might want to think about different ways people must behave in order to meet your goals. In other words, what behavioral innovation is required? What skills and competencies are required?

Operational Excellence

When a company starts with OKRs, there will most likely be many obstacles to overcome before the true power of OKRs can reveal itself. One of these is the need for operational excellence teams, preferably all equipped with a Lean or Agile mindset. Many companies starting with OKRs use them as an opportunity to clean house. They change their internal processes to prepare for the big change to come. During the first few OKR cycles, leaders use the momentum of OKRs to focus on process improvements or even innovations. Teams need a high level of operational excellence before they can start working on complex business problems. OKRs can help you challenge the whole organization to think about how the company should be structured and how processes could be improved. I always enjoy seeing hidden process constraints unfolded and solved when leaders set goals beyond what they thought was possible. When OKRs reveal these constraints, people can use the techniques described in Part 3 of this book to remove them.

OKRs as Strategy Communicators

The key to creating an organization that can innovate at scale is that it enables frontline workers, who solve customers' problems on a daily basis to make the best decisions possible, aligned with the overall company strategy. The authors of *Lean Enterprise* wrote: "To achieve this, we rely on people being able to make local decisions that are sound at a strategic level—which in turn relies critically on the flow of information, including feedback loops" (Humble et al. 2015, 9). However, to align people with the company strategy, to let information flow, to develop and let OKRs function, people need to understand what the underlying strategy is.

Research has found that "on average, 95% of a company's employees are unaware of, or do not understand, its strategy" (Kaplan and Norton 2005, 72–80), and that "one-third of the leaders charged with implementing the company's strategy could not list even one [strategic initiative]" (Sull et al. 2018). As a result, the following points are true of too many organizations (you may recognize a few):

- The Organizational Health Index (OHI) or similar employee survey results indicate a lack of clear direction.
- Employees say they lack clarity and focus, and they don't know where the company is going.
- The motivation of the employees is lagging due to a lack of purpose.
- There is little to or no innovation or learning initiatives going on.
- Repeated change initiatives fail.
- Too many constantly changing high priority projects distract people from the overall strategy.
- There are too many ad hoc issues and there's too much firefighting.

This list goes on and on. Now, if you think OKRs will solve all these problems overnight, I need to warn you. Even with OKRs, you can still have all the issues described earlier. However, when implemented with the guidelines provided in this book, you can eliminate most of them. I will show you how you can use OKRs as a great vehicle to communicate some of your company's strategic Objectives in a simple, compact way.

Surrogation

OKRs are never a replacement for solid strategy planning (and I dare say strong leadership and communication skills). It's just easier to communicate OKRs than a 100-page strategic plan. But remember that OKRs are only part of that plan. The HBR article "Don't Let Metrics Undermine Your Business" (Harris and Tayler 2019) expands on the concept of *surrogation* in corporate contexts, focusing on the tendency people have to mentally replace a strategy (or vision for that matter) with metrics. Make sure you don't make this mistake by "replacing" your strategy with just OKRs (and their cousin KPIs).

Focusing OKRs on Behavior Changes

Now that you know in which company contexts OKRs are the right choice, we will further specify how and where you should apply them. The processes, attitude, and culture changes that are required to revolutionize the execution of your company strategy often can only be achieved when people (customers, employees, your teammates, citizens, and so on.) change their behavior. A study by consulting firm Bain and Company (Litré et al. 2018) analyzed barriers to successful change management at 184 global companies and found that when executing strategic plans, a stunning "65% of initiatives required significant behavioral change on the part of front-line employees—something that managers often fail to consider." While I was researching this topic, a new world opened up for me. If you read between the lines of all books on building a successful business, you will discover a pattern. The one idea that stands out the most is behavior change. However, these are often not easy to administer.

Take the following example: At the time of writing, we are in the midst of the Covid-19 pandemic, and the strategy in my country to fight the virus is called a "smart lockdown." To succeed with this strategy, the government requires people to change their behavior by keeping 1.5 meters distance and wearing protective masks in public places. It's critical to change behavior of citizens, because the political leaders do not have the capacity to observe and control every act of these citizens. However, if the strategy is only addressed occasionally, it won't have as big an effect as a change in overall behavior, which is a shift at the basic or ground level, addressing something at the roots. Without true behavioral changes, the whole strategy to keep the virus contained will fail. Thus, behavior change is by far the most difficult component of any strategy execution, but also one of the most powerful, and should therefore be the main focus of OKRs.

To really leverage the power of OKRs, you need to carefully look at your current company strategy and ask: How can we use OKRs as a lever to execute our behavior change strategy? With which strategic Objectives do we really need a change in human behavior (both in employees and customers)? In which area do we need significant improvement? When this has become clear, you ask: Does it require a change in human behavior to get us to the desired result? If the answer to the final question is yes, then you know you should be developing OKRs in this space.

Distinguishing Behavior and Sign-and-Go Strategies

To gauge if a specific strategy or initiative requires behavior changes, I have developed a simple division that is inspired by *The 4 Disciplines of Execution* (McChesney et al. 2012), also known as 4DX. I'm a great fan of this set of proven practices aiming to execute your most important strategic initiatives. The concepts from 4DX and OKRs are quite similar, and I adapted some of the elements of 4DX to improve and streamline applied results of OKRs.

According to the 4DX approach, you can breakup strategies or initiatives that significantly move the needle for you team or organization into two categories:

- *Sign-and-go strategies* as I like to call them (in 4DX they are called stroke-of-the-pen). If you have the mandate and budget, place your signature at the bottom a document to get the ball rolling: a major acquisition, adding new employees, buying a new software tool, a new marketing campaign, or approving a project. The strategies will contribute to the growth of your companies, but won't (immediately) require a behavior change.

- *Behavior change strategies* are different, because they require people to change their behavior and habits. You cannot order your customers to use your product differently or to invite their friends to use your service. You cannot order your employees to do something different they have never done before. You probably know how hard it is to let people change their way of working (Figure 2.1).

This distinction is not absolute. For example, sometimes it can happen that a sign-and-go strategy evolves into a behavior change strategy. If you are a company building bookkeeping software and you want to change your licensing model from an on-premise perpetual model to cloud-based subscription model, you can sign and approve that strategy. However, all of a sudden, your employees need to learn new skills to make

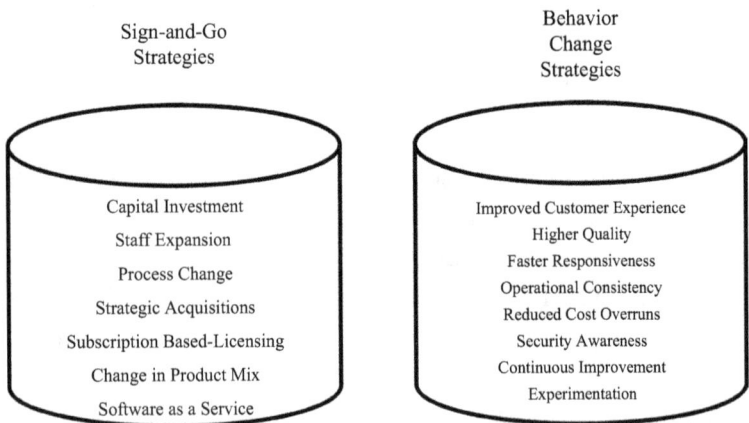

Figure 2.1 Different buckets of strategic initiatives. Sign-and-go versus behavior change

your software suitable for the cloud. More importantly, they now need to provide 24/7 maintenance support to keep the system running. This will require people to change their behavior. Your sign-and-go strategy has now become a behavior change strategy.

Over to You

Exercise: Divide and conquer (10 minutes)

Take a moment to look at your strategy and write down a list of all your strategic initiatives. Take a piece of paper and draw a line in the middle. Divide the list of initiatives of the two categories: sign-and-go and behavior change. Can you now select an initiative from the behavior change category that would make all the difference to your overall company strategy?

Difficulties With Behavior Changes

Often, management believes the reason teams struggle with strategy execution is obvious. As a manager once told me: "The team just lacks commitment and accountability." Some say that their teams don't have the right skills to make significant changes. Other reasons could be that people aren't feeling trusted, there are misaligned compensation systems, poor development processes in place, poor decision making, or people are simply not held accountable for results.

Although all above reasons might be valid, we can assign them to one root cause. It's the complete organizational system that is responsible for the inability to achieve strategic goals. To quote the authors of 4DX: "Any time the majority of people behave in a particular way the majority of the time, the people are not the problem. The problem is inherit in the system. As a leader you own responsibility of the system" (McChesney, et al. 2012, 5). More often than not, it appears that if people don't understand the strategy or the goals, they are not committed to it.

Old habits die hard, as they say, and just because teams have received word from management that they need to change or do things differently, this does not at all mean everyone will be jumping on board. Behavior changes might require more drastic means, such as shuffling team members and reassignments to expose them to other ways of doing things. This is going to be uncomfortable for everyone involved.

The Number One Enemy of Behavior Change Strategies

In many cases, the greatest enemy of failing strategy execution and thus OKRs is your daily work. BAU, or also the "whirlwind," pulls at us like a gravitational force. It distracts us every time and prevents us from achieving our goals.

BAU is all the stuff you do to sell, build, and make your customers and employees happy. To companies with software teams, I would like to mention that, yes, developing software features is BAU, too! What else would your development teams do? At the same time, it also prevents you from executing something new.

The whirlwind, BAU, old habits, status quo, and mediocrity are something that we humans love, no matter what we call it. Staying in our comfort zone, we go to work and do our "thing," day in and day out. We are on autopilot, doing what we know has worked before. As a consequence, we learn a little less every day and achieving ambitious goals is not even on our radar. It's the work and behaviors that people don't like or don't do yet that will boost their and the company performance.

Systems thinking theory (Meadows 2008) teaches that any time you try to change a stable system, you are likely to fail, because it always wants to go back to its status quo. It is the same with your organization and teams. Every initiative you launch that tries to change will be pulled back by the gravitational force of the system that we call BAU.

The Business as Usual Trap

Once you get started with OKRs, it is tempting to use them widely and indiscriminately. Every goal in your organization seems a potential candidate to transform into OKRs. Converting all of your BAU goals in your organization into OKRs is a natural response from many leaders who are new to OKRs. You *can* use OKRs wherever you use goals, but that doesn't mean you need to. Initially, it will provide value: Your goals will become more measurable and structured. They are also transparent and give you frequent feedback, but it's a trap. Before you know it, you are back to mediocrity, now managed by OKRs, and nothing significant has changed. Also, you end up with hundreds of OKRs throughout the organization, so it's no wonder you need OKR software to "manage" them.

I've visited many organizations where the label "OKRs" is used everywhere and has lost its transformative power within the organization. People start to "OKR" everything, resulting in generic and soul-less OKRs. If, instead, you want to make significant changes, you must use the label "OKRs" with care. Only use them for executing behavior change strategies, your breakthrough goals.

The Breakthrough Goal

Habits are hard to beat. Probably the most important limitation that needs to be considered when changing behavior is that you simply cannot change too many behavioral traits at the same time. It's for a reason that there are these 30-day challenges to get you back in shape, to quit smoking, and to change your diet. Changing human behavior takes focus, determination, and time, and you can only change a limited number of habits in a short period.

Therefore, breakthrough goals form a central component of the Lean OKR philosophy. If you don't focus, and if you don't make tough decisions, then OKRs won't have the impact they could have in your organization. You need to learn to say no, even to great ideas that come your way, in order to create real focus and see real results. As attention and focus are often totally wrapped up in the sign-and-go and BAU activities, the place where focus would truly make a difference too often gets pushed to the backburner. The focus needs to be on one breakthrough goal represented by a single set of companywide OKRs.

Breakthrough goals go under different names, for example, step change, crowbar, or booster. As we can also learn from 4DX author McChesney: "Breakthrough goals almost always require a change in human behaviour. This is not something you can demand from your teams; rather, you will require the commitment of their hearts and minds" (McChesney 2020).

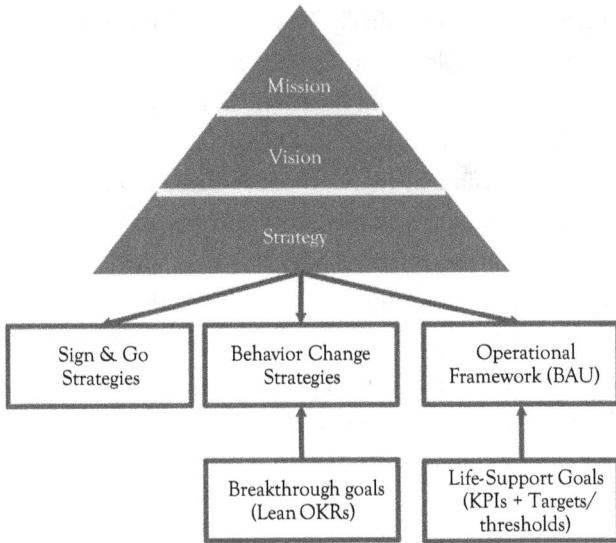

**Figure 2.2 Three buckets to divide your strategic aspects into.
Breakthrough goals (Lean OKRs) are part of your behavior
change strategy**

You reach this through granting them trust and autonomy. In Chapter 5,
you will learn how to select the right breakthrough goals.

The behaviors of your company's people may prevent you from achieving growth and executing your strategy, and this may include your own
past behaviors that have fed into the status quo. Any growth strategy that
creates significant breakthroughs eventually requires a behavioral change
strategy. This should be clearly distinct from sign-and-go strategies and
the operational framework of BAU (see Figure 2.2).

How can you achieve your growth strategy in the midst of day-to-
day operations? Hire more people? Maybe hire better people? Growing
and improving your workforce is only part of that strategy. You also
need to change people's behavior to adapt them to new ways of working.
You need an approach to align, engage, measure, motivate, and create
accountability in teams that enables them to execute your growth strategy. I am talking about complete enterprise agility, responding to market
change when it needs to. It is all about how your customers, employees,
co-workers, and teammates behave. OKRs are meant for this. They are

Example: Breakthrough Goal

Let's say that you are leading a SaaS company and decided to conquer a new market, in this case the health care market. This decision can be categorized as a sign-and-go strategy. However, it could be that you now require a breakthrough goal to open up this new market. You created the following OKR for your company:

Objective: Crack the health care market.

KRs:

- Increase total health care customers with a basic subscription from 0 to 200 per week.
- Increase total health care customers with a premium subscription from 0 to 20 per week.
- Increase number of daily active health care customers from segment XYZ to 100 per day.

Now it's time to challenge everybody in the company to move the needle on the KRs in the next 90 days. Because you are entering a new market, not only your new customers need to change their behavior to start using your product but also your employees need to change their behavior and habits in order to serve this new market. The Lean OKRs will compete with all your BAU goals to improve on your operational KPIs to make sure you stay in business. So to taking a chance against your BAU, you want to focus on only a single OKR and build in the OKR cycle to have a fair chance of winning.

the tool you can use to achieve this behavior change in and outside your organization.

Investing in Breakthrough OKRs

It has to be kept in mind that Lean OKRs are what teams must do *in addition* to their BAU activities, integrating into their daily working patterns. This doesn't mean people need to work harder, but they need to work smarter. Some companies allocate 20 percent of their annual budget to work on OKRs, while others make allocation of resources the responsibility of the teams. The amount of time and energy that teams need to spend on OKRs will be different each quarter, because the nature of the OKRs might be different. One quarter the OKRs may be about generating more leads and the next quarter they may be about customer satisfaction. This means some teams will barely spend 20 percent of their time on OKRs, while others may spend maybe 70 percent of their time on their OKRs (see Figure 2.3). As you will read in Chapter 5, sometimes teams cannot contribute to company OKRs at all—which is fine.

In product development, it's a different story. Since most OKRs will be focused on customers and products, most of your teams will spend more than 70 percent of their time on OKRs. That said, from my own experience I see that, especially in larger companies, in the first few cycles, the company OKRs tend to be focused on changing internal employee behavior. This internal focus allows leaders to make significant changes in internal processes, flow, and product quality. Even more importantly, they allow for experimentation within existing products as well as new markets. As a result of these improvements, the daily operation runs more smoothly and more time can be spent on (and experimenting with) change of customer behavior, which ultimately leads to growth and innovation.

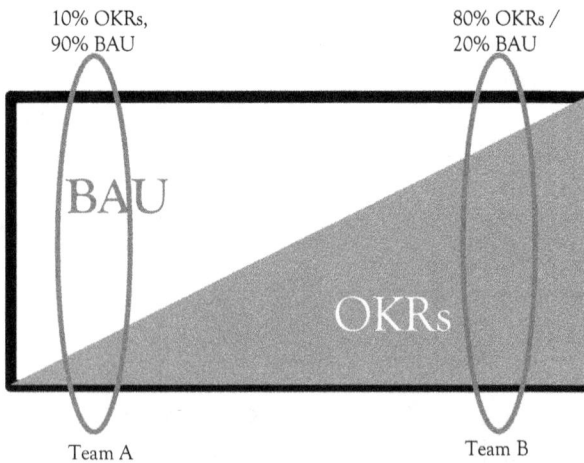

Figure 2.3 The distribution of BAU and OKRs "work" can change per quarter and per team

How Not to Use OKRs

In many cases, teams jump from OKRs straight into what are sometimes called "OKR initiatives." They believe they can define a whole list of action items upfront, at the start of an OKR cycle, to achieve the Objective. If it is possible to achieve your OKRs that easily, by simply defining initiatives, projects, or a to-do list, then it is probably safe to say that your Objective wasn't that much of a stretch to begin with.

The Horrible Action Item List

So, what are the specific reasons that an action item list approach is not recommended for achieving OKRs? Mike Rother, the author of *Toyota Kata* (Rother 2009, 30) provides a summary that explains it all:

- It is inefficient. Honestly, how many change initiatives or tasks have you been working on for the past months? Which of them have had significant results? It looks like a lot is happening, but in reality, there is little progress.
- We are in the dark. Running multiple action items at once doesn't give us a clear picture of what works and what doesn't. Admitting that you don't know what to improve to achieve your OKRs is perfectly fine, but often so hard to say.
- We are asking ourselves the wrong question. "What can we do?" is the wrong question. "What do we need?" is a better and more difficult question.
- We are jumping to countermeasures too soon. A lot of the time we jump to conclusions even before we truly understand the situation.
- We are not developing our people's capabilities. If it is easy and just part of their normal job, then people are not learning how to expand their problem-solving skills. If, however, you can equip your people with these skills, you will also reap the long-term benefits.

The more action items we have, the more "productive" we feel, but executing these action items doesn't require anybody to change their routines or habits. To achieve significant results, we need to systematically change the behavior of people (customers and employees). A list may work when you are in fact converting your BAU goals into OKRs. However, this means you would simply be defining a focused form of BAU work.

If OKRs are employed in this way, people will continue to complain about a lack of focus and direction. Even worse, if you try to capture all of your "business as usual" activities using OKRs, then what is the point of using OKRs in the first place? OKRs are not a tool to replace operational management tools and techniques; therefore, it is easy to predict that if this is your approach, you probably won't achieve any of your goals and, before you know it, OKRs will be the next management fad in your organization.

Project Portfolio Management

Larger companies often use project portfolio management (PPfM) to focus on doing the right projects at the right time, by selecting and managing projects as a portfolio of investments (Oltmann 2008). Managers can use company OKRs as a direction to help in selecting the right projects. This might seems like a good solution, and I've seen this approach many times in practice. However, projects actually aren't very suitable for achieving OKRs. There are four main reasons for this:

1. OKRs require stable, cross-functional teams to run small experiments. Often, project-based teams are created only for the duration of the project. This will prevent people to continuously learn as a team. In Chapter 6, we will explore in more detail how teams best function in the context of OKRs.
2. If OKRs are truly stretched goals, you will not be able to plan and estimate projects upfront, because you will be running into unknown territory all the time. You can only start projects if the risks are limited and the work is predictable, that is when you know how to achieve a certain outcome with a fair amount of certainty. Often achieving OKRs is the opposite, they are about taking risks, making

bets, learning, and experimenting. They are about achieving ambitious goals. In Chapter 12, you will find out more about how to run these experiments.

3. Sometimes people treat OKRs as a project in and of itself. For example, by having an Objective as "Finish project XYZ" or "Launch customer X on our platform." Then, these projects often are separated into phases: for example, an inception, elaboration, construction, and transition phase. Then, within these phases, you can have milestones such as "requirements defined" or "testing completed." However, these aren't necessary good progress indicators to track progress on a weekly basis, neither will they result in behavior change.

4. Projects run over and fail with disturbing regularity. In an alarming study, 1,471 IT projects were compared on budgets and their estimated performance benefits with the actual costs and results. When they broke down the costs running over, they found something that "the average overrun was 27%—but that figure masks a far more alarming one. Graphing the projects' budget overruns reveals a 'fat tail'—a large number of gigantic overages. Fully one in six of the projects we studied was a black swan, with a cost overrun of 200%, on average, and a schedule overrun of almost 70%" (Flyvbjerg and Budzier 2011).

If you would like to learn more, I recommend reading the mini book *#noprojects* (Leybourn and Hastie 2018). In it, the authors argue for the use of adaptive portfolios, which consist of initiatives that continuously deliver (customer) value, rather than a sequence of activities with no clear outcomes. The launch of a new website, the implementation of a new office application, General Data Protection Regulation (GDPR) compliancy, but also the implementation of OKRs themselves are examples of such initiatives. However, don't fall into the trap of adding "OKR initiatives" to your portfolio, because all your initiatives inside your (enterprise) portfolio will fall into the categories we discussed earlier: sign-and-go or BAU. In Part 3 of this book, you will learn how you can best achieve OKRs without the need to run long initiatives or projects.

Using OKRs to Describe ROI

Traditionally, Return on Investment (ROI) was used to justify the budget of a (large) project. Now, by employing OKRs, people are able to better describe the ROI in terms of the business outcomes. Although this is partly a very positive development, the true nature of OKRs starts to fade when they are used like this.

This can be illustrated by an example from software product development, which is on the rise worldwide. Many people suppose that describing an initiative, a feature or project goal in the OKR format will help software engineering teams to think in outcomes of the project ("Increase the conversion rate from free to paid accounts of 2%"), rather than blindly taking orders ("launch new feature X") from product managers or product owners—a phenomenon known as the "feature factory" (Cutler 2016). They are right that the latter could contribute to the conversion rate, but does this strategy help you to know if you are having actual success? Is the success of your features measured after they are released? By describing the outcome instead of taking orders (focus on output), you give the autonomy back to the team/engineers, so they can leverage their knowledge and skills to solve the problem. When you don't reserve the label "OKRs" only for big transformative changes, their transformative power is watered down.

Key Considerations to Solidify Your Success

Now that you know for which kind of companies OKRs are most suitable, what purpose they serve, and in which kind of cases they should be applied, I will give you some practical advice on what you should further consider to make your use of OKRs a success.

Emotional Management

Introducing OKRs requires significant change in employee behavior and an even bigger change in your workplace culture. OKRs require people to change both their way of thinking and their way of working (which is their own invented, time-tested, most-efficient method *for them*, not necessarily for the business). What you are asking of people isn't something small. Implementing OKRs isn't a project that you do. It's how you and everybody in the organization are going to work from now on.

To get people out of their comfort zone—which is what you do when you get them to change their behavior—you need to have a strong incentive. Without this, your OKR implementation will undoubtedly fail. The "why," as described earlier, will give you some guidance. People need to feel the urgency. This requires senior management to increase the emotional temperature in order to kick-start this behavioral change; otherwise nothing will change at all.

Multidisciplinary and Multidiverse Teams

In my experience, the best, most innovative, and ground-breaking results stem from multidisciplinary and multidiverse teams. This goes beyond people with different professional skills and diversity in gender and nationality. The Inclusive Collaboration, founded by Dr. Sallyann Freudenberg and Katherine Kirk, is about learning how to harness the benefits of broad neurodiversity rather than attempting to wedge everyone into a constrictive monoculture (Freudenberg 2016). This means that a broad variation in people's brains and how they function, for example, becoming manifest with regard to sociability, learning, attention, mood, and other mental functions, is approached as an asset. In my career, I've worked a lot with neurodiverse teams, and I have witnessed the most extraordinary solutions to really difficult to achieve (engineering) goals.

Ownership

Many executives make the mistake to hand over the OKR initiative to their HR department. Embedding OKRs into the DNA of your company should be the responsibility of one or more members of the executive team. Without their support, without their explanation of why it is important, implementing OKRs will fail. The reason is simple. OKRs are about executing strategy, and strategic planning is the task of the executive team. The executive team owns the strategic plan and also the highest level OKRs, the company OKRs. This does not prohibit you to involve other people to facilitate logistics and workshops when you cascade OKRs throughout the organization (see Chapter 5).

Old Habits Die Hard

For OKRs to flourish, existing cultural and operational patterns of the organization need to be upgraded. If all existing patterns remain, then the organization will simply do more of the same (with the same subpar results). Even with OKRs in place, I have still come across organizations with siloed departments, misaligned teams, low employee engagement, even lower commitment, and little to no innovation.

If you have seen the attempted implementation of Scrum or DevOps to become more "agile" and they failed miserably, then why do you believe OKRs are promising? If change initiatives fail within your organization, then there might be a structural problem—a pattern. Evaluate the roadblocks and fix those first before starting to implement OKRs.

The most successful OKR implementations I've seen are within organizations that are already fluent in Agile practices (see also Larsen and Shore 2018). That doesn't mean your organization won't be successful in implementing OKRs, it just requires momentous upfront dedication from senior management, including intensive investment in:

- Team development and work process design
- Acceptance of lower productivity during (technical) skill development
- Social capital expended on moving business decisions and expertise into the team
- Time and effort in developing new approaches to managing the organization

How to Start Implementation

To increase the likelihood that OKRs will launch well within your organization, you should try to limit the scope of the implementation at first. It is important to devise a plan whereby you can test OKRs within an isolated environment with a trusted team before you communicate your vision and behavior change strategies to your workforce. This way you can evaluate some solid results from practical issues, adjust your vision and scope, have a sketched-out plan for introducing OKRs, and anticipate what the workforce could expect (how their world would change) and what kind of team(s) would be required. There are a few options but here are some of my favorites that I often recommend to clients.

C-Level Team

If you're the leader of a company, on the board, or somehow in charge of the business, you might want to start with Lean OKRs with your executive team first. Since OKRs help you to execute corporate strategy, the ideal case is to start with all members of the executive team involved.

Perhaps, start by just setting a single OKR for a quarter to impact a critical metric within your organization. Don't announce or distribute the full roster of OKRs just yet. Try using them within your C-level team for a few OKR cycles first. If they work for your team, you can present your learning experiences and insights to the rest of the organization. Furthermore, test driving first also means you're talking from experience, not only theoretically. Leading by example is a management technique I favor and always recommend to my clients.

Pilot Project

Start a Lean OKR pilot project. Use a cross-functional team or department as your test group. When OKRs start to bear fruit, you can use this group as an example for other teams and departments. Alternatively, you can wait until other managers spot the team's superior performance and use this as the trigger to experiment with OKRs at higher levels within your organization (hopefully now with those managers' buy-in). It is important that you have buy-in from the executive team, since you will need their help to execute part of the strategy.

Educate and Scale OKRs

After you have booked some successes with the executive or pilot team, you can scale OKRs. Don't rush into demanding all teams to set and use OKRs. Instead, use a phased approach, where you first provide education, background, preliminary results, respond pragmatically to questions or concerns and only then ask people to start using them.

In Chapter 5, we explore how cascading OKRs work in more detail, but here is a simplified version of an OKR rollout plan:

Phase one:

- Educate leadership team.
- Leadership team develops health metrics (KPIs) at company level.
- Setup a pilot product team
- Leadership team sets first company OKRs.
- Leadership team silently uses OKRs.
- Educate middle management.

Phase two:

- Educate teams, leads and form ambassadors.
- Middle management provides coaching to cross-functional teams.
- Teams develop health metrics (KPIs).
- Teams set OKRs.

Over to You

Exercise: Envision the ideal

How would the world within your organization look with OKRs, from beginning to end, and how would you get there? What kind of customer or employee behavior is aligned with that vision? What would you expect from your workforce? How would you define the success of OKRs?

Chapter Recap

In this chapter, we've explored the fact that using OKRs is challenging and addressed the five key reasons why many organizations fail. Throughout the chapter, I explained strategies to avoid such pitfalls.

We've established when and where to employ Lean OKRs, highlighting that this tool is commonly used to achieve big results—results that can't easily be achieved at the normal rate of operation. We have addressed the importance of company culture, and the fact that a cultural, organizational, and behavioral shift is likely to be required for your company to implement OKRs successfully.

We've looked at how you might get started with Lean OKRs, by focusing on behavior change strategies, the breakthroughs that are required to make significant changes, how to keep things manageable, and how to foster companywide buy-in. The best application of OKRs is cases where a company or organization has reached a plateau and needs to essentially breathe a breath of fresh air into the way that they are doing things, both internally and externally, to reinvigorate teams, grow brand awareness, see their needle move, engage on a whole other level with their competitors, and achieve big, hairy, audacious goals that are thought to be impossible. They are ready to take risks, change behaviors, learn from mistakes, encourage regular communication through check-ins, and take front-end employee ideas to heart in improving the customer experience. OKRs are the cure for stagnation.

You should now realize that OKRs cannot magically solve problems with your company's strategy. However, OKRs can help you execute that strategy when your goals are realistic and you enable everyone to engage in the process.

Chapter References

Birkinshaw, J. December 11, 2017. "What to Expect From Agile." *MITSloan*. Winter 2018 Issue. https://sloanreview.mit.edu/article/what-to-expect-from-agile/

Cagan, M. December 11, 2011. "Measuring Innovation." https://svpg.com/measuring-innovation/

Cagan, M. June 17, 2019. "Product is Hard." Published by James Gadsby Peet Mind the Product Conference. www.mindtheproduct.com/product-is-hard-by-marty-cagan/ Video at: 08:07

Cagan, M., and C. Jones. 2020. *Empowered: Ordinary People, Extraordinary Products*. New Jersey, NJ: Wiley.

Cutler, J. November 17, 2016. "12 Signs You're Working in a Feature Factory." https://cutle.fish/blog/12-signs-youre-working-in-a-feature-factory

De la, Boutetière, H., A. Montagner, and A. Reich. 2018. "Unlocking Success in Digital Transformations." Survey by McKinsey and Company. www.

mckinsey.com/business-functions/organization/our-insights/unlocking-success-in-digital-transformations

Doerr, J. April 2018. "Why the Secret to Success is Setting the Right Goals." Filmed at TED Conference, Vancouver, Video, www.ted.com/talks/john_doerr_why_the_secret_to_success_is_setting_the_right_goals/transcript?language=en

Drucker, P.F. 1977. *People and Performance*. New York, NY: Butterworth-Heinemann.

Duhigg, C. 2016. "What Google Learned From Its Quest to Build the Perfect Team." *New York Times*, February 25, 2016 www.nytimes.com/2016/02/28/magazine/what-google-learned-from-its-quest-to-build-the-perfect-team.html?smid=pl-share

Flyvbjerg, B., and A. Budzier. September 2011. *Why Your IT Project May Be Riskier Than You Think*. Boston: Harvard Business Review. From the Magazine.

Freudenberg, S. 2016. "Inclusive Collaboration and the Silence Experiment." *InfoQ Article*, www.infoq.com/articles/inclusive-collaboration-silence-experiment/ (accessed November 14, 2016).

Godin, S. November 13, 2018. *This Is Marketing: You Can't Be Seen Until You Learn to See*. Portfolio; Illustrated ed.

Gothelf, J. 2018. "You Suck at OKRs. Here's Why." *Medium*, https://medium.com/@jboogie/you-suck-at-okrs-heres-why-84e7bf2836d3(accessed February 9, 2018).

Green, P. October 6, 2018. "Who Is Neri Oxman?" *New York Times*, www.nytimes.com/2018/10/06/style/neri-oxman-mit.html

Groysberg, B., J. Lee, J. Price, and J. Cheng. January–February 2018. *The Leader's Guide to Corporate Culture*, 44–52. Boston: Harvard Business Review Magazine.

Harris, M., and B. Tayler. September–October 2019. *Don't Let Metrics Undermine Your Business*. Boston: Harvard Business Review.

Humble, J., J. Molesky, and B. O'Reilly. 2015. *Lean Enterprise: How High Performance Organizations Innovate at Scale*. 1st edition. Sebastopol: O'Reilly Media.

Kaplan, R.S., and D.P. Norton. October 2005. *The Office of Strategy Management*, 72–80. Boston: Harvard Business Review.

Klau, R. 2018. "How OKRs Fuel Innovation." https://rework.withgoogle.com/blog/how-OKRs-fuel-innovation/ (accessed May 01, 2018).

Kohavi, R., and S. Thomke. September-October 2017. *The Surprising Power of Online Experiments*. Boston: Harvard Business Review. From the Magazine.

Larsen, D., and J. Shore. 2018. "The Agile Fluency Model: A Brief Guide to Success with Agile." Blog: https://martinfowler.com/articles/agileFluency.html (accessed March 6, 2018).

Leybourn, E., and S. Hastie. 2018. *#noprojects*. C4Media, publisher of InfoQ. com

Litré, P., D. Michels, I. Hindshaw and P. Ghosh. 2018. *Results Delivery®: Busting Three Common Myths of Change Management*. Bain & Company. www.bain. com/insights/results-delivery-busting-3-common-change-management-myths/

McChesney, C. July 16, 2020. *Executing in Complexity*. YouTube. https://youtu. be/vOYj_-pYpPc

McChesney, C., S. Covey, and J. Huling. 2012. *The 4 Disciplines of Execution: Achieving Your Wildly Important Goals*, 1st ed. New York, NY: Free Press.

Meadows, D. 2008. *Thinking in Systems: A Primer*. London: Chelsea Green Publishing.

Oltmann, J. 2008. "Project Portfolio Management: How to do the Right Projects at the Right Time." Paper presented at PMI® Global Congress 2008. North America, Denver, CO. Newtown Square, PA. Project Management Institute.

Osmak, I. 2017. "Why OKRs Fail." *Medium*, https://medium.com/@iosmak/why-okrs-fail-fc9ad804dde9(accessed June 9, 2017).

Sull, D., C. Sull, and Y. James. 2018. *No One Knows Your Strategy—Not Even Your Top Leaders*. Cambridge: MIT Sloan Management Review. February 12, 2018. Obtained from https://sloanreview.mit.edu/article/no-one-knows-your-strategy-not-even-your-top-leaders/

Sull, D., R. Homkes, and C. Sull. March 2015. *Why Strategy Execution Unravels—and What to Do About It*, 58–66. Boston: Harvard Business Review.

Willis, J. October 23, 2012. "Neo Taylorism or DevOps Anti Patterns." Portland: ITrevolution. https://itrevolution.com/neo-taylorism-or-devops-anti-patterns/

CHAPTER 3

How to Write Great OKRs

Never underestimate the power of dreams and the influence of the human spirit. We are all the same in this notion: The potential for greatness lives within each of us.

—Wilma Rudolph

Chapter Highlights

- From "comfort zone" to "learning zone"
- How to create "oarsome" Objectives
- Aspects of effective key results
- Magic questions and formulas

I once worked for a large retail company, and during one of the first OKR setting workshops, we tried to define the Objective for the next quarter. We agreed that the launch of the new webshop was our main Objective. Finishing it within 90 days was a major stretch for the company. All companies set goals, but defining meaningful and inspirational goals is a big challenge for many.

When we moved to set the KRs for our Objective, we realized we could only put in project milestones. How could we define KRs that track progress on a weekly basis toward our Objective?

In my car, on my way back to home, something resonated with me. The Objective was not to launch a new version of the webshop, building a new version is merely a means to an end. Why did we want to have a new webshop in the first place? Obviously, because of a bad customer experience (or at least that was the assumption here). But was that really so? Did we lose customers because of it? I couldn't tell. Now it became clear to me, the Objective was not to launch a new webshop at all. What we wanted was to decrease the number of customers that leave the website prematurely.

It's the outcome that matters and that is why we have such a hard time measuring the Objective. We changed the Objective to "keep all customers on board." Measuring the Objective became easy, and we defined "Decrease weekly customer drop-off by 20 percent" as one of the KRs. Now, the launch of the new webshop was under discussion. If the Objective was to keep customers on board, we might look into other means.

We could measure the success of our experiments every week. Without great OKRs, you cannot achieve great results. It took me several years to discover and master all the techniques you will read about in this chapter. I'm sure they will help you to write great Lean OKRs.

Great OKRs

In today's world, it is more important than ever that leaders understand how to inspire people. Creating powerful Objectives is more of an art form than a science. You can consult books and online resources for some inspiration, but just because an Objective inspires one organization or team, doesn't automatically mean it will inspire and motivate people in your company. This chapter provides you with guidelines and detailed explanations to create "good enough" OKRs.

Following the exercises in the previous chapters, you've hopefully managed to identify why you want to set goals (personal or business) and what you want to achieve by year-end. In this chapter, we transform one of those goals into an Objective, and subsequently we look at KRs.

Learning Zone

OKRs should be stretch goals, and the most ambitious of them are fondly referred to as moonshots. They should be a challenge for the organization, teams, and individuals. They combine Objectives, which are always qualitative and exist to inspire people, with KRs which are measurable and aspirational.

OKRs are meant to bring you out of your *comfort zone* (see Figure 3.1). When you are in your comfort zone, you come to work, you do your thing, and you are really good at it. You have developed the skills and competencies to be really good at what you're doing. You are fluent in it. Sometimes, you will face challenges in your job, but you can always rely on your skills and competencies.

When you set stretch goals with OKRs, the KRs involved should push you into what is called the *learning zone*; their aspirational nature is reflected in not-easy-to-reach targets. It should feel uncomfortable here; it's unknown territory.

If you have never learnt to do work in a different way, then the only way to navigate the learning zone is by experimenting, failing fast and hard, and probably disliking many of the new concepts because people naturally don't like to fail. However, it is in this zone that people develop new skills, new competencies, and get great ideas, which is the realm of OKRs. If you haven't learnt anything last quarter when you were working on your OKRs, they probably weren't that great.

Caveat: Be careful not to push yourself or other people too much, too hard, and too fast, especially in the first few cycles. Otherwise, you or your team could end up entering the *danger zone*. In this zone, the KRs are too ambitious, causing you or your team to get stressed, burned out, and probably demotivated. Don't tread in this territory. If people

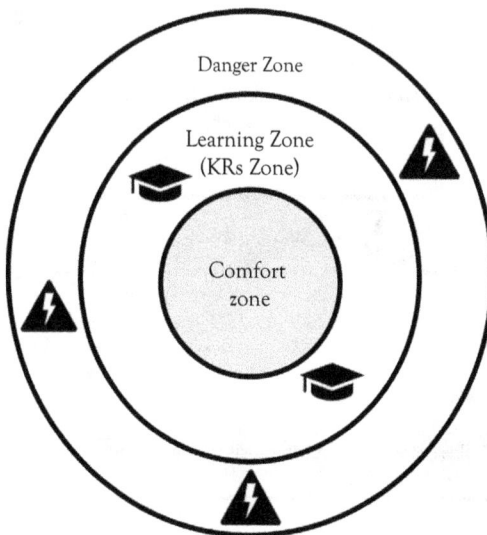

Figure 3.1 The comfort zone, learning zone, and danger zone

continue working over their weekends to achieve their OKRs, something is wrong. If halfway through the quarter people haven't yet moved any needle, you need to investigate. You need to work smarter, not harder.

In 2009, *Harvard Business Review* published a paper titled "Goals Gone Wild" (Ordóñez et al. 2009). The authors warned about aggressive goal setting, explaining that it is a "a prescription-strength medication that requires careful dosing … and close supervision." In the paper, they even had the following warning sign (Figure 3.2).

"There are many ways in which goals go wild: they can narrow focus, motivate risk taking, lure people into unethical behavior, inhibit learning, increase competition, and decrease intrinsic motivation" (Ordóñez et al. 2009). This widely cited paper has shaken up the world. However, as John Doerr wrote in *Measure What Matters*, "for anyone striving for high performance in the workplace, goals are very necessary components" (Doerr 2018). More than a thousand studies have confirmed the work of psychology professor Edwin Locke (Locke and Latham 2002). Hard goals drive performance more effectively than easy goals. Ninety percent of all studies confirmed that productivity is enhanced by well-defined, challenging goals (Doerr 2018).

Since OKRs should take you out into the learning zone, it sometimes can help to avoid using the term "success measures" for your KRs, but to rather call them "learning measures." By focusing on the learning aspect of OKRs, you stimulate the desired behavior: the willingness to experiment and to except that failure is okay. Or as Albert Einstein once said: "you never fail until you stop trying."

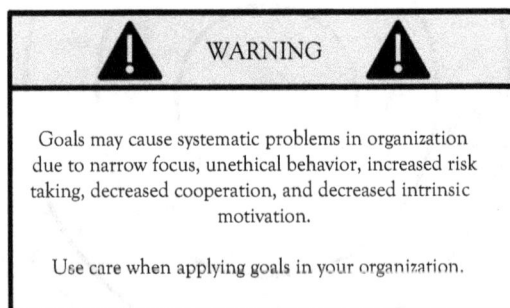

> ⚠ **WARNING** ⚠
>
> Goals may cause systematic problems in organization due to narrow focus, unethical behavior, increased risk taking, decreased cooperation, and decreased intrinsic motivation.
>
> Use care when applying goals in your organization.

Figure 3.2 The warning sign from the HBR article "Goals Gone Wild" (Ordóñez et al. 2009)

A common mistake is to attach compensation (raises and bonuses) to the achievement of OKRs. As by the above reasons, people will only stretch themselves if they feel safe and supported by their leaders. If you tie compensation and bonuses to OKRs, people will set lower targets and you lose the whole purpose of OKRs altogether. If people set stretch OKRs, you as a manager or leader should support them. If you wish to compensate people, do so based on continuous conversations, recognition, and feedback (CRF). In Chapter 6, we will look at this in more detail.

How to Create Effective Objectives

O Is for Oarsome

As you now know, an Objective is a short description of *what* you want to achieve, in "oarsome" words (i.e., describing something that is so outrageous that it approaches the borders of awesomeness). It states where you want to go in such an inspired way that people will remember.

A good Objective inspires and motivates everybody in your organization, so the challenge for leaders is to choose the right wording. What might be inspirational for you or your shareholders might not be something your employees will be sparked by. For example, "become profitable" and "become the market leader" are great inspirational Objectives—and they are probably the same goals that any company is after. However, not everybody in your organization will be as enthusiastic about or motivated by these Objectives as your senior leadership team. So, think back to the reason why your company exists, its purpose, often defined in a mission or vision statement (see Chapter 1). Its purpose is not to become a market leader, but rather to solve a specific (world) problem or to fulfil a job yet to be done for your customers or clients (Christensen 2016).

Consider these questions: What does this Objective even mean? Is there too much industry speak? Could you explain it to a third grader? What critical overall business metric do you want to improve significantly to drive your company forward? Describing your Objectives from a customer perspective is a very good start. What are the specific customer behaviors that will drive revenue, profit or your market leader position? Instead of "become the market leader," a better Objective might be "reduce customer drop-off during onboarding." When customer drop-off during onboarding decreases, then you are likely closer to becoming a market leader, which aligns with your company strategy. This approach to setting an Objective is motivational because it presumes that your staff are driven to serve your customers in a meaningful way. Finally, this new Objective starts with an action-oriented verb: "reduce." This will trigger action in people's minds. Avoid using weasel words, such as "leading," "competitive," and "client-driven" that will weaken your Objective (see the link in the Appendix to find more weasel words). Rather, make it action-oriented. Connecting your Objectives with your bigger "why," your strategy, and including a customer focus are the keys.

A good Objective always tries to improve a certain business metric (e.g., number of customers, EBIT, qualified leads, quality, churn rate, and cost to acquire customers). That is why you often see verbs like "increase" and "decrease" or synonyms in front of these metrics. To spice up your Objectives, you can use a thesaurus to make the words more inspirational. For example, to "boost" a certain metric sounds more inspirational than to "improve." Warning: don't fall into the trap of using weasel words. Inspire people, but don't be vague. In case of doubt, try to go for a less inspirational Objective, the key is to communicate intent.

Ideally, groups or small companies should have one Objective per cycle. Larger organizations may want two, but the idea is to zoom right in on the things that matter most to your business. More on this in Chapter 5.

Aspects of Effective Objectives

The more you practice, the better you'll get at writing effective Objectives. Over the years, through trial and error, I've cherry-picked key features of effective Objectives to create some guidelines for crafting fit-for-purpose Objectives. Feel free to use them to start you off and find out what will work best for you. At the initial stage, don't worry too much about the exact formulations you use; you can always rewrite them later.

Objectives should (ideally) be:

- *Inspirational*: Most Objectives start with a powerful verb to inspire everyone. Verbs describe impact and an Objective should propel the organization in a desired direction. Be careful here, verbs can also indicate actions or milestones. If you start writing Objectives, then it can be easier to start writing them with a noun (the subject) first, as I will explain in detail below.
- *Significant*: Concrete and result oriented. Is it an observable or detectable quality about the subject (noun) that you want more or less of? for example, accuracy, loyalty, and understandability. As a leader, what problem would you like teams to solve?
- *A number-free zone*: Avoid numbers, percentages, KPIs, or other measures, as the KRs will cover that. Not everyone has an affinity with numbers and you must inspire everyone. Objectives are ideally qualitative. However, sometimes a big number can inspire people. "Make 1 billion people happy" (Gawdat 2017) is more powerful than "Boost happiness around the world." In the end, you need whatever it takes to inspire people. It's a trade-off.
- *Measurable*: You track progress against your Objective with the KRs, but is your Objective measurable at all? Make sure your Objective contains a noun that can be measured: customers, employees, sign-ups, e-mails, and product usage.
- *Attainable*: Setting a challenging goal is fine, but be realistic.
- *Controllable*: By the group, team, or department.
- *Part of your culture*: Make them motivational and write them in the right tone and style.
- *Written*: Use down-to-earth, positive language. Avoid abbreviations.
- *Simple and short*: A maximum of seven words and easy to remember!
- *Specific*: Avoid woolly, generic, or timeless goals (e.g., "happy customers" or "revenue growth").

Two Recipes for Cooking Up Objectives

There are two recipes or formulas that help prepare a measurable Objective:

- Verb + adjective phrase + noun + adverb phrase. For example: "Grow high quality leads for Product X," "Acquire new customers at no expense," or "Boost daily watch time."
- Sometimes Objectives can be more powerful when they start with a noun. When starting with writing Objectives, it can be easier to think about the subject of the goal first. Measurement expert Stacey Barr has a different recipe for formulating a measurable goal: Noun + linking verb + adjective phrase or adverb phrase (Barr 2020). For example, "Retail customers promise eternal loyalty," "Leads are doubled for product X," or "Daily watch time grows exponential."

Common Mistakes

Writing good Objectives is hard. Here are some common mistakes you should try to avoid:

- Objectives as activities or milestones. For example, "Launch our new website." What would be the result of that launch? To attract more customers? Maybe you want more qualified leads. Then, that should be your Objective. Focus on the final result, the problem you want the team to solve, rather than the solution.
- Multiple Objectives in one. Don't try to squeeze in two or more Objectives into one: "Increase sales while reducing costs." Avoid using words like "while," "and," commas, and conjunctions. An Objective is about the achievement of one thing.
- Using woolly words that don't mean anything. Avoid using weasel words and clearly define *what* you want to improve. Can you explain it to a third grader?

Magic Questions for Objectives

In my in-house OKR trainings, I like to ask some of my magic questions to help guide people get on the right track:

- What is the number one constraint or bottleneck that prevents you from moving the needle? What does your company look like without that constraint?
- What critical business metric (KPI) requires a big boost? Avoid financial measures if possible.
- Where do you want to get to? What do you want to achieve?
- What do you want to focus on now? What problem will be solved with that?
- How can your group make an impact on your company's goal(s)?
- How can your group make an impact on one of the company's strategic priorities?
- What challenges do you currently face? Which one is the most pressing?
- How will the world look when you've achieved your Objective? What will have changed?
- How would you explain to a friend or your partner what you're going to do this quarter/year?
- What would you be proud to have achieved by the end of this year/quarter?
- What would be different 90 days from now? How would you observe that?

This list isn't comprehensive. If you can think of other magic questions, please add your own.

Examples of Good Objectives

Here are some examples of good business Objectives:

- Grow five-day active customers exponentially.
- Customers onboarded in the blink of an eye.

- Increase French client leads for product XYZ.
- Customers love how we support them.
- Boost the speed of delivering new features.
- Customers choose us over competitor X.
- Lightning fast batch payment transactions.
- Any service is restored in no time.
- European Customers advocate our product.
- Increase weekly sign-ups for our free trial.
- No more unplanned work.

Some OKR Examples Analyzed

Sometimes, it helps to learn from others' mistakes and successes. In the Appendix, you will find a link to more OKR examples including my feedback on their plus and minus points.

Timescale

It can sometimes be hard to determine the correct lifespan for your Objective. Sometimes, the Objective can be accomplished within one OKR cycle, but sometimes, it takes multiple cycles to see their effect. When an Objective spans multiple quarters or even years, it's important to note that only the KRs will change per OKR cycle, but the Objective remains the same.

Abstract or Operational: Finding the Balance

If an Objective is too abstract, people won't relate to it. If it's too operational, they may find it too directive (and dull). To see if your Objective has got the appropriate lifespan and level of abstraction, apply the Because & Why (B&W) technique. Let's discover how this works in more detail.

Can You Tell People the "Because … "?

When trying to define an effective Objective, it can help to add a "because" clause (O'Reilly and Miller 2018). This idea came from Barry O'Reilly and is useful for defining your Objective's lifespan. An example:

> **Business Objective Example:**
>
> Short-term tactical Objective: Decrease customer onboarding time.
>
> Because … ?
>
> Long-term strategic Objective: Grow our customer install base.

This "because" construction functions as the connection between the short-term Objective (boost my level of fitness) and long-term goal (win the 2020 surf competition). Linking long- and short-term Objectives helps motivate you and your group: Everyone *understands* the long-term Objective, but *focuses* on the short-term one.

Five Whys

The "five whys" technique can help you pin down your more important, underlying Objective and/or the right level of abstraction. It's a technique often used in Lean and root cause analysis. It's called "five whys" because by the time you have asked and answered why five times in succession, you have usually reached your underlying Objective. Here's a dialogue I recently had with a client:

> Sarah: Our Objective is to implement feature X in our online product before March.
>
> Bart: *Why* would that be beneficial for your customers?
>
> Sarah: Well, we have received a lot of complaints about the onboarding process.
>
> Bart: That's a pity. *Why* do they complain?
>
> Sarah: The onboarding process is just a mess at the moment; it confuses people.
>
> Bart: Your Objective might be to improve your onboarding process.
>
> Sarah: Yes, we should make our onboarding way more smooth!
>
> Bart: *Why* would you want to make it smoother?

Sarah: We want to grow our premium subscribers because we are currently losing new customers through the poor onboarding experience.

Note the real Objective we uncovered during this conversation: "grow our premium subscribers." Now it's up to the team to decide on the right scope by asking themselves this: "What can we do differently to grow subscribers within one quarter?"

Over to You

Exercise: Three Steps to Heaven
Use the previous tips, tricks, and examples to create your own Objective in three steps. Creating a good Objective requires a couple of iterations, so try to go over the checklist a couple of times.

Exercise 1: Decide on Your Single Goal (2 minutes)
In Chapter 1, you tried your hand at drafting your most important goal(s) for this year. If you defined multiple goals, try to pick just one of them. Only one!

Exercise 2: Write Down Your Objective (5 minutes)
Now write down that single goal as an Objective. Try to make it inspirational, keep it short and make sure it starts with a verb.

Use the magic questions and the B&W technique to check whether your Objective meets the criteria for an effective Objective. Give it some serious thought.

Exercise 3: Lifespan of the Objective (3 minutes)
What's the lifespan of your Objective? Try to use the "because" method to determine if there's any higher, longer-term Objective. Write down that higher Objective in a "because" clause.

_____ (your Objective) because _____ (reason for doing it)

If you end up with an Objective that's too abstract (e.g., "because I want world peace" or "because we want to make a profit"), then you went too far and need to bring that Objective back down to Earth!

Visualize Your Objective

If an Objective represents reaching the summit of a mountain, the finish line of a marathon, the moon or the B-state (Samuel 2018), you might want to use visuals that represent your end game. I like to call it your "picture of success."

Everyone is wired differently; some may not identify with all of the nice words you put in your Objective, no matter how much energy you've put into crafting them. In addition to your written Objective, it might be helpful to add a powerful visualization to help communicate with your team.

In my training sessions, I love to use LEGO® Serious Play® to help participants visualize an Objective by asking a participant to build a 3D LEGO model of their (company) Objective. This experimental process stimulates different parts of the brain, which often results in more imagination (Roos and Victor 1999). This method is also powerful to create alignment between department and teams Objectives. In Figure 3.3, you see one company Objective (the rocket in the middle) linked with multiple LEGO models which represent team Objectives.

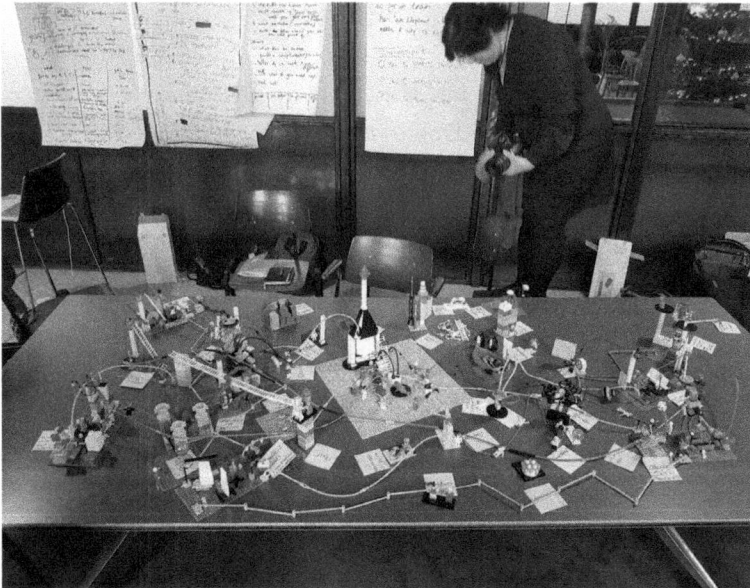

Figure 3.3 A LEGO© model representation of one company OKR (the rocket in the center) linked with multiple team OKRs

How to Create Effective Key Results

In the previous section, you learnt how to craft a concise and motivating Objective. Now we look at ways to measure progress toward your Objective using KRs.

Let's dive into KRs before finishing your picture.

Measuring Progress Toward the Objective

Remember, if the Objective is *what* you want to achieve, then the KRs measure whether you're on your way to achieving it (or not). KRs are a set of measures that show your progress toward the Objective. They describe *how* you're going to achieve the Objective.

There are many ways to measure progress toward your Objective. The whole next chapter is devoted to the creation of metrics and indicators for your KRs. The best source for finding a good progress indicator is by looking at the subject inside your Objective. If your Objective is to "Decrease customer onboarding time," then you should have at least one KR that says something about the time customers spent going through

---

Over to You

To create effective KRs, I find it useful to run the following exercise, which I learnt from Patti Dobrowolski during her talk "Draw Your Future" at TEDx Seattle 2013 (Dobrowolski 2013). First, think of an Objective, personal or business, either are fine. Next, take a blank piece of A4 paper and a pencil. Divide the paper in two by folding it horizontally, widthwise, making two A5 pages. Unfold it and draw a small picture of your Objective on the right-hand side of the sheet. Use some basic shapes like circles and squares, nothing too complicated. After that, on the left-hand side, draw a picture of today, your current state. Now draw three arrows from the left image (how things are currently) to the right image (your Objective). Done? Good. These three arrows will represent your KRs. In Figure 3.4, you see an example of three bold steps toward the desired new reality by Patti Dobrowolski herself.

Figure 3.4 An example of visualizing KRs as illustrated by Patti Dobrowolski, Up Your Creative Genius, creator of the process "Draw Your Future" in her strategy mapping exercise

your onboarding process. In this case, a good KR could be: "Reduce the average time customers spend on going through our onboarding process from 30 to 1 minute." Only having one KR isn't sufficient. You want to counterbalance the primary KR with a KR that says something about quality of the onboarding process (we call this "pairing"). For example, "Decrease the number of complaints about the onboarding user interface from 20 to 0 per week."

Aspects of Effective Key Results

Crafting good KRs is tough, so it's worth spending some time on it. Let's begin with some guidelines. Effective KRs should be:

- *Driving the right customer and/or employee behavior*: This is essential, and perhaps even the *MOST* essential point in this whole list. We will dive further into this topic in Chapter 5.
- *Trackable*: You should be able to track them over time (ideally daily or weekly) and look for improvement.
- *Quantitative*: Does the KR contain a number?

- *Outcome-focused*: Define the outcome, not what you need to do to achieve it. Try to avoid binaries, solutions, or milestones, which are output-focused instead of outcome-focused. Not helpful are, for example, "finish feature X," "launch the campaign," "the project is completed," and "the project has been migrated." Define the outcome by stating "Increase number of website visitors from X to Y" or "Increase number of product demo sign-ups from X to Y per week."

- *Few in number*: a maximum of four KRs per Objective.

- *Paired*: Try to pair KRs (e.g., have one KR on quantity and another on quality). You want to view the same results from different standpoints. This 1) reduces unethical behavior and the effects of measurements gaming. For example, increasing sales can be as easy as selling $100 bills for $50. Sales increase big time, but your profits not so much. So you always need to try to pair measures. Pairing also 2) helps to avoid an overemphasis on measures, by including measures of quality as a quantitative measure. For example, the number of defects in the software or the percentage of products not complying with standards.

- *Controllable*: Don't set KRs that depend on things outside your team's influence.

- *Aligned*: If you have dependencies on other teams to achieve your KR, have you talked to them about it? If you're dependent on another teams/departments, use an alignment workshop (see Chapter 8) to find consensus.

- *Aspirational*: This is an important characteristic of a stretch goal. For teams seasoned in OKRs, a KR should have a 50 percent confidence score at the beginning of the OKR cycle.

- *Owned*: Every KR should have a clear owner who is responsible for that KR. At the weekly check-ins (explored in Chapter 9), the owner is accountable for updating the numbers before each check-in.

Creating Specific Key Results

To be as clear as possible, make sure your KRs are as specific as possible. In fact, the more specific you can be, the better. If you want to grow your customer base, for example, a KR could be:

Grow our customer base to 2k.

This might look good at first sight. However, when other teams or individuals need to connect to these KRs, they might have questions like: How many do we have today? What kind of customers? All of them? Where do we grow them? So the more specific you can be, the better. An improvement could be to focus on a customer segment, add a baseline measure, and specify the timeline for the KR. For example:

Increase number of recurring customers in South America from 1 to 2k by March 25.

This one already looks better. Now you can add some demographic or psychographic information to scope it down even further.

Increase number of recurring South American customers in the 25 to 35 age demographic from 1 to 2k by March 25.

Of course, you can really go all out when crafting these, but try to find the right balance between simplicity and specificity. "Everything should be made as simple as possible, but not simpler," as Einstein is believed to have once said.

Progress-Based

One of the most important yet difficult criteria is to make your KRs progress-based. Most organizations struggle with this for many months or even years. That is why I've dedicated a whole chapter to measures in this book. For the impatient, have a look at Chapter 4 to find out more about measures.

If you make your OKR progress-based, you can track them over time, even checking on short-term Objectives. Many people starting with

OKRs believe tracking progress on a quarterly basis cannot be done. The approach in this book suggests otherwise. It is essential that you track progress on a weekly or even a daily basis. What is the point of having weekly check-ins if there are no measures to check against?

Measuring Weekly or Daily Progress

The rule of thumb is, shorter is better. Daily measures are better than weekly, and weekly measures are better than monthly. In fact, try to avoid monthly measures completely. Let me be prescriptive here: All measures that cannot be updated in less than a month's time are insufficient for use in your KRs. If you can't measure your performance on a weekly basis, then you won't receive any feedback from the "system," meaning people cannot learn from, act, or investigate it. Therefore, weekly or daily updatable measures are better. This is also in line with the "weekly" check-ins that we will discuss in Chapter 9.

Tracking OKRs With Confidence Scores and Grades

To track progress on your OKRs throughout the quarter, you can check the status of measures in your KRs on a weekly basis. In addition, you can use confidence scores. A confidence score is an indicator of whether a team or individual contributor believes a KR is achievable. When setting your KRs at the beginning of each OKR cycle, they should be challenging. A good rule of thumb is to assign a confidence score of 50 percent to each KR. Every week during your weekly OKR check-ins you update this score. This will hopefully trigger a discussion ("Hey Pete, your confidence in achieving this KR is low, why is that?"). This might seem counterintuitive, but as the saying goes, if it was easy, everyone would do it! OKRs, especially moonshots, are about achieving things that seem impossible. In Chapter 9, you will find how you can apply confidence scores to your KRs in more detail.

At the end of each OKR cycle, you will grade your KRs (see Figure 3.4) with the sole purpose of learning. If you've scored all of your KRs with 100 percent, you've achieved your Objective. It's that simple. However, if your KRs are really stretching your team, 70 to 80 percent achievement is considered a great accomplishment. In some cases (e.g., Google X, the moonshot factory), this number even goes as low as 20 to 30 percent. If the team achieved a KR with 100 percent, maybe they didn't stretch themselves too much. If the grade was 30 percent, maybe it was too ambitious and we need to lower our expectations for the next OKR cycle. Be careful that the 70 percent doesn't become the new norm. Teams should always strive for 100 percent achievement. In Chapter 10, we will look at how grading OKRs can play a role in the final OKR review (Figure 3.5).

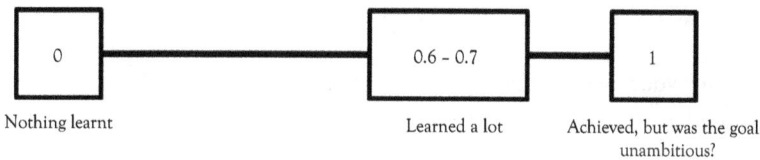

0	0.6 – 0.7	1
Nothing learnt	Learned a lot	Achieved, but was the goal unambitious?

Figure 3.5 Grading your OKRs

To track progress on your OKRs, you can also have a mid-quarter check-in and update the scores. In order to get faster feedback on past decisions and experiments, I prefer combining the scoring of OKRs at the end of the quarter with regular confidence checks during weekly OKR check-ins, which will be explained in Chapter 9.

Magic Questions for KRs

In my OKR workshops, I like to work with magic questions. Just as I illustrated earlier with Objectives, there are questions you can ask during the OKR setting workshop (Chapter 7) that help to elicit clear KRs.

Here are my magic questions for creating effective KRs for both executive and departmental teams:

- What are the customer behaviors that drive business results?
- What change in customer behavior will bring us closer to achieving the Objective? How can we measure that?
- What change in our own behavior will bring us closer to achieving the Objective? How can we measure that?

- How will achieving the Objective change our own and other stakeholders' experience and/or behavior? What would success look, feel, and/or smell like? How can we measure that?
- What could we do that we've never done before that might make all the difference to the Objective?
- What strength of this team can we use as leverage on the Objective?
- What do our best performers (i.e., staff, employees, and teams) do differently? How can we measure that?
- What weakness might keep us from achieving the Objective? What could we do more consistently?

Got your own questions? Feel free to extend this list and use them. It would be great if you would share them with me as well. Just e-mail me (my details are in the back of the book).

A Recipe for Cooking Up Key Results

Good KRs should contain a measure, baseline, and target numbers or values. This helps with tracking and seeing progress, a vital part of the OKR framework. The following formula will help you set a good KR:

[Increase/Decrease] [Statistic] [MEASURE] from X to Y by [WHEN]

Let's unravel the following KRs.

A business example: "Increase # of weekly sign-ups for our free trial from 3 to 20 per week by March."

Measure: weekly sign-ups for the free trail

Statistic: number (expressed as "#")

X (baseline): 3

Y (target): 20

When: by March

A personal example: "Decrease total body weight from 90 to 85 kg by June."

Measure: body weight in kg

Statistic: total

X (baseline): 90
Y (target): 85
When: by June

Using the formula might feel a bit artificial, but it helps develop good KRs. Use your creativity to find synonyms for certain words, like increase and decrease, to spice up your KR definitions. Forcing yourself to write KRs in this format will help you and your teams to think critically about the baseline (X), your target (Y), and, of course, the type of statistic and measure you want to use. Keep in mind that this formula is just a guideline and isn't a one-size-fits-all equation for all organizations.

Examples of Good KRs

Here are some examples of good business KRs:

- Grow total MRR from 2M to 5M.
- Increase number of positive reviews in trade publications to 5 per month.
- Increase number of five-day active customers from 200 to 2 k.
- Increase number of French-qualified leads from 2 to 10 per week.
- Increase number of weekly product demos scheduled from 2 to 10.
- Ensure average overall customer satisfaction is above 8 out of 10.
- Decrease the average time spent on training new hires from 40 to 20 hours.
- Reduce the average time on making a batch payment transaction from 30 minutes to 5 seconds.
- Increase the mean time to restore any service from 10 hours to 30 minutes.
- Increase number of French customers that advocate our product from 20 to 200 per week.
- Increase number of weekly sign-ups for our free trial from 3 to 20 per week.

- Decrease the percentage of unplanned work from 40 to 5 percent.
- Decrease the average lead time for small features from 20 to 1 day.
- Increase minimum frequency of deploying our software from once per month to 5 times per week.
- Decrease average usage of the 'Call me now' feature from 400 to 30 per week.
- Decrease load tested P99 latency across critical APIs from 2 seconds to 200 milliseconds.
- Improve maximum CreatePayment API transactions per seconds from 800 to 3,000 during a weekly load test.

Some OKR Examples Analyzed

Sometimes, it helps to learn from others' mistakes and successes. In the Appendix, you will find a link to more OKR examples including my feedback on their strengths and weaknesses.

Types of Key Results

There can be different types of KRs, and with them, differences of opinion. Ben Lamorte and Paul Niven were the first to categorize KRs (Niven and Lamorte 2016). They come up with three types:

- Baseline KRs
- Metric (positive, negative, and threshold target) KRs
- Milestone KRs

Others, for example, OKR expert Felipe Castro, simply say that there are two types of KRs: activity-based and value-based (Castro n.d.). Christina Wodtke suggests that start-ups focus on KRs based on growth, engagement, revenue, performance, and quality (Wodtke 2016, 111).

Many people have tried to put KRs into defined categories. I disagree with that. I believe it's better to focus on where to find the best measures to track your progress toward their corresponding Objectives. When you try to discuss when to use what type, you often end up in a semantic discussion. A simplified categorization of KRs may provide some support if you're just starting out and trying to understand OKRs. However, in practice, it is very hard to create good KRs for the long term when you restrict yourself to categorical thinking.

In the next chapter, we will jump into the wonderful world of measures and indicators so you can make the most informed decision about what will work best for you.

Chapter Recap

In this chapter, we've delved into OKRs as measurable and aspirational stretch goals and established that good KRs are a strong prerequisite for achieving your company's aspirations.

We've determined important characteristics of Objectives and explored guidelines for defining good (but not perfect) OKRs that will be challenging for the organization, teams, and individuals. We've taken a look at magic questions that can help to shape the process of setting Objectives.

By now, you should know that good KRs should push everyone out of the comfort zone and into the learning zone—that unknown and uncomfortable territory where real change happens—and you should be equally aware of the danger zone that awaits those that are pushed too hard.

Chapter References

Barr, S. 2020. "How to Make OKRs Measurable." www.staceybarr.com/measure-up/how-to-make-okrs-measurable/ (accessed February 19, 2021 and Last Modified January 28, 2020).

Barr, S. May 22, 2018. "A Recipe for Writing a Measurable Goal." www.staceybarr.com/measure-up/a-recipe-for-writing-a-measurable-goal/(accessed February 19, 2021).

Castro, F. n.d. "Success Criteria and Types of Key Results." https://felipecastro.com/en/okr/success-criteria-types-key-results/ (accessed February 19, 2021).

Christensen, C.M., T. Hall, K. Dillon, and D.S. Dunca. September 2016. *Know Your Customers' "Jobs to Be Done."* Boston: Harvard Business Review.

Dobrowolski, P. 2013. "Draw Your Future." *Recorded at TEDx Seattle 2013,* https://youtu.com/zESeeaFDVSw

Doerr, J. 2018. *Measure What Matters*, London: Portfolio Penguin.

Gawdat, M. 2017. *Solve for Happy: Engineering Your Path to Joy.* New York, NY: Gallery Books.

Locke, E.A., and G.P. Latham. 2002. "Building a Practically Useful Theory of Goal Setting and Task Motivation: A 35-Year Odyssey." *American Psychologist* 57, no. 9, pp. 705–717.

Niven, P., and B. Lamorte. 2016. *Objectives and Key Results: Driving Focus, Alignment, and Engagement with OKRs*, 1st ed. New Jersey, NJ: Wiley.

O'Reilly, B., and J. Miller. 2018. "What Is Excellence for a Team?" https://barryoreilly.com/explore/blog/what-is-excellence-for-a-team/ (accessed February 19, 2021).

Ordóñez, L.D., M.E. Schweitzer, A.D. Galinsky, and M.H. Bazerman. January 2009. *Goals Gone Wild: The Systematic Side Effects of Over-Prescribing Goal Setting.* Boston: Harvard Business School. Working Paper.

Roos, J., and B. Victor. 1999. "Towards a Model of Strategy Making as Serious Play." *European Management Journal* 17, no. 4, pp. 348–355.

Samuel, M. 2018. *B State: A New Roadmap for Bold Leadership, Brave Culture, and Breakthrough Results.* Austin: Greenleaf Book Group Press.

CHAPTER 4

Measures, Metrics, and Indicators

We find no sense in talking about something unless we specify how we measure it; a definition by the method of measuring a quantity is the one sure way of avoiding talking nonsense.

—Sir Hermann Bondi, Mathematician and Cosmologist

Chapter Highlights

- Measures—quantitative data and calculable information
- Indicators—tell us if we are making progress toward the Objective
- Lead and lag measures—what is the difference?
- How clear and deliberate KRs will inspire changes in behavior (tricky, but possible)
- Three steps to crafting good measures for KRs: methodology, defining, and formula

"We have Objectives that cannot be measured." This is probably the problem I hear most often by leaders in my training sessions. Another one is: "We have measures in our KRs, but we only see the effects months later." When you say OKRs, you say measures. Developing good measurements is challenging. Not because it's difficult, but because many have never learnt how to develop good measures, or they simply don't have the time for it.

One client asked me, "How can you measure progress when your measures are monthly as is the case when using Monthly Recurring Revenue (MRR) or Net Promoter Score (NPS)?" To answer this question, we need to understand how measures work, what they are made of and how different kinds of measures influence each other. The key is to understand the cause and effect relationship between different kinds of measures.

Through my trainings, I help leaders and their teams to develop measures with the help of some simple techniques. After every training, leaders and teams finally feel like they are in control. They know how to measure and track progress toward their goals. On a weekly and even daily basis, they can observe and understand the impact of their experiments and decisions. More importantly, they literally see the needle moving. In this chapter, I will show you what they have learnt.

Why Measures Matter?

In the previous chapter, you learnt how to craft your Objective and KRs. You are now prepared to zoom in on KRs, crafting effective measures. As you know, an Objective is only as good as its KRs. When it comes to KRs, the devil is in the details of how you write (or illustrate!) them.

The number of things you could measure is endless. Selecting a handful of meaningful measures that support your Objective well is hard. If you have defined a poor or weak Objective, you will get equally poor-quality measures and indicators which result in problems: demotivated teams, no observable progress, and certainly no achievements. Using the magic questions described earlier in the previous chapter, you can create a good list of candidates for KRs. Most important to remember is that the first and foremost function of KRs is to get you closer to your Objective.

Each KR should quantitatively describe a desired result that indicates progress toward your Objective. Former CEO of Yahoo, Marissa Mayer, once said: "It's not a key result unless it has a number" (Levy 2011, 163). But only using numbers won't help us much; we also need the context of these numbers. Ideally, when it comes to KRs, you want to include *indicators* to tell you if you are making progress, but you need *measures* before you can even begin to develop your indicators.

In the context of OKRs, we use measures, data, and information, for two reasons:

1. Tracking progress toward the Objective.
2. Informing teams about progress made, reflecting on past decisions.

Coming to Terms

Let's first get familiar with the terms we are going to use to carve out your clear and deliberate KRs.

Data are the simplest form of information possible. They are usually represented by a number or value. Seven, ten, true, high, and low all are examples of data. The data by itself are useless because they fail to relate any meaningful information. There is no comparison made, thus no story to be told.

Measure is a unit that relays the size, weight, or other quality or characteristic of something. Measures bring more clarity to the data by grouping them in true relationships and adding a little context. "20 percent" is more meaningful than "20." Better yet, "20 percent of 300 customers" tells us even more.

There are many different kinds of measurements, but in my years of practice, the one that stands out most is the measurement of behavior. We talked about this topic in Chapter 2, in terms of why behavior is important. We are going to look at behavior measurements closely in this chapter.

Information adds context in the form of meaning, thus making the measures understandable. "20 percent of 300 customers prefer to call us by video chat" adds context in the form of meaning to our measures. In your KRs, you always need information to add to your measures.

Indicators tell the story of how a situation will unfold, is currently unfolding, or has already unfolded. They're a set of measures over a period of time, using the same measuring methodology. You can use them to tell if you are making progress toward your Objective. The most important indicators tied to measuring organizational or team performance are what we call Key Performance Indicators (KPIs). Be careful not to take indicators as an absolute truth; they are one perspective that produces a certain version of the truth, but like any story, there are more sides than just one.

Metric(s) is probably the word people use when they actually mean (performance) measure or indicator. The word can mean a system of measurement (meters and grams), a standard of measurement or a mathematical function that defines the distance between each pair of point elements in a set. It can also mean a picture made up information, measure, and data in order to provide an answer to a root question (Klubeck 2011). I've decided to use both terms interchangeably in this book, because the term metric is so much incorporated in today's management literature and day-to-day management speak that it would confuse people.

Some prefer to capture the performance of measures visually, and graphs and charts are great formats to represent them. You will learn more about measuring performance and building charts in Chapter 12. Using pictures and drawings might also help. Use your creative mind here.

How to Craft Good Measures for KRs

Defining good measures for KRs is challenging for a lot of people, even for seasoned managers. Like the creation of powerful Objectives, crafting good measures is both an art form and a science. It's a skill you cannot learn from taking a course or reading a textbook, but the descriptions of my practical experiences can help to raise your proficiency more quickly. Nevertheless, you need deliberate practice, meaning you can only learn it by doing it a lot and often. Too many leaders jump eagerly into goal setting but rush through the measuring part, and therefore fail.

Measures can be developed at all levels of the organization. Some are at a visionary level, while others are at an operational level (see Chapter 5). All indicators, generated through measures, should ultimately answer the fundamental question of the team that uses OKRs: Did we achieve the Objective or not?

Select a Methodology

There's no doubt about it: Crafting good measures is hard work that requires patience and experience. There are several frameworks, techniques, and tools that could be of great help when looking for clues to isolate effective measures. Be aware that none of these methods and tools are magical; they will not provide you with any special secret for defining measures. Unfortunately, you will have to put in the work.

To help narrow down your search for a method that may work for you, I suggest you take a look at:

- Goal, Question, Metric (GQM) developed to find software measures (Basili, Caldiera, and Rombach 1994)
- Ishikawa diagram (Ishikawa 1968), better known as the fishbone diagram (see Figure 4.1)
- Obstacles or constraints in your system or process: Most managers know what is wrong in their system or know what bottleneck is preventing them from achieving great results
- DuPoint Model (Brown 1912) which breaks Return on Equity (ROE) into a three components and subcomponents
- Impact Mapping (Adžić 2012), a technique to find out how user outcomes are related to business goals
- The Program Logic Model (Mayeske and Lambur 2001) which consists of hypothesized descriptions of the chain of causes and effects leading to an outcome of interest
- The Agile Fluency Model (Larsen and Shore 2018) to map team-level behavior measurements of Agile teams

My guess is that there are some methods listed here that you recognized. Explaining each of them thoroughly and doing them justice would be a whole book on its own. I recommend you to research and experiment with them separately.

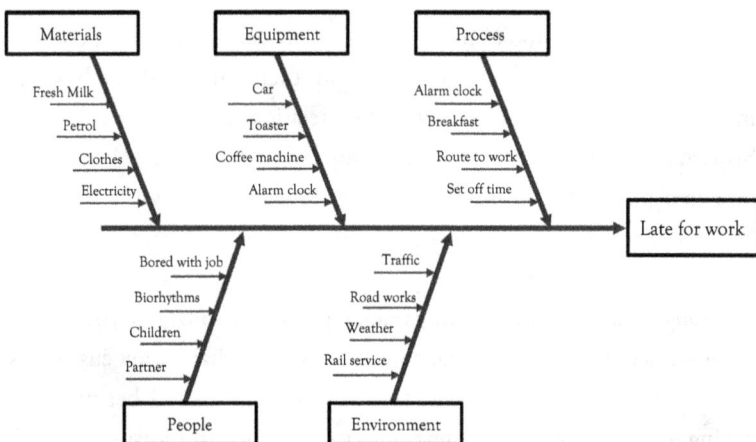

Figure 4.1 The fishbone diagram to discover cause and effect measures

Two of my favorite methods are GQM and fishbone diagram. With GQM you start with the goal (the Objective) and then start defining a question. For example, if your Objective is to "Increase the responsiveness of your service desk," the question could be: "Is the service desk responsive to our customers?" Sometimes you need to use the five whys technique from Chapter 3 to determine a good question. The metric (measure) could then be: "the number of trouble calls" or "The length of time before the caller hung up."

The complete example could look like this:

Goal (Objective): Increase the responsiveness of your service desk.

Question: Is the service desk responsive to our customers?

Metric (Measure): The length of time before the caller hung up.

With the fishbone diagram, you can start with defining the problem ("What prevents us from achieving the Objective now?") and write causes in distinct categories on each "bone." What "people" problems prevent us from achieving the Objective? Or what (software) systems prevent us from achieving the Objective? Probably, one of these causes is a candidate to become a measure of progress in one of your KRs. Even if you know how to measure progress toward the Objective, you probably find it hard to write it down. In the next section, I provide you with a helpful recipe to cook up a great KR.

Defining the Measure

Don't be tempted to look only at your current data. These days, companies collect hundreds of data points and put them into (big) databases. A smart data scientist can magically find correlations in any data set. Avoid this temptation and go back to your Objective first. What is it that you want to significantly improve? Then, you can try to develop a measure. If your Objective is to have "more happy customers," then how are you going to measure that? If you answer is Net Promoter Score (NPS), you are wrong. That measure will only track if people will promote your product or service. Instead, you might want to look at what happy customers *do* with your product or service. Can you measure that? I bet you can. Having an Objective with a clear object (the noun) to measure is a prerequisite for developing good measures for your KRs.

Once you know what you want to measure, you can define a measure for it: the object of your Objective. I like to use the recipe that Stacey Barr described in *Prove It!* (Barr 2017). A good (performance) measure contains:

1. A statistic: any quantity computed from values in a sample, like number (count), total (sum), average, median and maximum, or even a summary statistic (range, standard deviation). Examples are:

   Number of weekly website return visitors

   Average weight of apples

   Percentage of users that drop-off during onboarding

   Note: be careful not to use advanced statistics here. Remember, OKRs are about clear communication. Everybody needs to understand them.

2. Attribute data: What's the Object of measurement? Are we measuring apples, pears, or users? What are we applying the statistical methods to?

   Number of weekly *website return visitors*

3. Scope data: Can you limit or set boundaries to the data set?

   Number of weekly website return visitors *coming from the USA*

4. Temporal data: the frequency of measurement (per day, week, month, and so on)

   Number of *weekly* website return visitors

Once you have defined your measure, you can translate it into a KR. I suggest that you take this opportunity to make a number of KRs. You won't use all of them, but writing them down might help you in your crafting process, and be useful for the future. You will be able to define more meaningful measures for your KRs and thus your Objective. Do you remember the formula from the previous chapter?

[Increase/Decrease] [Statistic] *MEASURE* from X to Y [by WHEN]

Tip: Sometimes your measure can be a bit complicated. Some companies decide to include a separate description or illustration next to their OKRs. This could also be a place to explain the measure in more detail. What is even better is to keep the measure simple, especially since OKRs at company level need to be understood by the whole organization.

Measuring the Intangibles

I am sure you have this question on your mind: But how do we measure the intangibles? "Employee happiness" or "employee engagement" is the top ones many managers have asked me about. I'm a big fan of Douglas W. Hubbard. In his landmark book *How to Measure Anything* (Hubbard 2014), he has several approaches to measuring the intangibles. It will be beyond the scope of this book to explain that in detail, but his definition of measurement explains it all rather succinctly: "Measurement: A quantitative expressed reduction of uncertainty based on one or more observations" (Hubbard 2014, 31).

If you can observe it, then you can measure it. It's so simple, but so hard at the same time. Consider the following questions: What does "happiness" or "engagement" really mean? Why does it mean that to you? Is a happier workforce more effective? Will you receive less complaints about XYZ? By asking these kinds of questions, but also by using the five whys technique that we discussed in the previous chapter, you will be able to find observable and detectable things to measure. My advice is to practice. It takes time, but it can definitely be done.

Anecdote: Clarity is king

When I was working with a large bank in the Netherlands, the senior manager of a cross-functional department had one Objective, heavily inspired by Netflix and Spotify. It looked reasonable at first sight:

Objective: Grow an engineering culture

This Objective is clearly inspirational and compliant with most guidelines provided in the previous chapter. However, when you try to define measures for this Objective, you will soon find yourself in trouble. It's because the Objective isn't clear and measurable. How would you measure the object, in this case "culture"? When I asked him what he meant by "an engineering culture" he said: "I don't know. It's just a feeling." He continued: "Maybe I just want all engineers to continuously improve their own work. You know, like automating their own work process so they can spend more time on removing our legacy software." That answer gave me some useful clues toward defining a better version of the Objective. So the first step you need

---

to take, before you define any measures for your KRs, is to make sure the Objective is clear. A clear Objective contains an object that we can measure. Notice the relationship here: (Latin: *objectivus*, from objectum "object," meaning "impersonal, unbiased"). If you still need some help, go back to the previous chapter where we discussed "five whys."

Importance of Observation

After you have defined a clear Objective with a clear object to measure, your next step is to start looking at possible evidence that the Objective is really happening. This evidence can be in the form of observations. What could we observe if the Objective was achieved? During training sessions, I like to do a thought experiment with leaders: If you had a time machine and went 90 days into the future, what would you see (or observe)?

To use the "Grow an engineering culture" example:

- More time working on the removal of legacy software
- Work processes of manual engineering tasks are automated

The last step is to convert the above observations of the future into measures:

- Percentage of time a team spent on the removal of legacy software
- Number of manual work processes automated

Over to You

Your turn: Travel back in time

Let's do this thought experiment together. Pick an Objective, maybe the one you created in the previous chapter. Let's step into our time machine. We'll go 90 days into the future. What kind of things do you observe in your company, department, or team? Can you make a list of them?

The second step is to convert your observations into measures. Make use of the techniques discussed in "How to craft good measures" earlier in this chapter to define good ones.

A Simple Case Study to Illustrate KRs

The application of OKRs through measures is not always so clear-cut for users, and that is why here will go through the process with a personal example. Let's say you are getting married in six months' time. Congratulations! You've bought a nice outfit but you might want to lose some weight to really look your best. You decide to create a personal OKR for this challenge.

Objective: Fit nicely into my outfit before the wedding date.
KR: Loose some extra weight by June 1st.

In the above example, the object of measurement is you. We can observe your progress toward your Objective (to fit into your wedding outfit) by measuring your body weight. But the above example is too ambiguous, is it not? What does "some extra weight" really mean, how much is that even? It's interpretable in too many ways. According to the KR guidelines, you should add a number to it and try to pair it with another measure.

Objective: Fit nicely in my suit or dress before the wedding date.
KR: Decrease total body weight from 95 to 85 kg by June 1st.
KR: Decrease waist size from 85 to 82 cm by June 1st.

Now we are talking. Let's look at the first KR. You've added a measure (total body weight) to the KR. The number "95 to 85" is the data for the baseline and target, "kilograms" being then the unit of measure and "total" being the statistic. The other words like "decrease" and "by June 1st" provide us with information, even more context, regarding our KR, making it that much more specific. Notice that "by WHEN" defined a specific deadline for the KR. It's optional, but especially for longer-term OKRs, it can be helpful information to add. The more specific you can be, the better. The second KR tells something about the quality of your weight loss. You don't want to lose muscle tone; you can only fit into your wedding outfit by reducing some fat at your belly, making it extra difficult to cheat. Of course, there are more advanced techniques to measuring body fat, but this good (not perfect) KR will do the job just fine for us.

Some fun for the physicists among you…

Let's take a closer look at body weight—I hope you can recall your high school physics class. In the example, body weight is measured in kilograms. However, to calculate our weight on Earth, we actually need to multiply two measures: mass (in kilogram) and acceleration (meters per second squared). Weight is a force which is measured in newton, with the correct unit $kg{\cdot}m/s^2$) (Mathsisfun n.d.).

Technically, we need to rewrite our OKR like this:

Objective: Fit nicely into my outfit before the wedding date.
KR: Decrease total body mass from 95 to 85 kg by June 1st.

Frequency of Measurement

Body mass, measured in kilograms, is an indicator of our goal achievement. If we keep losing weight over a period of time, the measure will indicate whether we see a positive or negative trend toward our target.

However, if you measure your body mass only on the 1st of June, you will only get a binary indicator: Have you indeed achieved your Objective or not (yes/no)? The same holds true for milestone KRs (e.g., finish project x). At that moment, there is not much you can do if the result is negative, besides buying an expensive second outfit in a larger size.

In this case, the problem is not necessarily the type of measure, but the frequency of measurement. If we need to be informed about our decisions based on this indicator more regularly, we need more frequent measurements. For example, if we measure our body mass on a weekly basis, we get a better indicator of progress toward our Objective. We get more frequent feedback and can respond to a negative result much sooner.

The Complete Story

In our wedding example, do the KRs tell us the complete story of whether we are getting closer to our Objective? The combined measures inside the

Lost body mass per week until June 1st

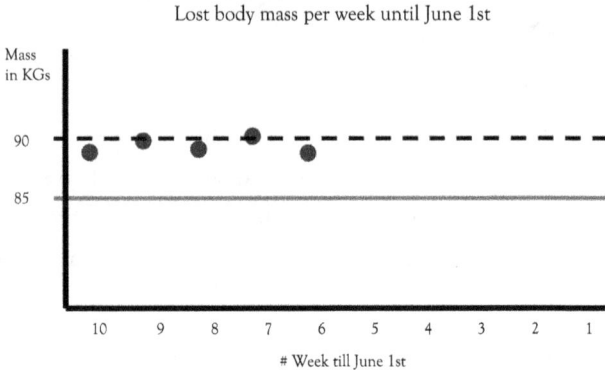

Figure 4.2 Lost body mass per week

KRs give us an idea that can help us to track progress and inform us about our decisions. The combination of measures over time helps us to develop an indicator. We might visualize the indicator, for example. Let's plot the data and measures in a graph (see Figure 4.2). In Chapter 12, we will go deeper into performance measure visualization.

We see that we do lose and gain mass every week that passes, moving up and down toward our target of 85 kg by 1st June. Only measuring body mass on a weekly basis doesn't provide us with a lot of direction on what we need to do to get us closer to our target of 85 kg. If we really want to achieve this goal of losing mass, then we need to change our habits and behaviors—things that we can influence directly. When standing on the scales the day before your wedding day, you know you have a problem when the only thing you can do is cut off your arm in order to reach your body mass goal. This does not only hurt, but the cure is worse than the ailment. What we are missing here are measures that can *predict* a decrease in body mass and that we can track on a daily basis. It's time to introduce lag and lead measures.

Lag and Lead Measures

Characteristics of good measures are that they change human behavior (for the better, I hope). Ideally, you, too, should include measures that change human behavior in your company. This could be customer behavior or employee behavior.

Using the wedding example, would weighing body mass once per week result in a change of behavior? Maybe, but it leaves a lot of room for sandbagging. A measure such as body mass is a measure of past behavior, making it lag behind in time; therefore, we can call it a lagging measure.

To decrease body mass, we need to change our lifestyle, our behavior, and habits. This is where I see most people and companies struggle. Finding good measures for your KRs takes time, patience, and the skill to isolate them. The majority of my work with clients exists in defining supportive performance measures.

In some cases, your OKR is just too big, is too abstract, or is simply too far in the future to understand what appropriate actions or experimenting will have the biggest impact (see Chapter 12). This is also true in our wedding example. Would it make more sense to break down our Objective into a smaller one? Maybe, the target of six months is too abstract. What could you do in say six weeks? Losing weight in six weeks is a big challenge, but can be done. I like to call these smaller goals micro OKRs, and you can read more about them in Chapter 11. Micro OKRs help us to break our larger goals into smaller, more manageable ones.

Luckily for us, we have learnt from science that reducing caloric intake and burning calories have a big impact on our body weight, making it a perfect candidate for a smaller OKR. With a high degree of certainty, we could say that they predict a decrease in body weight. Notice that these measures can also be easily updated daily or weekly. In this example, they make very good candidates to check during a weekly OKR check-in.

Let's go back to our wedding example, this time with an OKR that we can influence directly on a daily basis:

Objective: Cut down the calories.
KR: Decrease caloric intake per day from 3000 to 2300 kcal.
KR: Increase daily exercise time from 0 to 30 minutes.

We use "caloric intake per day" and "daily exercise time" as measures for our behavior. The simple fact that you will count your calories and exercise on a daily basis will already change your behavior. These measures predict our body mass, making them lead measures for our weight loss. If you repeat this for a period of six weeks, you will get the needle moving on your overall goal of reducing body mass and waist size. Once you isolate your leading measures, they can boost the performance of your goals.

Of course, it is a slightly different story when we work in highly complex environments like an enterprise business. Although there isn't a cookie cutter approach we can use to impact your OKRs, a simple example can instill the important underlying principles in your memory.

Lag Measures

Most measures tell you what happened. They are the result of past performance. Body mass is a lag measure; it lags behind in time. Jokingly, I tell people that if they can come up with a measure for an Objective within five minutes, it's probably a lag measure. This is because lag measures are easier to find. Most managers understand these types of measures, which is the reason why you will often encounter them in KRs.

Lagging measures can be best explained with another sort of example, one that I am sure you will also be familiar with. Take NPS, a favorite measure for product organizations and teams (for more measure examples, check the link in the Appendix). NPS reflects an answer to the question: "How likely is it that you, the customer, will recommend our product or service to a friend?" Customers are asked to provide a score from 1 to 10 (quantitative measure through a survey), and the average gives more information about how satisfied your customer is. Some companies like to use these measures as part of their KRs. In most organizations, the problem is that teams cannot influence the number directly. Even if they are true cross-functional product teams, they will probably not see any effect on these measurements on a day-to-day basis. The primary reason for this is that NPS is often measured on a monthly basis. By the time you get the results, you have missed the opportunity to respond. Of course, you could try to measure this score more frequently, but bothering your customers on a weekly basis might not be welcome nor appreciated.

NPS in this context is what we call a lag measure. It lags behind. The same is true for most financial measures, like MRR, or Earnings Before Interest and Taxes (EBIT). This is because of the nature of how they are reported: often monthly, and often tightly coupled to premium membership models.

Finding a good lag measure doesn't have to be hard. The examples provided earlier in this chapter should give you a good list of potential candidates to use in your KRs. Much to my dismay, the problem with most OKR "advice" is that it suggests only including lag measures in your KRs. As we have already learnt, however, that doesn't always tell us what we need to know.

Your Real Leverage: Lead Measures

"Never look back unless you are planning to go that way."
—Henry David Thoreau

To drive the performance of a team, you need a different type of measure that can lead, drive, or even predict lag measures. A measure that the team can influence directly and see the effects of almost instantly. This is where lead measures come into play. Lead measures are hard to find, and some consider them the holy grail in the land of measures. They are not forecasts or extrapolations based on historical data. Instead, they are a predictor of future performance.

Characteristics of good lead measures are:

- Predictive: Do they predict that the lag measure will move?
- Can be measured frequently (weekly or daily)
- Influenceable by the team or individual

To paraphrase W. Edwards Deming (1991), managing your company by only looking at lag measures, is like driving your car by only looking in the rearview mirror. Don't get me wrong, these numbers are important. At the end of the day, they will tell you how successful your strategy was. Investors and shareholders also love them. Lag measures ultimately measure the goal or the result (Figure 4.3).

In comparison, lead measures predict or drive future performance and greatly maximize your potential influence. They measure something that leads to the goal. Very few managers understand the relationship between

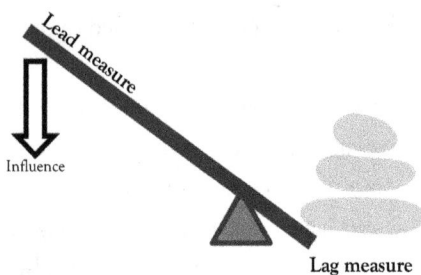

Figure 4.3 Lag vs. lead measure

lag and lead measures, and for this reason, I want to give them some special attention.

When you look at your system in terms of lead measures, you are finding ways to measure critical elements in your processes that will give you the leverage that your teams need. It may not surprise you that most lead measures are found in (internal) processes. Another powerful technique is to discover the constraints inside the process. Can we measure this constraint? I would recommend you read *The Goal* from Dr. Eli Goldratt (2014) where he explains the Theory of Constraints in the form of a business novel. It's a great resource to help you discover lead measures for your KRs.

A lead measure might be "the number of steps in a process that have not been automated yet." Another one could be "the mean time between acquiring a new lead and a follow-up call." In the wedding story, "caloric intake per day" and "daily exercise time" were our lead measures.

The main benefits of using lead measures are that they give you the opportunity to execute more frequent measurements and react faster with an increased influence.

Lead Measures for Teams

In business, achieving OKRs is a team sport. As described in *The 4 Disciplines of Execution*, there are two types of lead measures that are vital to understand when it comes to team behavior: small outcomes and leverage behaviors (Covey et al. 2012, 138).

Small outcomes are lead measures that have a frequency of measurement that focus the team on achieving weekly or daily results. In addition, they are formulated in such a way that they give each member of the team latitude to choose their own method of achieving it. Whatever actions they choose, with a small outcome lead measure, the team is ultimately accountable for producing the result.

Leverage behaviors are lead measures that track the specific behaviors you want the team to perform throughout the week or day. They enable the entire team to adopt new behaviors at the same level of consistency and quality and provide a clear measurement of how well they are performing. With a leverage behavior measure, the team is accountable for performing the behavior, rather than for producing the result that this behavior is meant to accomplish.

Let's look at an example:

Lead measure Example 1:
Objective: Involve customers in developing our products.
KR 1: Increase customer touchpoints per day from 5 to 10.
KR 2: Increase number of work items per week, in which feedback from real customers is asked for by the team, from 2 to 8.

Have you spotted the types of lead measures that are paired here? KR 1 is a small outcome, the result that employees are held accountable for being increasing touchpoints per day. KR 2 is a leverage behavior lead measure. The behavior that is measured weekly to keep employees accountable is asking for feedback from a certain number of customers.

Identify Team Behaviors

The best way to develop behavior measures is to look at one of your high performers, or to your high-performing teams. What are they doing differently than everybody else? Could you measure their behavior and apply it to other teams? How many times do they show this behavior? Can you count it? This technique is especially useful if you are looking for internal behavior changes but can also be applied when you want to observe how other teams interact with customers.

If none of your teams show the behaviors required to achieve the results, you need to develop new team behavior by answering three questions:

1. Whose behavior directly influences the results? Is it the marketing team, sales team, or maybe the product development team?
2. What is the specific behavior team members need to perform to increase the results? Can you objectively observe and measure it (by how often the behavior occurs)?
3. What supporting behaviors do leaders need to perform to support the teams? Can you objectively observe and measure it?

Generally, behavior is understandable and has a logic behind it, especially if you know what triggered it. The Antecedent–Behavior–Consequence (ABC) model, also known as three-term contingency, is an observation tool used by behavioral scientists (Skinner 1953, Pierce 2004 and Cooper, Heron, and Heward 2007) to understand the triggers (antecedent) behind behavior and the impact of behavior (consequences).

To influence behavior, you need to analyze what causes it. What are the triggers and impact of the behaviors on team members? For example, what happens immediately before the behavior happens? And do team members receive encouraging nudges after they have performed the desired behavior? (Figure 4.4).

You shouldn't measure team behavior in all situations regardless of costs, value, or practicality. You should measure behavior when doing so is feasible and clearly advantageous. Measuring team behavior makes sense when:

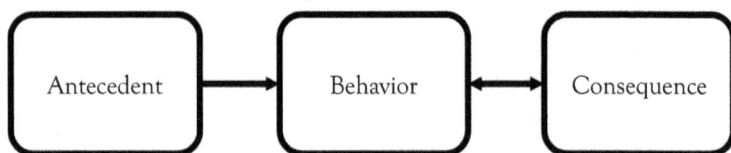

Figure 4.4 ABC Model for behavior analysis

- People are learning new skills.
- People need encouragement to keep behaving in the desired ways.
- It is critically important to change specific behaviors in order to achieve desired results.

10× Growth Lead Measures

In Chapter 1, we found that behavior change is the main focus of Lean OKRs, because the greatest challenge to the achievement of goals and visions through the successful execution of strategies is changing behaviors. From behavioral science, we see that we can measure behavior, and by using lead measures, we can achieve great leverage. So let's examine some lead measures that have changed the course of entire organizations and determine how exceptional success can be achieved:

- One billion hours of watch time per day. This was a game changer measure for YouTube in 2012 to 2016.
- Seven-day active users was a lead measure of the Google Chrome Browser Team. Fifty million was their target.
- Two thousand team messages sent is considered an active customer (Slack). At launch, in February of 2014, Slack had around 15,000 daily users. By February of 2015, the app boasted over 500,000 daily active users, with "tens of thousands" of new users added week after week, representing a 33-fold growth in just a year (Brown 2015).
- One file added to 1 folder on 1 device is considered an active customer (Dropbox). They grew from 100K registered users in 2008 to 33.9M registered users in 2017 (Mengoulis 2019).
- Using 5 of 20 features within 60 days is considered an active customer (Hubspot). They increased it from 3 in 2006 to 8,440 in 2013. In 2011, the company did $29M in revenue, which was a full 81 percent growth over the previous year (Brown 2014).

So, what do they all have in common? Well, what are they measuring? Indeed, each of the measures contains human behavior measures. In these cases, the high-level goals of the companies all measure behavior of their customers. These measures are often the "aha" moments for companies, and their correlation to long-term value was huge. That is how you end up with 10× growth!

Learn to Find Lead Measures

Finding good lead measures is hard. One technique that maps cause and effect is the Ishikawa diagram (Ishikawa 1968). Another is by looking how other companies use lead measures. In the Appendix, you will find a link to a list of measure examples. To apply the theory to a practical scenario, we will also take a look at the following example regarding online sales:

Lead measure Example 2:
Objective: Prevent "shopping basket" abandonment with online sales.
KR 1: Increase Weekly Customer Effort Score from 5 to 10.
KR 2: Reduce average number of guests' accounts abandoned baskets per day from 100 to 5 by June 1st.

In this example, we see two lead measures. The Weekly Customer Effort Score (CES) is an average score that measures how customers assess the effort they needed to invest to achieve their intended goal (Bryan 2020). You can use an (online) survey to ask your customers to rate the process they have been going through, in this case, an online shopping basket journey. Note: be careful with surveys, because they are often biased. An example of this response bias (Furnham 1986) could be the way the experiment is conducted or the desires of the participant to be a good experimental subject. The other measure is the average number of guests' accounts in which online shopping baskets have been abandoned. Are the measures in these KRs leading or lagging?

In this case, you can argue that an increase in the CES has predictive powers for the reduction of people leaving their baskets too soon. Less effort or a simplified "shopping basket journey" might result in less people abandoning their baskets. But do we know this for sure? This is something the team needs to investigate.

Maybe, the CES measure has predictive powers and then the team would have a real lever to achieve the Objective: Increases in the CES score could cause a reduction of shopping basket abandonment. It might also be the case that increasing the CES doesn't have the desired effect on shopping basket abandonment, and we need to investigate what behavior *will* predict customers abandoning their basket. Then, we ask if you could observe and measure that. As learning from your failures and improvement are often necessary, it is very important to reflect back at your OKRs regularly during the OKR cycle.

The Right Mix

The KRs should tell the complete story about the Objective. Measures can be lagging or leading. Lead measures can be small outcomes or leverage behaviors. The different angles, paired measures, and combinations are endless, so use your own judgment, experience, and skills to determine what kind of measurements serve the Objective.

When working with OKRs, you want to focus on both leading and lagging measures. It's the lead measures that are often used in operational teams. Company- or department-level OKRs tend to contain more lag measures in KRs. They are connected and linked throughout an organization (Figure 4.5).

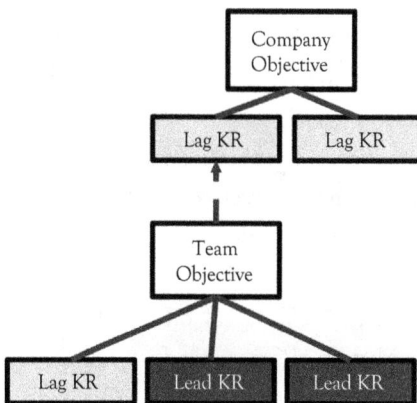

Figure 4.5 *How lag and lead measures are connected in the organization*

Over to You

Exercise: Measure for measure

With the lessons from the previous chapter, you have sketched out some OKRs. Let's put what you have learnt in this chapter to good use by refining your KRs. Don't forget to incorporate different kinds of measures.

Brainstorm some measures by using my magic questions from Chapter 3. Next, use the magic formula "[Increase/decrease] [Statistic] MEASURE from X to Y by DATE." This might feel a bit artificial, but it helps. Then the KRs for your Objective. Try using the following OKR format:

Objective: [What do you want to achieve?]
KR 1:
KR 2:
KR 3:

Sometimes, it helps to learn from others' mistakes and successes. For a little inspiration, check the link to the OKR examples in the Appendix which includes my thoughts and comments.

Measure Your OKR Success

How do you know if your OKRs work? Of course the needle of your KRs should have moved, but to see the success of your OKRs, you should also look at the impact they make on your company strategy. Did your OKRs have any positive impact on your business top or bottom line results? Did you actually make progress toward your vision? Is your business strategy working? Is your critical needle moving? To determine if your OKRs work, you need to have a few KPIs or critical measures that signals the entire organization if your efforts pay off (see Figure 4.6). For example, to find product market fit of a new product you've launched, you want to see an uptick in daily product usages. If OKRs work, you should see a significant improvement in performance of your KPIs. In Chapter 12, we will look closer how understand performance in more detail.

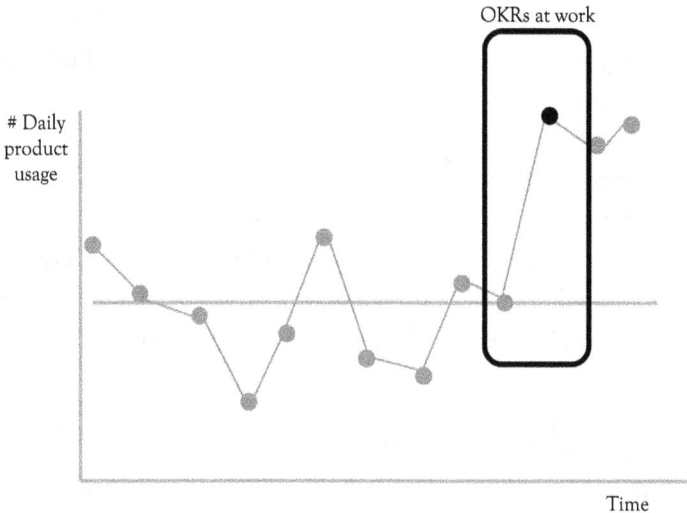

Figure 4.6 KPIs (e.g., number of customers using your product on a daily basis) are measures that track company performance over time. Here, OKRs are at work, making an impact on this critical needle

Well-Crafted KRs Are Conversation Starters

A client once told me: "OKRs really helped us to have data-driven discussions." I could not agree with him more. To quote Martin Klubeck in *Metrics*: "Metrics (and thus measures) should lead to discussions between customers and service providers, between management and staff. Conversations should blossom around improvement opportunities and anomalies in the data. The basis for these conversations should be the investigation, analysis, and resolution of indicators provided through metrics" (Klubeck 2011, 83–84). Understanding the concept of cause and effect on other company and team measures is key to implementing a good OKR system. This will be the topic of the next chapter.

Chapter Recap

In this chapter, we've explored measures and indicators, recognizing that any Objective is only as good as the KRs that let you know whether you are on track or not. We've drilled down into what good-quality, measurable KRs look like and how they can help you get a handle on progress.

We've learnt how good measures for KRs are crafted. We've seen that what's being measured must be clearly and precisely defined if it's to give us the evidence we need to track if progress is being made. We've looked at the difference between leading and lagging measures and the quality of evidence they can provide.

At this point, you should understand the value of clear and deliberate KRs for inspiring the changes in behavior that are required to meet your goals. You should have a clear picture of what measurable KRs are and what they could look like in relation to your organization's Objectives.

Chapter References and Notes

Barr, S. 2017. *How to Create a High-Performance Culture and Measurable Success, Prove It!*, 62. 1st ed. New Jersey: Wiley.

Basili, V.R., G. Caldiera, and H.D. Rombach. 1994. *The Goal Question Metric Approach, Chapter in Encyclopedia of Software Engineering*, 2nd ed. New Jersey: Wiley-Interscience.

Cooper, J.O., T.E. Heron, and W.L. Heward. 2007. *Applied Behavior Analysis*, 2nd ed. Upper Saddle River, N.J.: Pearson.

Hubbard, D.W. 2014. *How to Measure Anything: Finding the Value of Intangibles in Business*, 3rd ed. New Jersey: Wiley.

Klubeck, M. 2011. *Metrics: How to Improve Key Business Results*, 1st ed, 83–84. New York, NY: Apress.

Levy, S. 2011. *In the Plex: How Google Thinks, Works, and Shapes Our Lives*. New York, NY: Simon & Schuster. pp 163.

Mathsisfun. n.d. "Weight or Mass." www.mathsisfun.com/measure/weight-mass. html (accessed February 19, 2021).

Pierce, W.D., and C.D. Cheney. 2004. *Behavior Analysis and Learning*, 3rd ed. Mahwah, N.J.: Lawrence Erlbaum Associates Publishers.

Skinner, B.F. 1953. *Science and Human Behavior*. New York, NY: Macmillan.

CHAPTER 5

Cascading: Single OKRs to Rule Them All

Focus is the thing that makes the difference between excelling and flailing about in mediocrity.

—Christina Wodtke

Chapter Highlights

- The secret of high-performing organizations
- Lean OKRs
- Swarming around company OKRs
- OKR cadence and timelines
- Selecting single OKRs
- Integrating OKRs at all levels: ultimate, company, and team

While I was working for another FinTech company focused on private investment, the CEO asked me to help the executive team to implement OKRs and to roll them out throughout the entire organization. I knew they were missing a clear strategy and clear measures of success, and they couldn't explain their big, hairy, audacious goal (BHAG) simply, meaning they didn't understand it well enough.

Imagine a team of 500 to 1,000 people trying to connect with something no one completely understood. We needed to work on a way that facilitated every department would tie their work to the bigger picture.

First things first, for over half a day, we took the time to identify their most important needle. In their case, they wanted to attract new customers, meaning a 20 percent increase. From there, we could work on a plan to start changing behavior so everyone could reach that goal. "This is the first time I see how OKRs can help us achieve big results" one of the board members said.

The first and most important thing to improve was their customer onboarding process, because their research showed that new customers were dropping off to quickly during the initial signup phase. When this became the focus, we could cascade with a different and clear direction. The process was simple, everybody understood what the priority was and frontline employees could see how their work directly contributed to the big picture.

In the past decade, many ideas and best practices on how to cascade and scale OKRs have been described. However, there isn't a cookie-cutter approach that you can simply apply. An approach that works great for one organization, can work destructive for another. That is why this chapter explains varied approaches and alternatives. I advise to not blindly adopt one approach and stick to it, but rather start small, learn and adjust as you go.

The Secret of High-Performing Companies

In the previous chapters, we looked at defining your mission and vision and crafting your OKRs. If you and five people start up a company in the garage, you should be able to set and align your OKRs now, by putting them on a whiteboard and off you go. It's a different game when you are a company of say 1,000 or more people. It is in this chapter that I address how to use OKRs to boost performance, especially in larger, more complex, and multilayered environments.

But before you start cascading your OKRs down in your organization, I need to tell you a secret.

After working with dozens of companies in all shapes and sizes, and supplementing my knowledge by studying literature, I discovered an important goal-setting pattern that characterizes high-performing companies.

If we look within an organization, we see goals everywhere. Project goals, roadmap goals, initiative goals, personal development goals, Scrum goals, Key Performance Indicators (KPIs) with targets, and Quarterly Business Review (QBR) targets.

The highest level goal of a company is often put into a BHAG (which technically is an Objective). In the book *Build to Last*, Collins and Porras (2004) described the BHAG that is typical for highly visionary companies. This one bold goal is a powerful mechanism to stimulate progress. The authors wrote: "A BHAG engages people—it reaches out and grabs them in the gut. It is tangible, energizing, highly focused. People "get it" right away; it takes little or no explanation" (Collins and Porras 2004, 117). A BHAG is a long-term goal, sometimes lasting for many years.

One famous example would be the goal President Kennedy announced to the nation. In his speech on September 12, 1962, he said: "We choose to go to the Moon in this decade and do the other things, not because they are easy, but because they are hard; because that goal will serve to organize and measure the best of our energies and skills, because that challenge is one that we are willing to accept, one we are unwilling to postpone, and one we intend to win, and the others, too" as quoted in *John F. Kennedy and the Race to the Moon* (Logsdon 2010, 1–4). It's was a clear visionary goal that spoke to everybody's hearts. It was not an incremental change; it was one focused, bold goal.

It is no coincidence that in his book *Measure What Matters* (Doerr 2017), John Doerr deems "focus" as the first superpower. The examples from his book all contain single bold OKRs. David Kopf, cofounder from the Remind App, had this 10-week goal: "to interview 200 teachers across the United States and Canada." The team behind Google Chrome had this single Objective: "50 million seven-day active users." Together with the executive team behind the successful dating app The Inner Circle created, we created their long-term bold goal of "Every second a member gets together."

In *Scaling Up*, the author Verne Harnish suggested to have one "critical number" for the year or quarter to help you get closer to your BHAG (Harnish 2014, 152). Harnish defined a list of ten habits that companies must peruse to scale up, known as the "Rockefeller habits." One of these habits is the number 2 on that list: "everyone is aligned with the #1 thing that needs to be accomplished this quarter to move the company forward." In the book *Lean Analytics* (Croll and Yoskovitz 2013), the authors suggested a critical metric called the One Metric That Matters (OMTM, which technically is a KR). In the book *Four Disciplines of Execution* (Covey et al. 2012), they also talk about focus on the One Wildly Important Goal or the WIG as one of the four disciplines. In the book *North Star Playbook* (Cutler et al. 2019), we see One North Star Metric for one to three years into the future.

It's not a coincidence that we can observe a pattern here, which is a pattern that is characteristic for high growth companies. They exploit the ability to radically focus on *one* single goal to rule them all. However, focusing on a single goal with a single metric is generally a bad idea for reasons discussed in Chapter 3—Goals Gone Wild. To quote Casey Winters, chief product officer at EventBrite: "Fooling anyone at the company that only one metric matters oversimplifies what is important to work on, and can create tradeoffs that companies don't realize they are making" (Winters 2016). That is why frameworks such as the North Star Framework also include three input metrics that will support the single north star. Many companies favor capturing their long-term goal as an OKR, which gives them the flexibility to include two or three key measures. This will reduce unethical behavior, the effects of measurements gaming, and avoid an overemphasis on metrics.

Notice the variation in the duration these goals have. Some of them are 10 weeks long, others last four years. Let's look at how these goals relate to each other.

Goal Hierarchy

A long-term BHAG is often too abstract for people to determine what this quarter or year should be about. Therefore, organizations break down the long-term strategic goal into mid- and short-term tactical goals. In Figure 5.1, I've categorized some of the goals we discussed into three levels. Level 1 are long-term goals, level 2 are mid-term goals, and level 3 are short-term goals. Traditionally, OKRs are level 3 goals, but as you will read in this chapter, they can also be a great way to define level 1 and 2 types of goals. For now, we will continue to focus on level 3 goals.

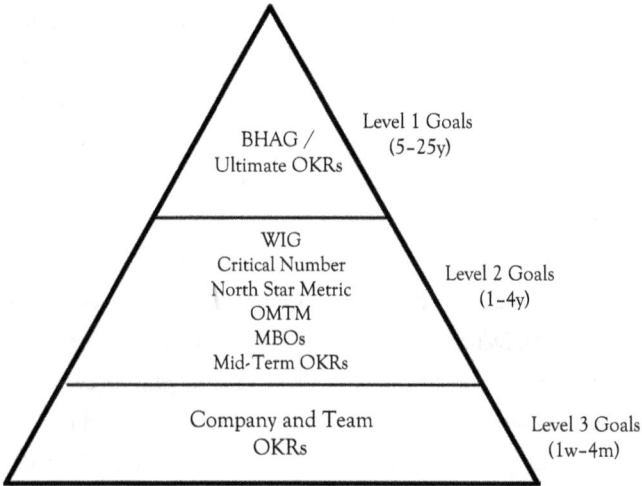

Figure 5.1 Goal hierarchy. From long-term OKRs to tactical short-term OKRs

Lean OKRs: Focus on Single OKRs

Some of your OKRs might have a modest stretch in them to make some small improvements in your market share; however, this will not reveal the benefits of OKRs. You won't see any significant change in any of your level 1 needles. Therefore, this approach is what I call the operational OKR approach. John Doerr (2017, 135) calls them "committed OKRs," others call them "roofshots" (instead of moonshot goals), because they are goals you expect to 100 percent achieve, and therefore, they are not much of a stretch. This approach to OKRs might work well for organizations that cannot take too much risk or don't have the budgets. Don't get me wrong, this approach might be a good match for your organization and situation, but if you want to do more than just run your business smoothly, you might be interested in the approach that follows. It might sound radical, but it changes the status quo, continuously. This is the realm of one Objective (Wodtke 2016), or what I like to call the Lean OKR approach.

How many OKRs would you need? *ONE.* With your (executive) team, you should only focus on one Objective and a handful of KRs per cycle, no matter how large your organization is. If OKRs are truly about breakthrough goals that require behavior change, only one Objective per department or team can be effective. Did you ever try to change your own behavior and habits? Then, imagine how hard it will be to change hundreds, thousands, or even millions of people's behavior at the same time! Maybe if you are using OKRs for a long time, like Google, you can have more at some point. However, I advise to always start with one Objective per cycle, no matter where your team is located on the organizational chart. That will force you and your team to make tough, risky, sometimes bold, decisions. But don't worry, it's only for one quarter.

On average, each person makes 30,000 decisions every single day (Hoomans 2015). What if they had the ability to base these daily decisions on *your* vision and business goals? Frontline employees work with your customers every day. Think about the impact you could make if they memorized your goals, keeping them at the forefront of their decision making. While slogging through the day-to-day activities can blur company goals, imagine the powerful, task-driven "army" you could mobilize if you managed to get one strong goal in their heads. You might get your company on course toward achieving something big.

In an enterprise setting, this is applied slightly differently, because you probably have very different business lines (Facebook has Instagram, WhatsApp, and Oculus VR) with their own business models. In this case, develop one corporate company OKR and one OKR per business line. Make sure they all contribute to the company OKR.

In *High Output Management*, Andy Grove wrote: "The art of management lies in the capacity to select from the many activities of seemingly comparable significance the one or two or three that provide leverage well beyond the others and concentrate on them" (Grove 1995, 58). Peter Drucker wrote: "Innovation requires knowledge, ingenuity, and, above all else, focus" (Drucker 2002, 95–100). In *Measure What Matters*, John Doerr wrote: "Top-line Objectives must be significant. OKRs are never a catchall wish list nor the sum of a team's mundane tasks. They are a set of stringently curated goals that merits special attention and will move people forward in the here and now. They link to the larger purpose we're expected to deliver around" (Doerr 2017, 56–57).

The law of diminishing returns also applies to goal setting. If you have one to three goals, you probably will be able to achieve them. If you have 4 to 10 goals, you might achieve 1 to 2 goals. If you have more than 11 goals, you will probably achieve none. If you don't understand what the true goal-throughput of the system really is, your organization's excess inventory of goals is likely to increase. Thus, I strongly suggest to start with *one* set of OKRs.

OKR Swarming

So far, we only talked about company OKRs, which are fine if you are a start-up. In larger companies, these OKRs cannot be achieved by a single group of people alone. Most of today's organizations are structured around business functions—which isn't a model I recommend. These functions are called the business units or departments of a company. Examples of these are finance, marketing, sales, product, IT, engineering, or customer success. Then, within these business functions, you find one or more groups of people or teams.

First, let me explain what I mean with a team: We can only call a group of people a team when the following conditions are met:

- The group of people has the same common goal.
- There is mutual dependency on each other to achieve that goal.

In all other cases, people are a group, not a team. There is nothing wrong with being a group or team, but as you will learn in Chapter 6, this requires a different way of leading. From a recent publication in *Nature* magazine, we can learn that that small teams are critical for disrupting (Wu, et al. 2019). In my experience with tech companies, I can confirm that small teams (5–10 people) are better in achieving OKRs than larger teams, but critically evaluate if this will work in your context. Since OKRs are a team sport, I like to call a group of people working on OKRs a *team*.

To break down company OKRs, many companies use their organization chart to determine how to link and connect OKRs to each other. Executives set company OKRs, and department heads set OKRs that will be connected to the company KRs. Then, leaders in close collaboration with their groups or teams create OKRs that connect to the KRs of their department. Figure 5.2 schematically shows a simplified version of how this hierarchy of OKRs might look like.

Connecting OKRs via the direct reporting lines of an organization chart might seem like a sound approach; however, most ambitious company OKRs require very close collaboration between all business

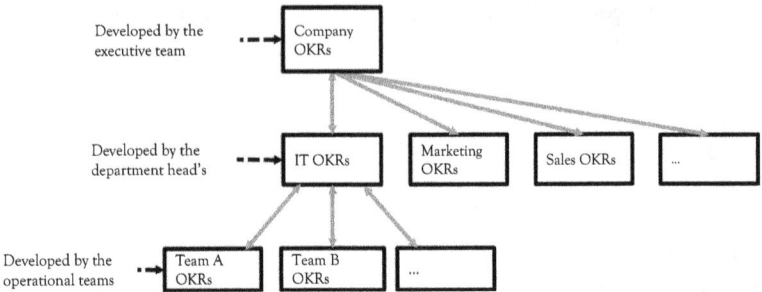

Figure 5.2 Hierarchy of company OKRs, department OKRs, and team OKRs

functions. For this reason, some organizations decide to create different organizational structures, like interconnected networks. A common approach is to use cross-functional/multidisciplinary teams that are teams that combine people from various business functions. These teams go by different names, most common are: product teams, squads (Kniberg and Ivarsson 2012), circles (Buck and Sharo 2017), and BusDevOps (business, development, operations). These teams are equipped with all the necessary skills to work autonomously on OKRs, which then contributes directly to the company OKRs. For example, a product team can be comprised of a business analyst, software engineers, quality assurance engineers, designers, and other experts. Imagine if you have hundreds of these teams, all having their own OKRs, contributing to your single company OKRs, then achieving remarkable results won't be far away.

By using this network structure, you can remove the complexity of hierarchical organizational structures. In Figure 5.3, you see a single company OKR at the center and teams *swarm* around it, each trying to influence the company KRs.

Not all companies, whether established or not, will have the flexibility to scale out OKRs as described earlier. What I described is an idealized model, because each company is different with its own unique set of challenges and thus asks for adaptations and exemptions. Therefore, I'll still mention and refer to departments as a logical grouping of multiple teams in the sections that follow.

With that said, OKR expert, Christina Wodtke suggests that at the end of the day, the most important thing when rolling out OKRs

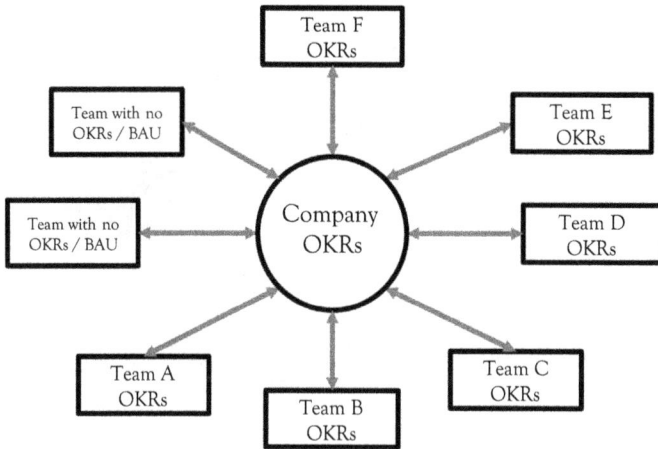

Figure 5.3 *Cross-functional teams connect directly to the company KRs*

companywide is to make sure that the company OKR remains the central focus, so that teams, departments, and even business as usual (BAU) activities revolve around the company's main strategic priority (Wodtke 2020). Accept that not all teams can always contribute to the company OKRs. In the section about team OKRs, I've made some suggestions about what approach teams can take when they cannot contribute.

OKR Cadence and Timelines

The default 90-day OKR cycle is also called the quarterly cadence, because it creates a pattern that will be repeated every quarter. Using this tactical approach, people can still feel that they missed the "big picture." Therefore, it is considered best practice to embed this 90-day cycle in a more encompassing and enduring cadence by adding an additional annual OKR cycle that supports strategic planning. Some might include an even longer cycle, as YouTube did, which had a four-year cadence (level 2). Even longer-term OKRs can be used to describe the ultimate Objectives a company wants to achieve. We call them the *ultimate OKRs* (level 1). Ultimate and annual OKRs and their corresponding cycles are there for one thing: To provide context (see Figure 5.4).

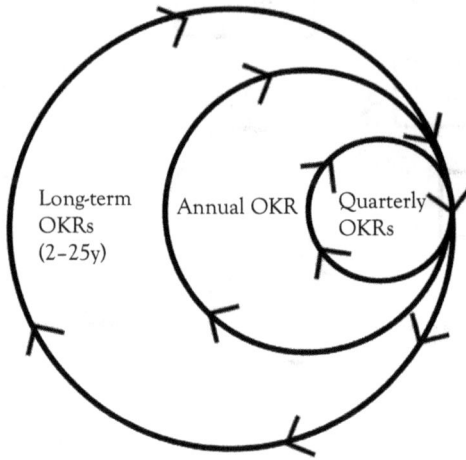

Figure 5.4 Different OKR cycles to create context for the small cycles

Dual Cadence OKRs

When you have an annual OKR cadence in combination with a quarterly cadence, we call this a dual cadence approach to OKRs. The executive team sets the annual company OKRs, while multidisciplinary teams use quarterly OKRs to move the needle of the annual OKRs. Some executive teams also decide to use both annual and quarterly OKRs, as this gives

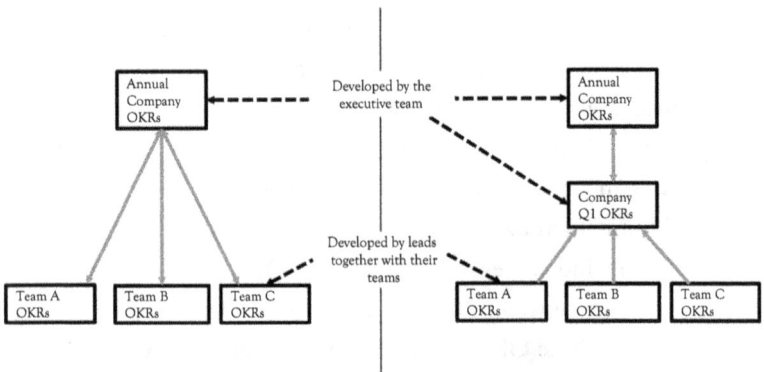

Figure 5.5 Two options for a dual cadence approach

them more agility. Which combination works for you depends on your company size and the level of agility you require (Figure 5.5).

An Alternative Approach: Mixed Frameworks

Although considered best practice, you don't have to use these longer-term OKRs and cycles, they are optional. If you find a better alternative to create a longer-term strategic context for your department and teams, that is fine, as long as you can communicate this effectively and consistently. Some companies prefer to keep OKRs only for strategy execution and use a different framework to define their strategic context.

Some successful combinations I've encountered are:

- Scaling Up's Critical Number (Harnish 2014, 152) plus quarterly OKRs: In the book *Scaling Up*, the author describes how companies should focus on the critical number and define OKRs (rocks) to move the needle.
- BSC plus quarterly OKRs: Another approach would be to use the Strategy Map (Kaplan and Norton 2004) from the Balanced Scorecard (Kaplan and Norton 1992) and select one Objective with its companioned measure that requires behavior changes.
- North Star Framework (Cutler et al. 2019) plus quarterly OKRs: Use team OKRs only to influence the input metrics.
- The 4DX's Wildly Important Goal (McChesney 2012) or the WIG plus quarterly OKRs: Use team OKRs to influence the company-level WIG.

If you choose one of the above alternatives, I recommend you to define your goals in the format of 4DX's Wildly Important Goal (WIG): *from X to Y by when* (McChesney 2012, 38).

In the upcoming sections of this book, I will outline the best practice solution in detail, including how to design and work with longer-term

OKRs in relation to your quarterly OKRs and team-level OKRs. The intricacies of the OKR cycle and how to execute the workshops and events that constitute it are the subject of Part 2 of this book.

Cascading OKRs: Trickling Down

All models are wrong, but some are useful

—George E. P. Box

Throughout history, there have been many attempts to create the perfect cascading model for goal setting with OKRs. I also found myself in the same pitfall, running in circles for many months, until I realized that the perfect model doesn't exist. All businesses are different, and there is no cookie-cutter approach when cascading goals or OKRs. There are just too many variables you need to consider. However, I will share with you the underlying patterns of success I have discovered, in order to help you accelerate your implementation of a cascading model that suits your specific business.

Much like an actual waterfall, the term cascading OKRs implies that there is a source and direction, but there is also the influence of an ecosystem that feeds back into the OKR cycle. Cascading implies top-down goal setting; however, setting and achieving OKRs in practice require both top-down and bottom-up efforts, as it is a collaborative and integrated process. This is also called bidirectional goal setting (see Figure 5.6), and this is why some prefer to call this process "connecting" or "linking" OKRs, instead of calling it cascading. You should cascade the intent (what are we trying to achieve), rather than copying the Objectives or KRs from the level above.

At the highest level, we have the BHAG or ultimate OKR (level 1), with an average time span of 5 to 25 years. The ultimate OKR acts as the true north for your organization. To get closer to your ultimate OKR, the executive team develops a strategy and they will inform what is the best bet to get closer. That bet is called your company OKR (level 3). These company OKRs are normally only set by the executive team, because they are companywide, even though there are some bottom-up techniques which I will also shed a light on subsequently. Annual company OKRs are optional (level 2), but can help provide more context. Working

Approach #1	Approach #2
Developed by the executive team	Developed by the executive team

⇩   ⇩

```
┌─────────────────────┐    ┌─────────────────────┐
│    Company OKRs     │    │    Company OKRs     │
└─────────────────────┘    └─────────────────────┘
```

↕   ↕

Leaders bring a candidate Objective ⇨
```
┌─────────────────────┐    ┌─────────────────────┐
│     Team OKRs       │    │     Team OKRs       │
└─────────────────────┘    └─────────────────────┘
```

⇧   ⇧

Teams create KRs for the proposed Objective	Objective and KRs are developed by the teams reviewed by their leaders

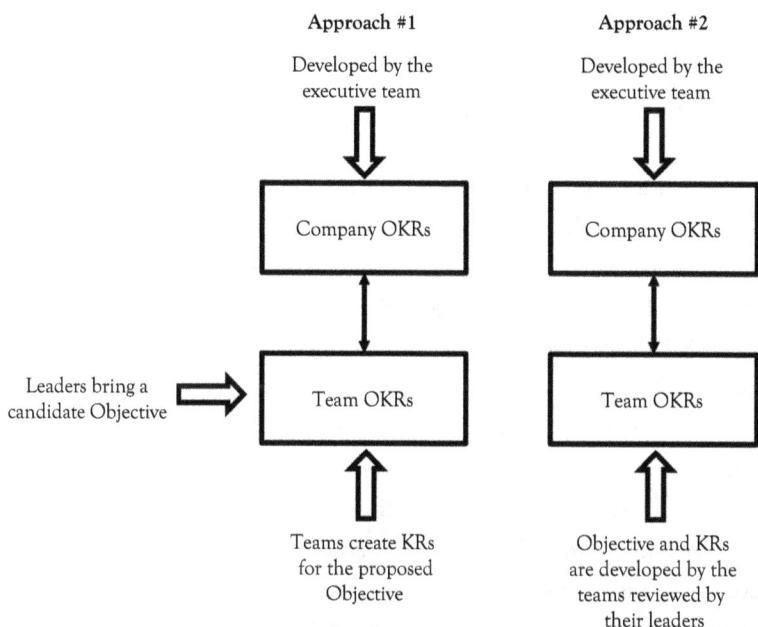

Figure 5.6 Two approaches for bidirectional goal setting. Top-down and bottom-up OKRs

exclusively with quarterly company OKRs gives you more focus and agility. Experiment with which approach works best for your company. If your company size is up to 30 employees, this model should be sufficient. Every employee in your organization should try to move the needle on the quarterly company OKRs.

For companies between 30 and 300 employees, you should also set quarterly team OKRs. The idea is that your quarterly company OKRs are *influenced* by the quarterly OKRs set by empowered teams (Figure 5.6). There are two common approaches to set OKRs at team level:

1. Leaders (CXOs, VPs, product managers, and engineering managers) create draft Objectives (optionally with candidate measures for the KRs) and bring them to the teams during the OKR setting workshop (see Chapter 7). The team can then provide feedback and determine to "accept" the Objective. Now, the team is invited to create KRs that will measure progress toward the Objective.

2. Teams themselves set the OKRs and ask their leader(s) to review the OKRs. Leaders can bring strategic context or any other information to the table that can help the team to create good OKRs.

Which approach works for your situation depends on the skills of your leaders and the maturity of your teams. My advice is to experiment with different approaches and see which one works best. It's important to get buy-in from the team, so don't dictate the rules, but try to coach. In Figure 5.7, you can see what a full cascading model could look like for an organization of ±300 people.

If your organization is bigger than 300 employees, you probably have more layers of management, for example: regions, countries, business units, or divisions. In such a scenario, you want to replicate the team-level pattern for every layer. Simplicity is key here. Be aware that the more levels of OKRs you create, the more overhead you will have to manage communication, alignment, and planning. To reduce the complexity, you want to keep your cascading as lean as possible. That starts by focusing on one company OKR per year or quarter.

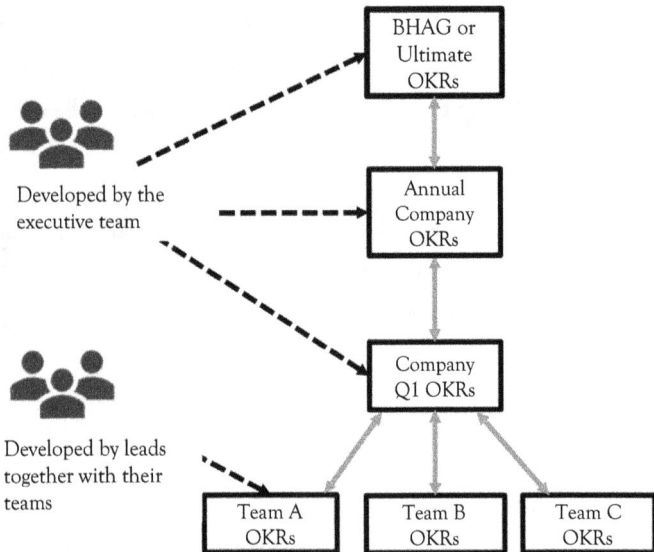

Figure 5.7 Ultimate OKRs, annual and quarterly company OKRs, and team OKRs linked together

As with any other tool, adjust OKRs to your company's needs. If ultimate or annual OKRs help to create context for your executive team, use them. Experiment and employ the reflection workshop (described in Chapter 10) and the end of the OKR cycle to evaluate your process and make improvements.

Selecting a Lean OKR

So how do you select a single company OKR for the year or quarter? First, remember the different categories of strategic initiatives from Chapter 2? To find a single OKR, you should use the following categories to divide all the aspects of your strategy (Figure 5.8):

- Sign-and-Go: These initiatives only require money and authority, that is, your signature of that of your boss, for example, to buy a new HR software system or acquire a new business.
- Breakthroughs or behavior change: This is the realm of OKRs. This is where significant change in human behavior is required (customers or employees). On what important Objective would you spend 20 percent or more of your company's effort in order to create a significant impact on your results?

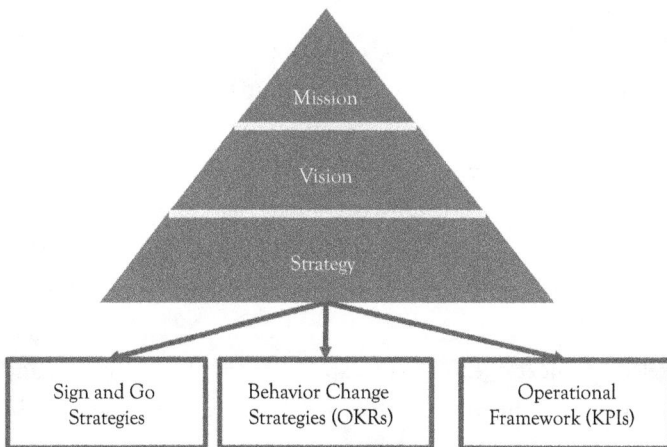

Figure 5.8 Three aspects of strategy

- Life-support or BAU: The processes and daily work that will keep the lights on in your organization and accounts for circa 80 percent of your workload. This is often managed using KPIs, for example, customer satisfaction score, number of new clients, or MRR.

Now look at all aspects of your strategy or plan. Can you put them in any of the aforementioned buckets? Is there one aspect of your plan that is not urgent enough, but is the thing that you always wanted to happen, but never got done? Maybe it is the one that has the potential to move the needle and bring significant changes to your organization? That is your candidate for your company OKR. Often, it is that type of goal that is not necessarily essential, as the goals in life-support are, but it is an important matter that no one ever gets to, despite the fact that everybody knows it needs to be done to move your company forward. In 4DX (McChesney, et al. 2012), they use the metaphor of war. The company OKRs is the war you need to win in order to achieve significant results. All your operational teams will then need to fight their battles (team OKRs) to win the war.

By using the three different buckets, your executive team should be able to select one company-level OKR for the quarter ahead. Next, with the same technique, your operational teams should now be able to also select single OKRs that connect to the company KRs.

Uncertainty of the Future

Using the different buckets to identify your most important quarterly company, OKRs have helped a lot of executive teams to select single quarterly OKRs. However, some like to also plan OKRs for a whole year. After the executive team has crafted their company strategy and defined their strategic priorities, they will probably have a list of company OKRs, each one with its own set of KRs. The company OKR that has the highest priority goes first, then, at the end of the quarter, they select the next one. This is an approach that I recommend, and it's discussed in the Christina Wodtke article "Cascading OKRs at Scale" (Wodtke 2020). This methodology works well when we consider the Cone of Uncertainty (Bauman 1958); that is to say, no one can predict

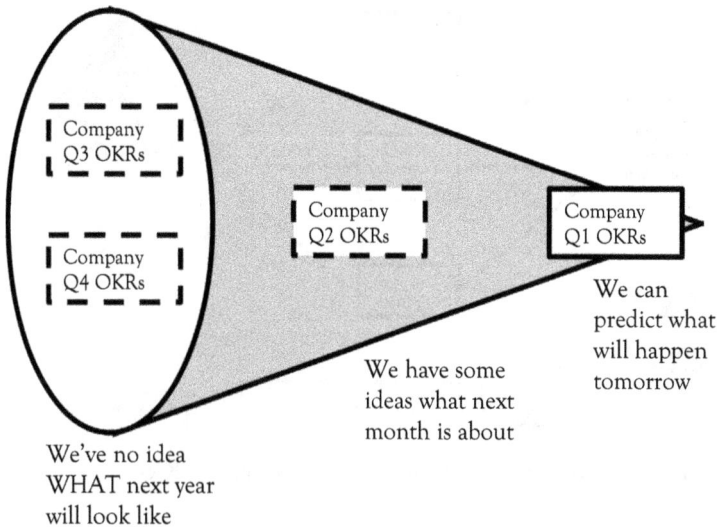

Company
Q3 OKRs

Company
Q2 OKRs

Company
Q1 OKRs

Company
Q4 OKRs

We can
predict what
will happen
tomorrow

We have some
ideas what next
month is about

We've no idea
WHAT next year
will look like

Figure 5.9 The Cone of uncertainty

the future, and the further into the future we attempt to predict, the less accurate our predictions are. With just-in-time delivery of OKRs (another Lean concept), you reduce risk and create options to pivot later when needed (Figure 5.9).

With that said, we also need long-term goals, those ultimate and annual OKRs. Without them as a guide, it is difficult to make (tentative) plans for the long haul. Regardless, this approach also saves leadership plenty of time and energy sketching out KRs at the end of each quarter.

Ultimate OKRs

Duration: Long term, 5 to 25 years
Who: Executive team
What: Visionary goal
How: Crafted off-site (for focus)

As you can see in Figure 5.10, the source for any company OKR is the company's mission, vision, and business strategy. Sometimes, an executive team chooses to reflect their vision of a BHAG in an ultimate OKR,

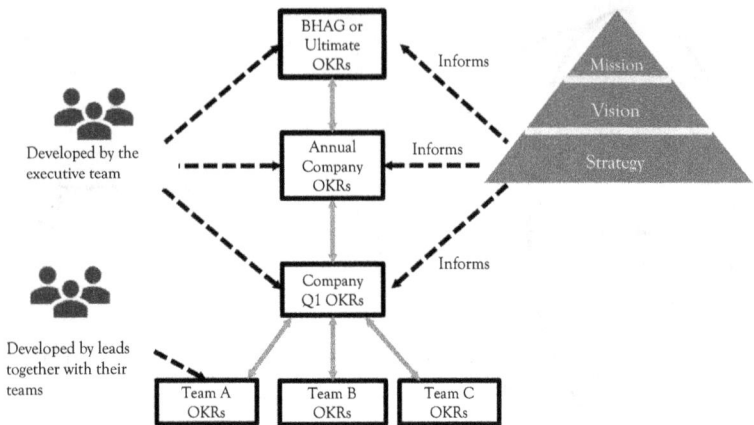

Figure 5.10 Ultimate OKRs are the highest level OKRs

creating a long-term Objective that will help to keep everybody focused on the coming year(s). These types of OKRs tend to be more bold, progressive, and aspirational in nature. Although these long-term OKRs are optional, they can be great to help you inspire and define multiple measures of success, instead of just one as is the case when you use a BHAG.

When you frame your visionary goal as an ultimate OKR, you can have multiple KRs (measures) that will counter the effects of a single measure. These KRs shouldn't be directly tied into financial measurements, like Annul Recurring Revenue (ARR), but should be focused on making an impact in the world (e.g., improving the lives of your customers). I do believe all companies are in business to make money, but try to avoid putting monetary metrics in your OKRs and focus on customer value instead.

Just like a BHAG, you want your ultimate OKR to inspire people. Don't be religious about not putting a number in the Objective. At this point, it is fine to use some bold number as long as it is an exciting motivational source for people.

Examples of Ultimate OKRs

Some companies prefer to use the OKR format to state their bold, long-term goal, the most famous one is from YouTube (Doerr 2017, 163):

Over to You

How to define an ultimate OKR:

- Arrange an off-site visionary workshop.
- Help your team define visionary OKRs. Some ideas can come from questions like:
  - What is your BHAG?
  - How can you tell a compelling story that will excite and engage the people to go after your vision?
  - What do engaged customers do with your product?
- Turn them into OKRs.
- Revisit your ultimate OKR every quarter or year.

Objective: Reach 1 billion hours of watch time per day
KRs:

- Search team + main app(+XX%), living room (+XX%)
- Grow kids' engagement and gaming daily watch time from X to Y hours
- Grow total VR catalog from X to Y videos

Health Check Metrics

While you and everybody else is focused on this ultimate OKR, you should also keep an eye on your health metrics. These bold goals are often accompanied by another bold goal: the "profit per X" measure as described in more detail in the book *Scaling Up* (Harnish 2014, 120–121). Usually, the denominator (X) sets the context for this measure; some examples are "profit per plane" to "profit per booked appointment" or "profit per premium customer." This denominator is also a great candidate to put in your ultimate OKRs. Creating ultimate OKRs doesn't have to be difficult. You could use the same workshop format as setting regular OKRs (see Chapter 7).

> **Exercise**
>
> Sketch out what an ultimate OKR could look like for your company.
> Could you define a BHAG and turn that into an OKR?

Ultimate OKRs are representative of the goals everybody is dreaming of: goals that achieve exponential growth. Ultimately, this is the realm of OKR moonshots (the ultimate stretch goals). If you want everybody in your organization to focus on a single OKR, ultimate OKRs could be a great place to start. Developing OKRs at this level is very powerful and I recommend that you craft one.

Alternative Models

Ultimate OKRs are the highest level goals you will have in your organization. Alternative goals that can be used at this level are Kept Promise Indicators related to your brand promise. An example of a Kept Promise Indicator (also KPI) goal would be from Rackspace, a company offering cloud solutions. Their KPI was: "Fanatical Support: Over 1,400 trained cloud engineers" (Harnish 2014, 115). If you prefer to only use a BHAG at this highest level, that is also fine.

Annual Company OKRs

Duration: One year
Who: Executive team (with input from multidisciplinary teams)
What: Annual goal, informed by your strategy
How: Crafted off-site (for focus)
When: 1 to 2 weeks before the fiscal year ends.
Must have before proceeding:

- Mission, vision, and strategy, preferably a BHAG or ultimate OKRs
- Health KPIs
- The "critical number" as defined by the Rockefeller habits #2 (Harnish 2014, 152)

Whether you are a Small- to Medium-Size Enterprise (SME) or an established multinational, you need to have a strategic plan. Your strategic plan will inform your annual OKR. Can you pick one critical performance measure from your strategic plan that is the most important one? Subsequently define one breakthrough goal that requires a change in human behavior to make significant impact on this critical metric. Try to convert it into an annual OKR. That would be your *war*.

To develop a longer-term, behavioral-change OKR, consider this question: "If every other area of your operation remained at its current level of performance, then which is the one area where change would have the greatest impact?" Another question could be: "Where in your company/team is a significant change in performance required to make all the difference?" Next, ask: "What behavior (customer or employee) needs to be changed that would make all the difference to this Objective?"

Example

Let's say you are in the mobile phone business. Your annual company OKR might look like this:

Objective: Customers promote Acme Model X to their friends.

KRs:

- Increase weekly number of customers that promote us to their friends from over 10K by June 1st.
- Increase the average product rating of model X from 3.4 to 4.8 by November 21st.

If you are a FinTech company handling online payments, then your annual company OKR could be:

Objective: Boost the customer lifetime value (CLTV) of large and SME customers.

KRs:

- Increase CLTV of enterprise customers from 200K to 2M.
- Increase CLTV of SME customers from 20K to 50K.

These questions will force you and your leadership team(s) to think about the outcome they want to achieve in the near future. Sometimes, you need to ask these questions twice to get to the real behavioral change you seek. Use the OKR setting workshop format in Chapter 7 to define your annual OKR during your off-site event. By the end of this event, you will have an annual OKR, and it will probably be one that will make all the difference in your company.

You should review the annual OKR with your executive team every quarter or month. Adjust this OKR as you go, since it only acts as a line in the sand. Some include the discussion around annual OKRs in their Quarterly Business Review (QBR).

Health Check Metrics

While focusing on this annual OKRs, you should also continue to be aware of your company's health metrics. Use the perspectives from the Balanced Scorecard to develop KPIs that you want to monitor on a continual basis. Health metrics at this level could be related to shareholders, employees, customers or processes and financial outcomes. Some examples of health metrics are profit per month, gross margin per month, MRR or ARR, EBITA, employee and customer engagement, number of leads, lead time of processes, costs, and accuracy of data.

Some find it useful to also target the expected financial outcomes to give more context to their OKRs. Be careful with communicating these financial goals, before you know it, these will get more attention and urgency than your OKRs.

Over to You

Define where you want to be one year from now. It's okay to have an OKR that takes even longer. Most extraordinary results take time. What are the main capabilities that your company must pursue over the next year?

Alternative Models

If you don't need long-term planning—when you are a start-up, for example—you can skip this annual OKR phase and go directly to company OKRs every quarter. Alternately, you can replace the annual OKR with one of the alternative approaches mentioned before. Other powerful ways to motivate and inspire people are to experiment replacing the annual OKRs with the following:

- Replace the qualitative Objective in your annual OKRs with a quantitative statement to make it more inspirational and powerful. Use quarterly team OKRs to influence the KRs.
- "One Critical Number" (Harnish 2014, 152), plus quarterly team OKRs. Use quarterly team OKRs to influence the critical number.
- One Objective from your Strategy Map, with its companioned KPIs, that requires behavior changes. Use quarterly team OKRs only to influence the KPIs.
- Use the North Star Framework and define one north star metric and develop two to four input metrics. Use quarterly team OKRs only to influence the input metrics.

Quarterly Company OKRs

Duration: Quarterly (90 days)
Who: Executive team (with input from multidisciplinary teams)
How: Crafted off-site (for focus)
What: Recommended: a single company OKRs per quarter
When: 1 to 2 weeks before the quarter ends
Must have before proceeding:

- Mission, vision, and strategy, preferably a BHAG or ultimate OKRs
- Annual company OKRs
- Health check metrics

The annual company OKR helps the executive team to inform their company quarterly OKRs. For focus reasons, you really want to zoom in on only one company OKR per quarter: the 90-day challenge as I like to call it.

Setting quarterly company OKRs is optional, but highly recommended if you need more company agility. When you do use quarterly company OKRs, you might want to skip the annual company OKR. When executives start out with OKRs, they like to stay in the comfortable position of doing annual planning and let the departments and teams decide where, when, and how to contribute to the annual KRs. However, too many annual OKRs can be perceived as too abstract. This can result in sandbagging, because teams will always find a KR in the list of annual OKRs that will suit them. To avoid this, you can set more concrete quarterly company OKRs that are aligned with higher-level OKRs or business metrics. In Chapter 7, about OKR setting workshops, we will dive deeper into how to do this practically.

If the executive team likes to do a bit more upfront planning, they can choose to develop four OKRs for the upcoming year. Pick only one OKR for the first quarter. The others are just a line in the sand for the future. Don't spend too much time on future OKRs as the idea is to remain flexible the farther into the uncertain future you look and attempt to predict (although they might help other teams with their long-term planning). Just like with an annual OKR, you want to focus on changing people's behavior, but this time in the short term. Quarterly company OKRs can help to bring back the agility your company needs. If you only define annual OKRs and jump into team OKRs, you might lose the possibility to correct course or pivot when your market is changing.

You should review the quarterly OKRs with your leadership team every week during a weekly check-in.

Bottom-Up OKRs

In some organizations, the leadership team installs a practice where department leaders or even all employees can make suggestions for the company OKRs. This can be done via a (digital) poll system. If you install this practice, make sure you treat the outcome of the poll with respect and seriously consider the result. Communicate about this openly.

Example

Let's go back to FinTech business example. Your annual company OKR might look like this:

Objective: Our customers stay longer with us.

KRs:

- Increase CLTV of enterprise customers from 200K to 2M.
- Increase CLTV of SME customers from 20K to 50K.

Based on the company's strategy to increase CLTV, the executive team agrees to focus on the "Increase CLTV of SME customers" KR for this quarter since this is the most problematic problem. A quarterly company OKR might look like this:

Objective: SME customers stay with us their whole life.

KRs:

- Increase CLTV of European SME customers from 20K to 50K.
- Increase CLTV of North American SME customers from 20K to 60K.
- Increase CLTV of APAC SME customers from 20K to 45K.

Health Check Metrics

The employed health metrics on a quarterly basis will be the same as on an annual level. You want to keep an eye on them while you focus on quarterly results.

Alternative Models

The alternative models from the annual OKRs can be also be used for quarterly company OKRs, but then for a shorter time.

Team OKRs

Duration: Quarterly (90 days)

Who: Departments and/or teams

What: Recommended: a single tactical team OKR per team per quarter

How: Crafted autonomously through team negotiation

When: Before the quarter begins, immediately after the company OKRs have been announced

Must have before proceeding: Annual or quarterly company OKRs or a critical business metric (Figure 5.11)

Now that all the long-term and company OKRs are developed, they need to be announced to the whole organization. This happens in the OKR kick-off meeting. You can see how that works in more detail in Chapter 8. After the announcement of the quarterly company OKR, all leaders together with their teams will try to define team OKRs that aim to impact the company's OKR. The idea is to *influence* the quarterly company KRs, or if you are working in a large company, this could also be the country, region, or department KRs. See more on connecting and aligning OKRs in Chapter 8—the alignment workshop.

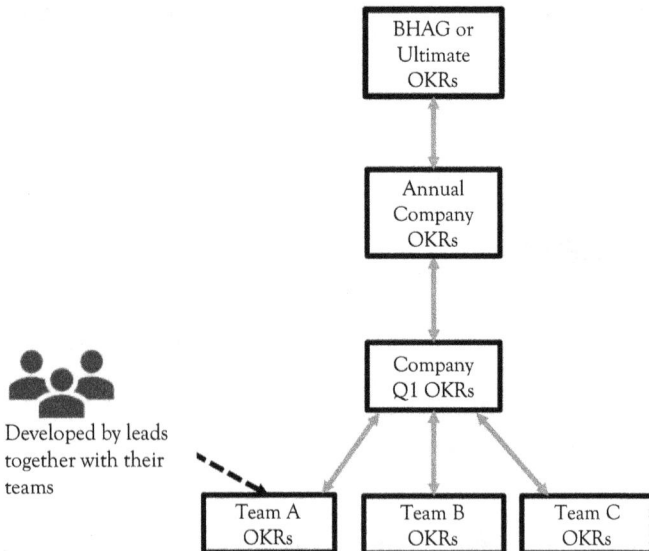

Figure 5.11 Team OKRs that contribute to the company's first quarter OKR

If the company OKR is the *war*, the team OKRs are the *battles* as they are called in 4DX (McChesney 2012, 40–41). Single OKRs for teams are best rolled out on a quarterly basis. The more OKRs you try to enforce, the less focus and engagement you can expect, and the higher chances are you will need to deal with demotivated team members. A team can only achieve one Objective with excellence in such a short timeframe. I wouldn't recommend deviating from this standard, because it will blow up your OKR complexity. So, let me be very prescriptive here: *Teams should only use one single OKR at a time.* No team should have more than one OKR. You should review the OKRs with all team members every week during a weekly check-in.

What If Teams Cannot Contribute?

The following question often arises: What should my teams be doing if they cannot contribute to this single company OKR? This is especially true for service teams like finance, IT, legal, and customer service. It can also happen that the current (product) strategy is more important to follow than focusing on the company OKR. There can be three solutions:

1. Some quarters, teams can contribute more than others (see Figure 5.12). However, it's a leader's job to convince teams that they CAN. Try to spark some creativity in the team. Challenge them to think outside the box. Five percent contribution is better than nothing. For example, if the company OKR is about an increase of new customers leads and you are product team, you might think this OKR is mainly for the sales teams. However, maybe the product team can collaborate with the sales teams (this often requires a change in their own behavior) to the product demo's. Always challenge teams to contribute to the company OKRs.
2. Accept the fact that not all teams can contribute to the company OKRs. Let the team measure their performance though the help of KPIs. Setting BAU goals in the form of KPIs with targets is perfectly fine. Having a radical focus on a single OKR doesn't mean you should forget about your other BAU activities. Most teams are still responsible for keeping the lights on (e.g., customer support,

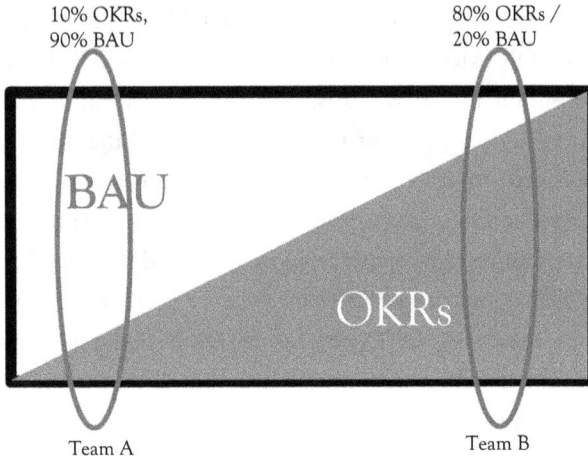

Figure 5.12 BAU work (managed and monitored with KPIs) vs. OKRs work. The distribution is different per quarter, department, and team

sales and marketing, and product development teams). Just like KPIs at the company level, teams should also use KPIs to monitor the performance of their BAU work. *Remember: You measure your team performance with KPIs, not with OKRs.*

3. Teams that fall outside of contributing to the quarterly company OKRs can also develop their own OKRs to improve their service or process. However, if no breakthroughs or behavior change is needed, fall back on KPIs to improve speed and quality of their BAU.

What If We Cannot Finish an OKR Within the OKR Cycle (e.g., Quarterly)?

I get this question a lot. The answer is simple. You learn! Learn why you didn't move the needle enough on your KRs. Were you too optimistic? Too pessimistic? Did you use the correct measures in your KRs? Incorporate what you learn into the setting of the next quarterly single company OKR. Repeat.

Sometimes, it happens that the Objective itself cannot be achieved within one OKR cycle. Then, the leaders with their teams can decide to bring the Objective to the next OKR cycle and define different KRs.

We Have More Layers in Our Organization

If your organization is more complex and contains multiple layers (e.g., country, region, business unit, and teams), you can repeat the team OKR pattern. Where possible, don't let OKRs reflect your hierarchical organizational structure. Don't set them on all possible reporting lines. Instead, use the introduction of OKRs as an opportunity to flatten your organization, or change the way you can be organized in the future (e.g., decentralized organizational structures like a sociocracy). See the section "OKR Swarming" to learn how company OKRs could be used as a network rather than a hierarchy.

Health Check Metrics

Health metrics on team level can vary from quantitative KPIs like team happiness to quantitative metrics like the health of the codebase, number of customer complaints, API performance, process lead time, and throughput. What is important for your team to monitor on a continuous basis? Henrik Kniberg, Agile Coach at Spotify, developed the Spotify Health Check for teams (Kniberg 2014). It's a qualitative self-diagnosis that teams can conduct every quarter or so to check how healthy they are with regard to aspects like collaboration, fun, skills, and more.

Examples or team-level health metrics are as follows:

- Qualitative measures: quality of the codebase, are we having fun, how fast are we delivering to customers, how suitable is our process, are we autonomous in our decision making, and do we still learn?
- Quantitative measures: new monthly leads, costs, net promoter score, average conversion time per lead, average process lead time, average process throughput, product or output quality, mean time between failure, and mean time to recover.

Team-Level OKR Examples

Based on the quarterly company OKRs from the previous section (increase CLTV of SME customers) and the product strategy, the leaders of several teams took the challenge to improve the customer lifetime value. Their strategy was to focus on the support of additional currencies, as to enable their customers to increase their conversion options. Based on new customer insights, this would then entice SME customers to stay with the company longer, because they are unlikely to leave for competitors which support only a smaller variety of foreign currencies. The leaders of the credit card team, debit card team, charging team, and marketing team created Objectives for their teams. The final OKRs for these teams looked like this:

Credit card team

Objective: Customers worldwide can use their credit card with their local currency.

KR 1: Increase number of supported credit card currencies in APAC from 5 to 35.

KR 2: Increase number of supported credit card currencies in Europe from 3 to 25.

Marketing team

Objective: Clients write positively about our products.

KR 1: Increase number of big client testimonials on new currencies from 5 to 20.

KR 2: Increase number of SME testimonials on new currencies from 5 to 20.

Debit card team

Objective: Support all major currencies for our debit cards.

KR 1: Increase number of supported debit card (settlement) currencies in APAC from 2 to 20.

KR 2: Increase number of supported debit card (settlement) currencies in Europe from 3 to 25.

Alternative Models

There is also a model where the executive team sets no OKRs, but only defines a critical business metric with an ambitious target (see section "An

Alternative Approach: Mixed Frameworks"). After the announcement of this metric and target, teams set their quarterly team OKRs. The idea remains the same, teams should influence this critical metric with their OKRs.

Individual OKRs

Some organizations cascade OKRs even further down to individual OKRs. On this level, employees are asked to contribute to the team, department, or even the company KRs. However, I've never seen this model work well in practice. Individual OKRs are almost always related to personal development goals, which may not be in the best interest of the team. If you want to achieve significant change in a company, you cannot do this alone; achieving OKRs is a team sport. Moreover, changing individual behavior works better with group pressure and group commitments. If you are a start-up company and your marketing team is one person, I believe you can still use OKRs for the "team." However, I generally recommend avoiding the hassle of setting individual OKRs and stop the cascading process at team level. If you insist on tracking individual employee performance, use the tools and techniques from Chapter 4, but do me a favor: never refer to them as OKRs.

Chapter Recap

In this chapter, we've looked at the bigger picture. We've explored cascading Lean OKRs in detail and established a clear view of how aligned OKRs can work on different levels and time frames to help your organization achieve its most ambitious goals.

We've learnt about ultimate OKRs that communicate your mission and vision, company OKRs that capture annual or quarterly goals for everyone, and team OKRs that ensure ownership of the OKRs at every level of the organization.

By now, you should have a clear picture of how Lean OKRs can work on a number of levels to bring about real change. Importantly, you should recognize the importance of being realistic in selecting your (number of) goals and you should feel informed and prepared to navigate the process of cascading your OKRs.

Chapter References and Notes

Bauman, C.H. 1958. "Accuracy Considerations for Capital Cost Estimation." *Industrial & Engineering Chemistry* 50, no. 4, 55A–58A, Doi:10.1021/i650580a748

Buck, J.A., and S. Villines. 2017. *We the People: Consenting to a Deeper Democracy*. Washington, DC: Sociocracy.

Collins, J.C., and J.I. Porras. 2004. *Built to Last: Successful Habits of Visionary Companies*, 10th revised ed. New York, NY: Harper Business.

Croll, A., and B. Yoskovitz. 2013. *Lean Analytics: Use Data to Build a Better Startup Faster*, 1st ed. Sebastopol: O'Reilly Media.

Cutler, J., and J. Scherschligt. 2019. *The NorthStar Framework*. San Francisco: Amplitude. https://amplitude.com/north-star

Drucker, P.F. August 2002. *The Discipline of Innovation*, 95–100, 102, 148. Boston: Harvard Business Review.

Grove, A.S. 1995. *High Output Management*, 2nd ed. New York, NY: Vintage Books.

Harnish, V. 2014. *Scaling Up: How a Few Companies Make It...and Why the Rest Don't (Rockefeller Habits 2.0)*, USA: Gazelles, Inc.

Hoomans, J. March 20, 2015. "35,000 Decisions: The Great Choices of Strategic Leaders." The Leading Edge. Roberts Wesleyan College. https://go.roberts.edu/leadingedge/the-great-choices-of-strategic-leaders

Kaplan, R.S., and D.P Norton. February 02, 2004. *Strategy Maps: Converting Intangible Assets into Tangible Outcomes*, 1st ed. Boston: Harvard Business School Press.

Kaplan, R.S., and D.P. Norton. January–February 1992. *The Balanced Scorecard—Measures that Drive Performance*. Boston: Harvard Business Review Magazine.

Kniberg, H. September 16, 2014. "Squad Health Check Model – Visualizing What to Improve." *Spotify Engineering*, Blog. https://engineering.atspotify.com/2014/09/16/squad-health-check-model/

Kniberg, H., and A. Ivarsson. November 14, 2012. "Scaling Agile @ Spotify with Tribes, Squads, Chapters & Guilds." https://blog.crisp.se/2012/11/14/henrikkniberg/scaling-agile-at-spotify

Logsdon, J.M. 2010. *Prologue: We Should Go to the Moon*. In *Race to the Moon. Palgrave Studies in the History of Science and Technology*, ed. J.F. Kennedy. New York, NY: Palgrave Macmillan. doi:10.1057/9780230116313_1

McChesney, C., S. Covey, and J. Huling. 2012. *The 4 Disciplines of Execution: Achieving Your Wildly Important Goals*, 1st ed. New York, NY: Free Press.

NASA. 1962. Transcript of John F. Kennedy Moon Speech - Rice Stadium. https://er.jsc.nasa.gov/seh/ricetalk.htm (Last accessed February 20, 2021).

Winters, C. 2016. "Chief Product Officer at Eventbrite, Don't Become a Victim of One Key Metric." Blog: https://caseyaccidental.com/one-key-metric-victim

Wodtke, C. February 16, 2020. "Cascading OKRs at Scale. 2020." https://medium.com/@cwodtke/cascading-okrs-at-scale-5b1335812a32 (accessed February 10, 2021).

Wodtke, C. September 02, 2016. "One Objective to Rule them All." http://eleganthack.com/one-objective-to-rule-them-all/ (accessed February 10, 2021).

Wu, L., D. Wang, and J.A. Evans. 2019. "Research: Large Teams Develop and Small Teams Disrupt Science and Technology." *Nature* 566, pp. 378–382.

CHAPTER 6

Empowered Teams Make the Difference

An empowered organization is one in which individuals have the knowledge, skill, desire, and opportunity to personally succeed in a way that leads to collective organizational success.

—Stephen Covey

Never tell people how to do things. Tell them what to do, and they will surprise you with their ingenuity.

—General George S. Patton

Chapter Highlights

- Creating urgency for OKRs
- Empower teams with OKRs
- Building trust and psychological safety
- Advise on leadership skills
- Teaching teams how to use OKRs

During an intake conversation, the CEO of a 200-employee technology company proudly showed me all the OKRs within the company. His main concern was that he didn't see any positive impact on the bottom-line results (revenue, cross sales). He created five Objectives at the company level, each with five KRs, resulting in 25 KRs. Then, he personally created (with good intentions) all the team-level OKRs for his 15 teams, most of them with output focused KRs, such as "Build feature X," "Start working with Scrum," "Call 25 prospects per week," and "Publish the first blog post by August." I told him that OKRs are not to micromanage, command-and-control what teams should be working on. Instead, he should try to bring problems to the teams so they have the freedom to make their own choices to solve them. His response: "Are you crazy? How on earth could I then control what my teams are working on. This is a typical example of a manager that doesn't trust his teams to do the right thing. OKRs do not necessarily prevent dysfunctional leadership styles, because the OKR system only helps you with structure and process, not with instilling trust in your teams. That needs to come from you.

If you are going for ambitious OKRs, you need to trust and empower your teams. Of course, you should also support and coach them and provide help when needed. Never push teams and employees into what we have identified as the danger zone. OKRs are always about challenging people to learn, to make discoveries, and to get them out of their comfort zone, into the learning zone. It's in that learning zone where people need to feel secure and know that it is safe to experiment.

In my trainings, I help companies to (re)charter their teams. I help leaders to understand how to trust, build a psychologically safe environment, and create urgency to start using OKRs. I found that when leaders embrace this new way of thinking, they empower their teams to thrive. Their performance will improve and innovation increases.

OKRs are a big cultural shift for companies and their leaders. In this section, I will answer the question of how to empower your teams with OKRs.

In the previous chapter, I explained the difference between a *team* and a group, but didn't explain why it is important to make the distinguishment. People that are working on the same tasks or assignment are not necessary a team if they are not mutually dependent on each other to achieve a mutual outcome. How people communicate and behave is also different in a group than in a team.

Leading a team is different than a group of people. For example, you approach a team member as a representative of the entire team. You approach a member of a group individually, and they speak for themselves.

Whether or not you are a team in the context of OKRs is important to understand. Sometimes, it can be better to not create a team, but simply align a group of people toward the achievement of OKRs. For example, you can set OKRs for a customer support desk department where each individual needs to promote a new product. The whole group can check-in on this OKR every week, but they are not a team. However, I've seen the greatest successes when cross-functional and empowered teams work together to move the needle on their KRs. A stable and diverse team that is end-to-end responsible for an outcome is one of the most effective organizational structures to achieve customer centric OKRs. That's easier said than done as it turns out that 75 percent of most cross-functional teams fail (Tabrizi 2015). The common root causes are unclear governance, lack of accountability, unclear goals, and by organizations' failure to prioritize the success of cross-functional initiatives. It shouldn't surprise you that having clearly established goals and deadlines (OKRs) is among the top four reasons to succeed with cross-functional teams.

I've met many leaders that said they want to change their organization to have self-organized and cross-functional teams, but never made the jump. With the three alignment strategies as discussed in Chapter 8 and the proposed practices from this chapter, you have all the tools to turn this into a reality.

OKRs as a Team Sport

I have never seen individual OKRs work well in a company context and in my method I do not cascade OKRs down beyond the team level, for the reasons described in Chapter 5. In my eyes, achieving Lean OKRs is a team sport. Consequently, when you are the leader of a single team or multiple teams working with Lean OKRs, you need to be in a coaching role. Managing involves telling, directing, tending to immediate needs, and exerting authority. Coaching is about exploring, facilitating, partnership, and long-term improvement. I even dare say that true cross-functional and high-performing teams don't need to be managed. However, they do need someone who takes on a leadership role and provides them with the strategic context and a complex problem to solve, so they can make the best decisions possible to solve this problem and are held accountable to the results.

If your company is a start-up or scale-up, OKRs can help to develop your new leaders. When you have junior managers in your organization, then OKRs provide a great tool to give a boost to their competencies and skills. OKRs can help managers to develop boundaries and constraints for *empowered* teams. Not that you can dictate the rules, but together you can set priorities and help them to understand what is most important for the organization. They can act as the guardrails for the team.

Team Chartering With OKRs

Before you create a new team to work on OKRs, you need to develop a plan on how the team will work together. That plan is called a *team charter* or the orientation phase. It helps to set direction and formalize agreements. A team charter not only works well for operational teams, but executive teams can learn and get value from a team charter as well. Chartering a team is the first step in building a high-performance and empowered team.

How to Charter a Team

During a workshop, a team needs to agree on a common mission, vision, and team values. Next, they should define norms, rules, working agreements, and the context. Then, you as a leader need to provide the team with a clear Objective to work on. The team will then create KRs to measure progress toward the Objective. They will do this in close collaboration with you as the leader. If you have existing teams and you never created a proper team charter, it can bring a lot of value to do redo the charter. You can do this through a team charter workshop prior to your OKR setting workshop, or you may even combine them. I suggest you read the book *Liftoff* (Larsen and Nies 2016), where they describe in detail how to facilitate a team charter. Ask a skilled facilitator to prepare this workshop to get the most value out of the team charter.

There are multiple team charter formats available, some of the common elements are as follows:

- Mission statement: the reason why a team exists.
- Values: how team members treat each other.
- Norms: how team members interact, behave, resolve conflicts, and share information.

- Goals: What are the team OKRs?
- Scope or context: What is the team going to do, but more important, what are they *not* going to do? What is our sandbox?
- Roles, responsibilities, weaknesses, and strengths? What skill-set does the collective have? How will each member contribute, what are unspoken roles (e.g., who brings coffee, who schedules meetings)? What are we really good at and what skills do we lack?
- Celebrations: What do we celebrate and how?

Most of the elements we already covered in this book, but some we didn't discuss and are worth explaining in the context of team empowerment.

Values

Many executives and managers mistakenly confuse core values with aspirational goals for the future. Unlike goals, values are the core principles your organization or team needs to live by. Committing to core values isn't an easy job. Years ago, Patrick Lencioni wrote: "If you're not willing to accept the pain real values incur, don't bother going to the trouble of formulating a values statement" (Lencioni 2002), and this is still applicable today. Don't make setting values an HR effort, because executive and operational teams need to own the process of setting (core) values. Value setting is not about building consensus, it is about defining a set of fundamental, strategically sound beliefs on a broad group of people. If you set the right values for the right reasons, for a team or even the entire company, it can be a powerful addition to your OKRs.

Team Values, Norms, and Behavior

Team values inform your team norms. Norms are a set of (ideal) rules and behaviors the team holds its members accountable for. One very useful exercise is to measure the performance of your team norms and behaviors. During training sessions, I ask a team to do the following:

1. For each of your team values, cocreate a list of rules or behaviors that belong to these values. Put them on a (digital) whiteboard.

2. In a survey, ask each team member to rate each behavior on a Likert scale (agree–disagree). The score 1 means we are not performing this behavior and 5 means we show this behavior constantly. This will be your baseline.

3. Collect all survey responses. During a retrospective, determine what behavior improvements are required and define clear action items. Could they be leading indicators to improve team performance?

4. After three months, repeat steps 2 and 3.

Note: If your company has core values defined, you can use the same set of questions to define and improve on companywide behaviors. If you have regular one-on-one meetings with your team members—and I hope you do—then gauging how much people show these behaviors throughout the week can be a very helpful device for leaders to measure performance. If team members don't show the expected behavior, you probably want to retrospect, determine obstacles, and run experiments (see Chapter 12) to learn how to remove them.

Roles, Responsibilities, and Strengths

In Chapter 1, we touched on the formula for motivation: Autonomy + Mastery + Purpose = Motivation. One important aspect to achieve OKRs is mastery. Teams need to have the right skills and to have mastered these skills to achieve their goals. Therefore, you need to hire strategically and equip teams with the right skillsets. During team chartering, a team can establish an overview of the (unspoken) roles, responsibilities but also their skills and competencies.

By using a team skill self-assessment, you can determine if you are missing any skills to achieve your OKRs. The "Dreyfus model of skill acquisition" (Dreyfus and Dreyfus 1980) shows how learners acquire skills through formal instruction and practice, used in the fields of education and operation research. This model can be useful to map the current team skills as well as identify gaps in the skillset. Subsequently, teams can use the analysis to define criteria for job profiles or find ways to expand the skills of their existing members.

Trust

Absence of trust among team members is the most fundamental dysfunction within a team (Lencioni 2002, 188). You simply cannot have a team without trust. Lencioni wrote that team members need to be genuinely open with each other about their mistakes and weaknesses in order to build a foundation of trust.

In my experience with management, I noticed that managers are often reluctant to use an experimental approach to OKRs. They often believe that experimentation is an expensive exercise. Most likely, they are afraid to expend resources, or they just don't trust teams to do the right thing. As you learnt in Chapter 12, experiments don't need to be an expensive undertaking. The lack of trust most leaders have in their teams concerns me, because *without trust, your OKR implementation is doomed.* A working OKR implementation is built upon trust and psychological safety.

When the Objective is not understood, commitment or accountability is lacking, or talent and skills seem to be missing, we often think that "our people" are the problem. However, these points mainly indicate "people problems" that are generally the product of the processes and not inherent to the persons involved.

Hopefully, this book makes this point very clear: People aren't the problem; the system (e.g., the organization or team) is the problem! If you do closer analysis of the system, you will notice the root cause of not achieving your stretch goals; it is actually in plain sight: your BAU. It's your job as a leader to prevent your teams from getting pulled into it. You need to coach them and *trust* them to do the right thing.

Learning Zone and Psychological Safety

When the pressure is on, the whirlwind sucks people back into the center, into their comfort zone of BAU. However, this prohibits the opportunity to learn and grow (Figure 6.1).

It is the role of the leader to monitor and provide the boundaries that keep people out of the danger zone, and let them know they are safe to play.

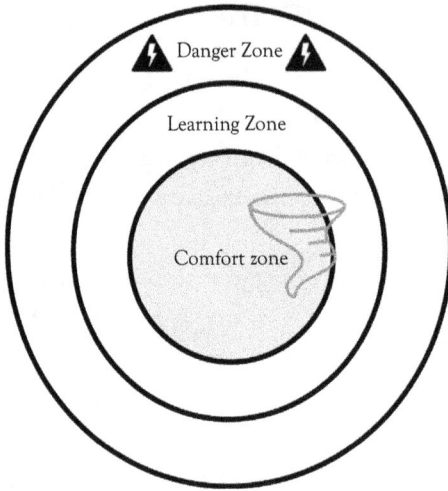

Figure 6.1 The comfort zone: the whirlwind pulls you back in

Fixed and Growth Mindset

In her ground breaking book *Mindset*, Carol Dweck describes the difference between people with a fixed mindset and those with a growth mindset. In a more recent article, she wrote:

Individuals who believe their talents can be developed (through hard work, good strategies, and input from others) have a growth mindset. They tend to achieve more than those with a more fixed mindset (those who believe their talents are innate gifts). This is because they worry less about looking smart, and they put more energy into learning. When entire companies embracing a growth mindset, their employees report feeling far more empowered and committed; they also receive far greater organizational support for collaboration and innovation. In contrast, people at primarily fixed-mindset companies report more of only one thing: cheating and deception among employees, presumably to gain an advantage in the talent race (Dweck 2016).

Many people have a fixed mindset, meaning they will not automatically think that they can achieve something extraordinary. However, your role as a leader is to change that and make sure people have a growth mindset. This can be done by challenging them on their behavior and habits. OKRs give you the opportunity to finally have these conversations.

You might believe that the following variables have an influence on the effectiveness of a team:

- Colocation of teammates (sitting together in the same office)
- Consensus-driven decision making
- Extroversion of team members
- Individual performance of team members
- Workload
- Seniority
- Team size
- Tenure

According to research project Aristotle that was done by Google on highly effective teams, actually none of the above attributes are significantly important (Duhigg 2016). This research determined that only the following five key dynamics have a significant influence on effective software teams at Google:

- Psychological safety
- Dependability
- Structure and clarity
- Meaning
- Impact

Although the outcomes of the research project don't necessarily mean that these dynamics always apply or are beneficial to every organization, it is striking that a lot of these aspects have to do with a safe and stable environment. However, the key takeaway from project Aristotle in my eyes is that the behaviors and norms that are important in growing highly effective teams are not always what you expect. I thus advise you to find out which aspects play a role inside your own organization, and codify the behavior and norms you want to foster. Are there any aspects relating to psychological safety?

Measuring Psychological Safety

Organizational behavioral scientist Amy Edmondson used a list of statements to measure psychological safety. Think of a team you work with closely. How strongly do you agree with these five statements on a scale of 1 to 5?

1. If they take a chance, and screw up, it will be held against them and me.
2. The team has a strong sense of culture, and it can be hard for new people to join.
3. The team is slow to offer help to people who are struggling.
4. Using their unique skills and talents comes second to the objectives of the team.
5. It's uncomfortable to have open, honest conversations about the team's sensitive issues.

Creating Urgency for OKRs

For some organizations, it will always require a crisis to make sustainable change. Covid-19 is a good example in our current society. As a result, remote working is now the norm for many companies. The good news is that OKRs can act as a catalyst for change, and they can create the same urgency as a crisis, without the need for an actual crisis.

In Chapter 2, we went over the five main reasons why OKR implementations fail. The number 2 reason is that leaders insufficiently explain why they want to use OKRs. However, once their purpose is known, often it still isn't easy to get everybody on board. As with any other change initiatives, you need to articulate the urgency of the change. There are two ways you can create urgency for OKRs (Thiecke and van Leeuwen 2018):

1. Based on ambition: we have to, because we don't want to do anything else except solve this problem. For example, *we believe our product will increase the speed of carbon dioxide reduction in the air. We owe it to society to make it a success. OKRs will help to execute that mission.*

2. Based on necessity: it must happen, we must do something differently. Our current way of working isn't sufficient anymore. If we don't change now, we won't survive another year.

Signs that you haven't increased the temperature of the urgency for OKRs might include responses such as:

- "We've already tried methods X, Y, and Z, and they didn't work either."
- "You are the third manager that will try this."
- "Maybe now isn't the right moment."
- "This is just how it works in our organization."

The OKR Mechanism

There is an interesting paradox in how OKRs work, which you can use to your advantage here. You need to create urgency to implement OKRs, and they can simultaneously help you to create urgency, as well. OKRs can be used to create urgency by a) conveying the ambition (going to the moon and back) or b) exposing the necessity (we need to do this, or we will lose customers). By using OKRs, you can communicate the urgency to people's hearts (using Objectives) and minds (KRs).

What You Can Do as a Leader

Once you've identified the urgency to implement OKRs within your organization, your work is still far from done. To facilitate the change, you could use one of these ideas:

- Repetition is your friend: Repeat the urgency for OKRs as many times as you can.
- Hold on: Don't let the system undermine your actions.
- Change the working environment: Make sure everybody attends the OKR events and workshops. Stick to the process until it becomes second nature.

- Enthuse people: Bring in your own emotions about implementing OKRs. Be vulnerable and share what worries you have about the current situation.
- Confront people: Maybe you need to confront people with the reality of the way your organization currently operates. Show them what other organizations do in comparison and what it brings them.
- Provide boundaries. Say, "Next quarter, we will stop working with our Quarterly Business Reviews. From then on, we will use OKRs and health metrics as our new standard."
- Change your own behavior: For example, don't report the way you always have. Instead, try to include OKRs in your weekly e-mail reports.
- Question yourself: How important is the change to OKRs for you? What will change for you if the organization starts to use OKRs? Do you have that clear? If it isn't urgent for you, then it's very hard to make it urgent for anybody else in the company.

The latter points in this list indicate that there is more to introducing OKRs than just making changes in your company. Are you, the leader, prepared to change your own behavior? Are you ready to give up the way *you* used to work, and venture out into new territory?

Leadership for Winning Challenges

Helping teams to define a good challenge is hard. The challenge shouldn't be too easy, nor should it be impossible. Mr. Toshio Horikiri, the CEO of Toyota, once proposed that both "easy" target conditions—those that we can envision achieving from the very start—and "impossible" target conditions do not provide us with much sense of motivation and fulfillment. In *Toyota Kata*, Mike Rother explains: "When you have a challenge that lies between these extremes (easy and impossible) and it is achieved, an adrenaline-like feeling of breakthrough and accomplishment is generated ('We did it!'), which increases motivation and the desire to take on more challenges" (Rother 2009, 111). For leaders, the most important role you have when it comes to OKRs is making sure you provide the team with a good challenge or a "problem to solve." This is why the OKR setting and alignment workshops (see Chapters 7 and 8) are so important; they are opportunities for leaders to collaborate with the teams on defining a great OKR that will motivate and engage everybody for the next period ahead.

The Progress Loop

Like most things, we find that our lives have a cyclical pattern. Day in and day out, we work or think about work-related matters, and this behavior is influenced by and has an influence on our performance in a loop. A "good day" (or bad day or mediocre day), on which we feel satisfied (or dissatisfied or ambivalent), drives our performance, which gives a new set of results that, in turn, have the power to enhance (or diminish, or otherwise impact) our work life. This reveals the potential for self-reinforcing benefits. Basically, it's the "self-fulfilling prophecy," where our thoughts and beliefs impact our actions and they, in turn, enforce our beliefs and subsequent actions, and so on.

So, in relation to OKR check-ins, the concept of progress is illustrated nicely by the words of Amabile and Kramer: "By supporting people and their daily progress in meaningful work, managers improve not only the inner work lives of their employees but also the organization's long-term performance, which enhances inner work life even more" (Steven and Kramer 2011). Can you coach and mentor people to find good measures to track progress?

Discipline

As a leader working with OKRs, you are in the business of changing people's behavioral patterns. The problem is that most managers and leaders have never learnt how to change others' behavior. The discipline that is required is highly connected to interest and enthusiasm. The assumption from leaders and managers is often that these should manifest spontaneously in the team, but this is a tall order. Why? Because of the second law of thermodynamics, or entropy, which states that any process will eventually become more complex, and more problems will occur when left alone.

This is the reason why leaders must follow the OKR methodology and stick to it, specifically this Lean OKR approach. It is necessary to implement the OKR cycle with regularly scheduled check-ins where attendance is mandatory. Your role as a leader and manager is to teach people how to apply the outcomes of the OKR check-ins, to frame current and target conditions, to define experiments, and to overcome obstacles together (more on this in Part 3). Through this approach, interest and enthusiasm are spurred, leading to challenges being accomplished and a progress loop leading to the positive anticipation of subsequent challenges.

Guidance and Support

When you roll out your OKRs in your company, everybody in the organization should have an OKR mentor or coach. That coach is the manager or (team) leader, and their responsibility is to ask the following five questions when working with teams or individuals:

1. What is your set of OKRs?
2. What is your baseline now? Are we improving?
3. What obstacles are preventing you from getting closer?
4. Which obstacle are you working on now?
5. What is your next experiment? What do you expect to learn?

Some organizations prefer to install dedicated OKR coaches. It's fine to have a handful of these people helping the executives with the initial roll out, but after OKRs have landed in the organization, it's the role of the leaders to create Objectives for teams and coach them to achieve these. Hiring an OKR coach that has a lot of experience with OKRs can definitely help to increase the success of your OKRs, but in the end, it won't replace strong leadership skills.

Chapter Recap

In this chapter, we've been reminded of the significant cultural change that's required of the teams as well as leadership levels for a company to experience the maximum benefit of OKRs. We've recognized that a big-change initiative like OKRs can be challenging to implement within an organization and that careful emotional management is key when challenging people to change the way they work.

We've explored how OKRs can empower teams by providing a tangible context for their actions and instilling trust. We've established effective starting points for your company's OKR journey to make it aspirational yet manageable for all stakeholders.

You have come to the end of Part 1, and it is great you have done all the work to provide yourself with a solid foundation. Part 2 will take you through the process of running successful OKR workshops so that you can apply the OKR cycle practically, and make sure people are going to use the OKRs that are so carefully developed, boosting their engagement and accountability.

Chapter References

Amabile, T.M., and S.J. Kramer. May 2011. *The Power of Small Wins*. Boston: Harvard Business Review.

Cutler, J. 2017. "Psychological Safety: The Secret Weapon of Awesome Teams." https://medium.com/smells-like-team-spirit/safety-makes-awesome-possible-97acb601ff59 (accessed February 23, 2021).

Doerr, J. 2018. *Measure What Matters*. London: Portfolio Penguin.

Dreyfus, S.E., and H.L. Dreyfus. 1980. "A Five-Stage Model of the Mental Activities Involved in Directed Skill Acquisition." Available Online at www.researchgate.net/publication/235125013_A_Five-Stage_Model_of_the_Mental_Activities_Involved_in_Directed_Skill_Acquisition (accessed February 09, 2021).

Duhigg, C. February 25, 2016. "What Google Learned From Its Quest to Build the Perfect Team." *New York Times*, www.nytimes.com/2016/02/28/magazine/what-google-learned-from-its-quest-to-build-the-perfect-team.html?smid=pl-share (accessed February 09, 2021).

Dweck, C.S. March 22, 2016. *What Having a "Growth Mindset" Actually Means*. Boston: Harvard Business Review.

Dweck, C.S. 2007. *Mindset: the New Psychology of Success*. New York, NY: Ballantine Books.

Edmondson, A. June 1999. "Psychological Safety and Learning Behavior in Work Teams." *Administrative Science Quarterly* 44, no. 2, pp. 350–383.

Larsen, D., and A. Nies. 2016. *Liftoff: Start and Sustain Successful Agile Teams*, 2nd ed. Raleigh: The Pragmatic Bookshelf.

Lencioni, P.M. 2002. *The Five Dysfunctions of a Team: A Leadership Fable*, 1st ed. Hoboken: Jossey-Bass.

Lencioni, P.M. July 2002. *Make Your Values Mean Something*. Boston: Harvard Business Review Magazine.

Rother, M. 2009. *Toyota Kata: Managing People for Improvement, Adaptiveness and Superior Results*, 1st ed. New York, NY: McGraw-Hill Education.

Tabrizi, B. 2015. *75% of Cross-Functional Teams Are Dysfunctional*. Boston: Harvard Business Review. https://hbr.org/2015/06/75-of-cross-functional-teams-are-dysfunctional

Thiecke, M., and B. van Leeuwen. 2018. *Systemic Transition Management*. Nijmegen: Het Noorderlicht.

Tools:

ReWork, Google. n.d. *Foster Psychological Safety*. https://rework.withgoogle.com/guides/understanding-team-effectiveness/steps/foster-psychological-safety/

PART II

Running Successful OKR Workshops

Introduction to Part 2

A goal without a plan is just a wish.

—Antoine de Saint-Exupéry

Now that you've identified your single Objectives and the KRs to identify whether you've achieved them, it's time to think about a system for achieving them. Having no system is a bit like most New Year resolutions: great ambitions that quickly fade away in the midst of our busy lives.

Forget About Goals for a Moment

In his book, *Atomic Habits*, James Clear says: "Forget about goals, focus on systems instead" (Clear 2018, 23). What he means by that is that we can use OKRs to describe the result we want to achieve. Only describing your OKRs won't bring you very far. Putting systems in place to be the vehicle for OKRs will set you up for success. Therefore, this part of the book will focus on the system that is required to achieve your OKRs.

The system to increase your likelihood of success with your OKRs is called the *OKR cycle*. It's no shortcut to success and still requires hard work and long-term commitment to implement. Typically, OKR adoption takes one to three years. If you're ready for that, let's go.

The OKR Cycle

I will describe the OKR system focusing on a quarterly OKR cycle, as this is probably the most relevant to most leaders. Following the initial company kickoff meeting, both the company and team-level OKR cycles are in store for a series of workshops, events, and activities:

- Goal-setting workshop
- Alignment workshop
- Kickoff event
- Frequent (weekly) check-ins
- Reflection workshop

In the following chapters, we will look more closely at each of these workshops and events. In each chapter, you will find a practical agenda that can help you get started, regardless of the size of your organization.

OKR Timelines

Both company and team OKR workshops (set, align, and kickoff) are normally held shortly before the next cycle (a quarter, in this case) starts (Figure 2.0.1). The company OKR workshops come before the team OKR workshops, unless the teams are more operational in nature (finance, HR, development), in which case the OKR workshops might run in tandem. The OKR check-ins are performed weekly throughout the quarter. Just

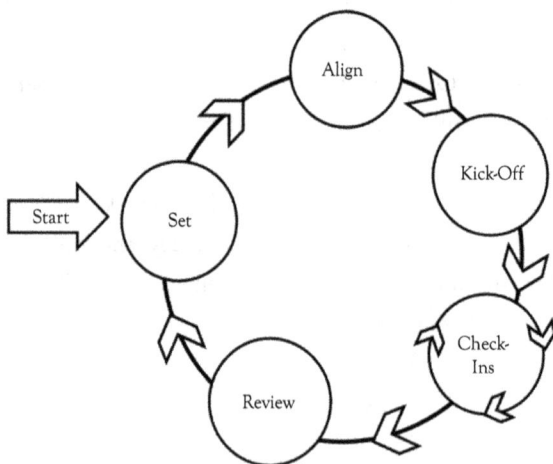

Figure 2.0.1 The OKR cycle overview

before the quarter ends, the review workshop is planned. Make sure the review workshop is always planned *before* the setting workshop of the next cycle, because you want to use the learning and results from this workshop in the next setting workshop. Figure 2.0.1 schematically represents what an OKR cycle looks like, plotted over time.

Planning OKR cycle workshops and events can sometimes require a lot of coordination and logistics (meeting rooms, available people, and off-site locations). Try to schedule one or two days for all of the set, align, and kickoff workshops, for all teams. Make sure it takes no more than one week to keep the momentum. Some companies have an "OKR week" each quarter, in which the company and team OKRs are set, aligned, and announced in the kickoff. This way, everybody understands what is expected of them (Figure 2.0.2).

OKR Themes

Some companies like to make achieving OKRs a little nicer by creating a fun theme around them. These themes can be linked to a book, sport, series, or movie. Really anything can be used here to enthuse people. By drawing a name from a hat, select someone to facilitate, and organize your quarterly theme. If your objective is about giving a big boost to generate more leads, maybe the theme could be around a series or movie. You want to make more new "friends" with potential clients. Then, the series *Friends* could be a quarterly theme for your company, where your

OKR Timeline
Quarterly OKRs

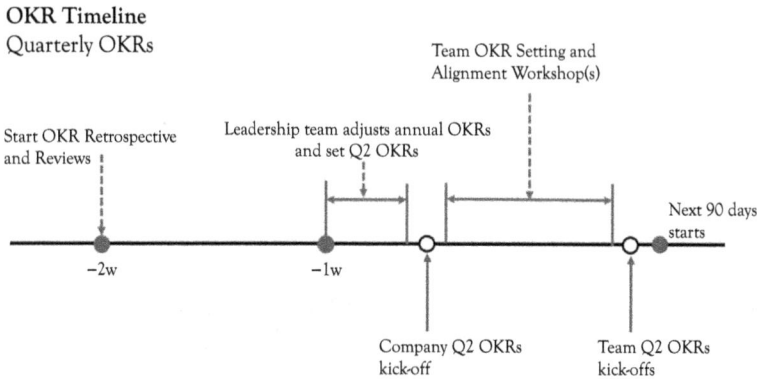

Figure 2.0.2 An OKR workshops and event timeline

departments or teams can play the role of the characters like Rachel, Monica, or Ross. Use your creativity here. Use posters in your workplace, presentations where these characters pop up. Achieving OKRs can be a lot of fun.

CHAPTER 7

Running a Successful OKR Setting Workshop

Chapter Highlights

- Three stages of setting OKRs
- Facilitation techniques
- Setting remote OKRs

I still remember my first OKR setting workshops of my own team. In the back of the conference room, I heard one of my team members talk to his colleague sitting next to him: "This stuff is easy, you describe a goal and slam some metrics in. How hard can this be?"

A few hours later, we were still discussing, arguing, and debating what the objectives should be for this quarter. It all felt chaotic, somehow this goal-setting meeting got out of control, and people randomly suggested objectives, following their gut feelings. We were deep down in discussions about semantics, the objective format, and how to make it more inspirational. Defining the KRs was even harder. We couldn't decide on the best measures for our objective. After four hours, the meeting ended and was to be continued the next day.

What we were missing was a structured way to set and agree on our OKRs. A format that we could finish in time with good results.

Setting OKRs by yourself is already tough, but imagine setting good OKRs in a group. Throughout the years, I've learned and experimented with multiple techniques and formats. When you have a good structure, setting OKRs in a group can be fun, bring surprising insights and generate creative and inspirational OKRs. Given the incredible effectiveness and consistent results of this workshop format, I was able to help set great OKRs with hundreds of teams.

Setting OKRs

Setting OKRs works the same at all levels of the organization and for all types of OKR levels (company, department, team, etc.). Although I will focus on team OKRs here, the principles of the described workshop can thus be applied to other levels and types of OKRs, too. The only important difference is the starting point, or context (see Figure 7.1). As explained in Chapter 5, Cascading, the context of team OKRs is usually the annual or quarterly company OKRs.

Let's assume that the leadership team of your company has already set and aligned the quarterly company OKRs based on the strategy of the company. The next stage is announcing the company OKRs to the whole organization so that teams can define their own. After the announcement of company OKRs, the senior team leaders (e.g., the engineering manager together with the product manager) create candidate Objectives for each team and bring these to the OKR setting workshop to discuss with the teams (see Chapter 5). Some companies prefer to let each team develop their own OKRs in close collaboration

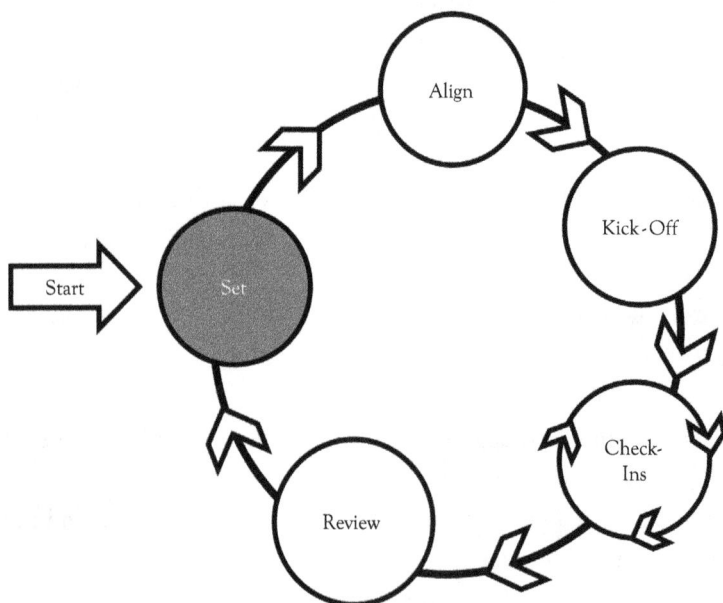

Figure 7.1 The OKR setting workshop

with their leaders. Which approach works best for your teams depends on their team maturity and your own leadership skills and preferences. Regardless of which style you choose, you need to actively coach and manage the teams. OKRs are about better management, not less management.

After you defined a final Objective together with the team, it is up to the team to decide how to measure progress toward the Objective and set the baseline (X) and target (Y) for each KR. Of course, as a leader, you can bring your experience and skills to help them defining good measures, or even propose your candidate measure.

Company OKRs are also set during an OKR setting workshop, but we will focus on team OKRs only in this chapter.

The OKR setting (or goal setting) workshop is the first in the OKR cycle. Its purpose is to create draft OKRs, aligned with one of the company's KRs for the next OKR cycle. The key is that teams, together with their leader(s), define OKRs that *influence* the KRs of the level above. In this chapter, we look at when and how you should run this workshop and who should participate.

The OKR Setting Workshop

When

Either straight after the announcement of the company's OKRs or one week before the start of the new quarter.

Duration

For the first workshop, schedule 4.5 hours. As you get better at setting OKRs, you'll need less time. Teams that have been using OKRs for some time often need no more than two hours for this workshop.

Prep Work

Preparation is key. Let all team members know beforehand the purpose of the session, for example, by sending a calendar invite with a description of the workshop.

There are two approaches to prepare for this workshop that I've seen working:

1. Before the OKR settings workshop starts, the (senior) leader creates candidate Objectives for each (product) team, aligned with the Company KRs, the (product) strategy, and other leaders. Defining good candidate Objectives for your teams requires time and good strategic planning. Don't rush this preparation phase and make sure you have enough room in your calendar to work on it. Some leaders spent weeks for this activity. Sometimes, it makes sense to also develop candidate measures for the KRs. The leaders will bring the candidate Objectives to the workshop. The leader can choose to attend the OKR setting workshop in person (preferred) or, if they serve many teams, they can present the candidate Objectives for each team during an all-hands session prior to this workshop.

2. This option is only for senior product teams. Let everyone in the team know beforehand what the purpose of the session is. Ask them to prepare by thinking about and jotting down how their team can influence the company KRs and, specifically, what might be a good team objective to achieve this. If you are working in a larger company, a team might only influence the department or regional KRs. Decide in advance to which KRs you are going to contribute. Try to focus on one company KR, only choose two if you can really hit two birds with one stone.

Who

All team members should attend, plus the leader(s) that created the candidate Objective. If your company has one, invite an OKR coach, especially the first time, to challenge and guide the teams. Ideally, you also want a skilled group facilitator to guide the process. The facilitator doesn't need to have experience with OKRs to guide the workshop, but this experience certainly does help when people have questions related to OKRs and the process.

Agenda

The workshop has two or three stages and a break:

1. (optional) Identify the appropriate company KRs that fit the individual teams best (30–60 minutes).
2. Define or refine the objective (30–60 minutes).
   BREAK (15–30 minutes)
3. Define the KRs (30–120 minutes).

Stage 1: Identify the Appropriate Company KRs

This stage is optional for team OKRs. If the leader did bring a candidate Objective to the workshop, you can skip this stage. In all other cases, the leader and the team can discuss which company KR should be impacted.

1. Set the stage by quickly running through the company OKRs. It is useful for the leader to refresh everyone's memory on the company OKRs and explain one more time the intent behind them.
2. The leader discusses with the team which company KR(s) they believe they can best support and influence.

Once you've agreed which company KR the team can best influence, it's time to develop the Objective.

Stage 2: Define or Refine the Objective

If the leader brought a candidate Objective to this session, then the intent and reason for selecting this Objective needs to be explained to the team, together with the possible impact on the company KRs. In addition, the leader should explain any strategic context the team should be aware of. After the explanation by the leader, the team has a chance to ask questions and challenge the Objective. They should also check on the feasibility of the Objective. In case the Objective is very ambitious (a moonshot), the leader should express the reasons behind stretching the team and that 100 percent achievement is not required. If the team "accepts" the leader's

Objective, you're done and you can proceed to the next stage. In case the team doesn't accept your Objective, you can refine the existing one, create a new one or follow the steps below.

In case the leader did not bring any team Objective, or if the workshop is about crafting a company OKR, ensure you complete stage one and follow these steps:

1. As you asked everyone to start thinking about a good Objective, you now list and discuss their ideas. Maybe you also want to generate new ideas for Objectives. You can try a technique called free-listing (see boxed text in the following) to generate a list of objectives that can influence the company KR.

2. Now the tough part: Decide on the best objective for the quarter (it could be a mix or variant of the ideas listed or something new). First, let everybody present a one-minute pitch of their Objective, then select the best one. A useful technique here could be affinity mapping and dot-voting. Remember, your goal is to select *one* Objective. You might want to store some good candidate Objectives that fell off the bandwagon for next quarters.

3. Use the guidelines from Chapter 3 to check whether the objective is good and will be effective. Is it inspirational? Will it challenge the status quo? Make the necessary adjustments.

4. Double check with all participants if the Objective is doable within the quarter. If the Objective is a stretch one, then, of course, it will be less doable than one that you commit to for 100 percent. The leader should have a conversation with all team members to discuss how attainable the Objective is within the 90 days. Good OKRs have a 50/50 percent of achievement (Wodtke 2016, 147), unless you are just starting off.

5. List any dependencies you might have on other teams or departments. If so, then make sure you have conversations with them. Schedule meetings accordingly or make sure they participate in the alignment workshop (see Chapter 8).

Although the creation of the Objective is a collaborative process between the leader and the team members, it's not a democracy. The leader always has the final say in the Objective. As a leader you have the right to veto. In some cases, the outcome of the previous steps might lead to an inappropriate/unsatisfying Objective. This often happens if the team is new to the process. The leader can then ask the team to refine or select another Objective.

Stage 3: Define the KRs

1. Having defined the Objective that will impact the company KR for that quarter, now brainstorm a list of measures for the Objective. Sometimes, the leader that created the draft Objective also has some ideas on how to measure progress toward the Objective which can be brought to the table as well. You can use the free-listing technique in combination with the magic questions and techniques from Chapters 3 and 4. If you are an operational team, can you think about the lead measures?

2. Select the top three or four measures. Again, you can use affinity mapping and dot-voting to select the best measures.

3. Agree on the baseline (X) and target (Y) for each measure and convert them into KRs. Check out the guidelines and tips in Chapter 3 on setting good KRs. If you currently don't have the data for these measures, you should exclude them. You shouldn't spend weeks to get the first results in. Decide if collecting the data manually might be an option.

4. Double check with all participants if the KRs are doable within the quarter. Are they stretched? What are the chances you will make them within 90 days?

Free Listing, Affinity Mapping, and Dot-Voting

Techniques that I frequently use in OKR setting workshops are free-listing, affinity mapping, and dot-voting. If you have been in an Agile Retrospective before, this might be familiar to you. Free-listing is a technique for gathering data about a specific domain. Affinity mapping is a technique to group results from a free-listing exercise.

Finally, dot-voting is a prioritization technique. Combined, they can be very powerful to select an objective or set measures:

1. Ask all participants to write down on a sticky note what they believe to be the most important objective for the next quarter (for objectives, you can also gather input from all employees in the company). Just one objective per sticky note.
2. Group similar sticky notes together. For example, you could group objectives in the following categories: objective, task, motto/slogan, measure, or wish. Ignore all the non-Objectives for now. The others could be great ideas to move the needle on your OKRs later on. Alternatively, group them based on the perspectives from the Balance Scorecard: customer, financial, process, people, and product.
3. Dot-vote. Give each participant three "votes" in the form of marker dots. Ask all participants to stand up and create a (virtual) circle. Walking clockwise, every participant sets one marker dot on any group of stickies. Repeat this three times. You may vote on your own objective. Consider using an app for anonymous voting to avoid people voting strategically.
4. The group objectives with the highest number of votes wins.

You can repeat this to select measures for your objective as well. Then, select a top three or four. These will be the input for your KRs. Remember that you need to try to pair KRs, so ideally you select one or two quantitative and one or two qualitative KRs.

There are other techniques to gather data and set priorities in a group. Feel free to experiment with them and decide what works best for your team.

Facilitation Techniques

There are a lot of formats available to keep people engaged and motivated throughout a workshop. Also there are several tools to discover good objectives and KRs. Following, I've listed some techniques that I have used and come to appreciate over the course of my career. Feel free to add in your own techniques.

- Increase participant engagement: Liberating Structures (Lipmanowicz and McCandless 2014).
- Decisions making and prioritization: Dot-voting, Lean Prioritization (2x2 matrix), MoSCoW method (Clegg and Barker 1994), Kano Model (Kano et al. 1994), Eisenhower Method, RICE method, and ICE model. The website *gamestorming. com* is a great resource for finding out workshop formats to keep people engaged.
- Information gathering: Free-listing, space saturate, and group (affinity mapping).
- Metrics discovery: User experience and elicitation techniques. For example: Impact Mapping (Adzic 2012), outcome mapping (Earl et al. 2001), current reality tree (Dettmer 1997), and the techniques discussed in Chapters 3 and 4, like Because & Why.
- Process bottleneck discovery: with Lean techniques like Value Stream Mapping (Martin and Osterling 2013) and root cause analysis (Wilson 1994) to spot waste and bottlenecks in processes.

If these techniques don't ring a bell, you might find it helpful to do some additional research into them. Some of these techniques aren't described in books or research papers, but are described extensively online.

Remote OKR Setting

When you work with online teams or a mix of onsite and online teams, you need to do the OKR setting workshops remotely. There are great online tools available to facilitate OKR setting workshops. When you facilitate online OKR workshops, it is very important that everybody can contribute. Make sure everybody has a high-quality Internet connection, a webcam, and a headset. There are online whiteboards available where you can simulate a physical workspace. I've positive experience with online collaboration tools such as Miro, Mural, or Google's Jamboard, but any tool with a similar feature set will do the job.

Over to You

Maybe you're not using OKRs at work yet, but you do probably "work" with certain teams in your private life. So, let's improvise:

1. Identify a team. This could be your family, a small group of friends with whom you do a specific sport or hobby, some people you always wanted to go on holiday with, and so on.
2. Arrange a "workshop" time and venue (e.g., the kitchen table, in a cafe, and on Zoom).
3. At the goal-setting meeting, start by explaining:
   a. OKRs: this is a good exercise for checking how familiar you have come with OKRs.
   b. The purpose of this "workshop": to decide on a common goal (e.g., how to plan more quality time together as a family, a fun run the group could do together, and your proposal to go on holiday together).
4. Lead the workshop broadly, as described in this chapter. Obviously, you can do things much less formally where appropriate. Don't worry, your session will still involve many of the key components and processes that a workshop at your work would.
5. At the end, ensure you have your agreed objective and KRs and have identified who is responsible for each task.

The result of this workshop is a draft of your team OKRs. Some teams use the time left to generate some initial ideas about how to move the needle of their KRs. In Part 3 of this book, we will explore what tools teams can use to move the needle in more detail. For now, don't commit to the ideas just yet, because things might change after the alignment workshop.

CHAPTER 8

Align and Kickoff

Chapter Highlights

- Three strategies toward alignment
- Facilitating the alignment workshop
- Kicking off your OKRs

A big benefit of OKRs is that they will create alignment between all teams involved. That this doesn't happen by itself was the conclusion of a company specialized in developing mobile apps. Their teams created OKRs, put everything in their OKR software system, but missed the mark with the alignment stage.

Leaders didn't feel they could influence the OKRs or help teams find alignment. They felt overwhelmed because they didn't only want to have alignment on their company goals (vertical alignment), but the teams also wanted to align with each other (horizontal alignment).

To make sure teams really understand how they can influence the company KRs, to be really aligned with management and other teams, they need to collaborate with each other during the alignment workshop. Companies often skip this vital step in the OKR cycle (Figure 8.1). When I teach people how to run the alignment workshop, they discover that aligning with others can be easy.

By running alignment workshops, managers and teams feel they are in it together. This sense of togetherness can truly spark great things.

Strategies Toward Alignment

Setting OKRs in isolation will keep your organization working in silos (engineering, sales, marketing, and customer support). When you want to achieve ambitious goals you have never achieved before, you need to

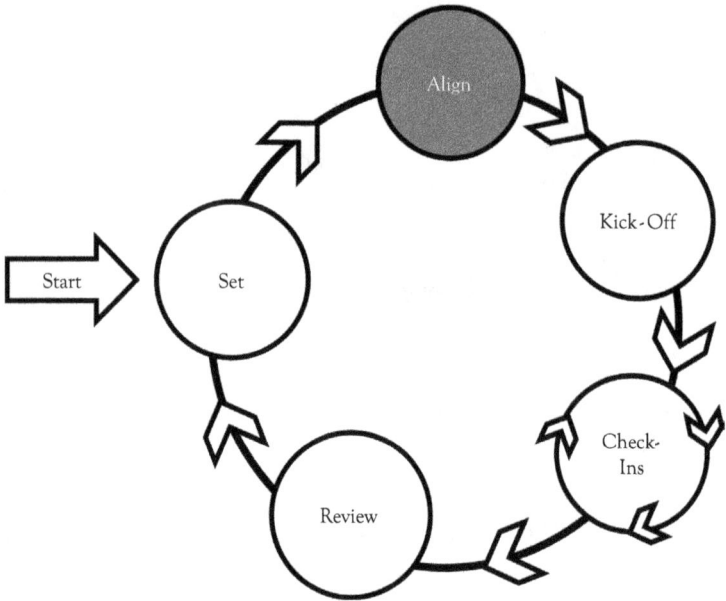

Figure 8.1 The OKR alignment workshop

work closely with other departments and teams to find out whether you are going in the same direction and whether resources are spread out based on the same priorities, and to understand how dependencies work.

The OKRs between teams and the overall company OKRs need be aligned also. How else do you make sure all the small battles will help to fight the bigger war? Therefore, the OKR alignment workshop is a perfect opportunity for leaders to challenge teams on their OKRs and how they are aligned to the company OKR.

There are three common ways you can achieve alignment when working with OKRs:

1. Through transparency
2. Through 360-degree alignment with the representatives from the following teams: leadership, functional, and operational
3. Through shared OKRs

Alignment Through Transparency

The concept of alignment through transparency is simple and, ideally, there is no workshop required: You publish your draft OKRs in a shared environment via a common channel (e.g., e-mail, intranet, wiki, Google Docs, or OKR software). Then, other teams will look at your OKRs to see if there are any conflicts and will contact the team for conversations about the dependencies and resources. As perfect as it sounds, in reality, many teams will skip this step, especially teams new to OKRs. Teams actively contacting other teams to discuss OKRs is something I rarely find in organizations. If every team is working on their own goals, why would they even care about other team goals? However, if teams are transparent and proactive, the alignment workshop could be skipped.

Alignment Through 360-Degree Alignment

If your company is like most organizations and you have multiple functional teams in your company or departments (e.g., marketing, sales, IT, and customer support), you need to ensure the teams are aligned to ensure the following:

- Resources (monetary, human, and machines) are
  available.
- Your team OKRs contribute to the company's KRs.
- You have addressed any dependencies you have with other
  teams.

OKR expert, Felipe Castro, likes to call this 360-degree alignment (Castro n.d.).

The 360 alignment normally happens during the alignment workshop, which will be described in the following. During the alignment workshop, you bring in people that represent their organizational function. In the example in Figure 8.2, there will be five people in the workshop: one representative from each team.

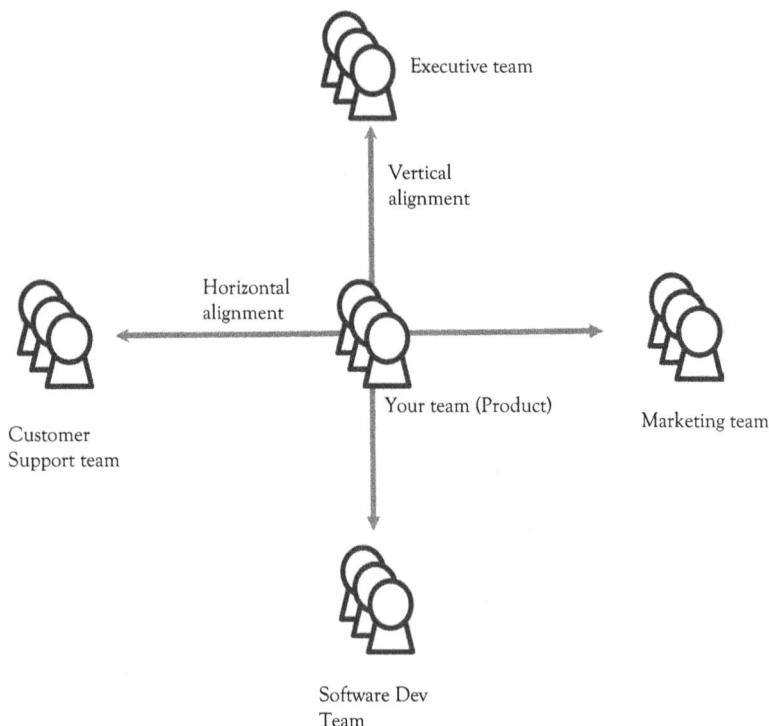

Figure 8.2 360-degree alignment

Alignment Through Shared OKRs

Having OKRs per organizational function will still keep your functional silos intact. The same is true if you would like to set a hierarchy of OKRs that mirrors your organizational chart. If you don't have any issues with that, then use the 360-degree alignment approach described earlier. However, most organizations would like to change their organization structure to be more aligned with what is called their value stream.

A value stream is a concept from Lean Thinking (Womack and Jones 2003). The period between the moment a customer orders a car and the moment it leaves the factory floor is called a value stream. In between, all employees perform value-adding activities. OKRs can be a great transformative tool to help you get closer to aligning your organization structure with your value stream. Instead of having teams per organizational function, you want people from each function or department to form a

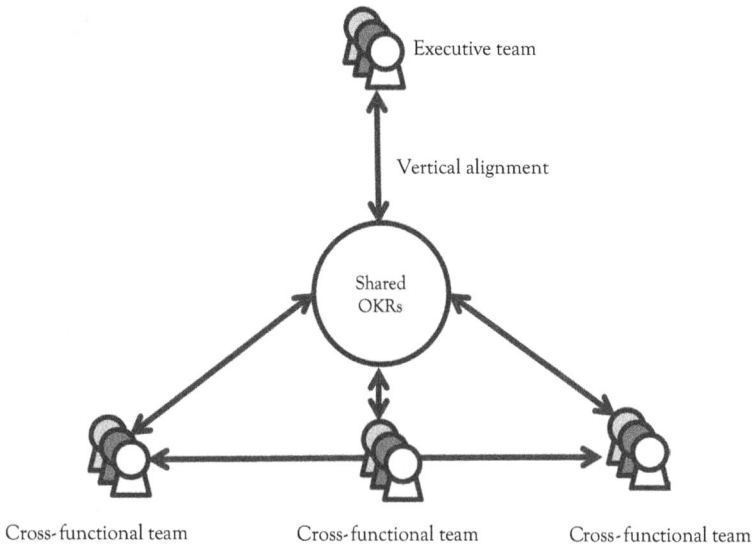

Figure 8.3 Using a shared OKR with cross-functional teams

multidisciplinary team (also called a cross-functional team) that will work together on a value stream, focused by using a single OKR.

Creating alignment across functional teams can be achieved by using a single shared OKR. So, instead of using an OKR per functional area, you will create a single shared OKR that spans across these functional teams (Figure 8.3).

Using shared OKRs also provides that little push that you always wanted to form new organizational structures (e.g., tribes and decentralized groups). Did you ever dream of product teams or cross-functional teams? Now is the time to create them by using the single shared OKR option which provides a mechanism to give it traction.

For alignment with other "shared OKR groups" and/or the executive team, you can use the same OKR alignment workshop described in Figure 8.3.

The Alignment Workshop

In the alignment workshop, you use the feedback received from other (executive) teams' representatives to finalize your team OKRs before publication via your preferred channel. This feedback could be that your measures are not correct or that your targets within your KRs are too optimistic or pessimistic. It could be that your objective is not aligned enough with the company OKR. Maybe the quality of your OKR is not what it should be or there might be conflict with other teams' OKRs. You probably know that giving feedback on OKRs you haven't written yourself is always easier. You want to bring this healthy dose of criticism into the workshop to help others improve their OKR writing skills.

When

After the OKR setting workshop and before the next OKR cycle starts.

Why

The alignment workshops will help if your team has dependencies on other teams. During the workshop, the OKR owners learn if there are dependencies and how to handle them.

Example: The marketing team needs IT support to achieve their OKRs. So it makes sense to have an open discussion with the IT team (e.g., about the specific support needed, what's feasible for IT in terms of resources, and the smartest arrangements for delivering that support).

Frequency and Duration

Schedule as many alignment meetings as necessary to resolve all of the issues. Allow two to six hours for an alignment workshop. The more team representatives, the more discussion and time needed.

Who

It's important to find out which teams or colleagues you're dependent on and which are dependent on you. You also have a responsibility to the higher level OKRs, generally this is the company OKRs, to which you're contributing, so usually you'll invite the relevant company KR owner(s). Depending on your company's size, you can also invite one of your department's senior managers.

It isn't very productive to align with other teams when the full teams are in attendance. Therefore, I suggest that each team sends someone to represent their voice and can be referred to as their OKR's "owner."

Rotating this role within the team ensures that everybody will become familiar with the process. This also includes leadership teams, although the nature of their OKRs requires different people with expertise. If the company OKRs are all about product development, it might not be too productive to send the chief financial officer to the alignment meetings.

Remember: It's OK to make demands on the time and resources of other groups, teams, or individuals. After all, there'll be times when others ask you to help achieve their objectives.

Alignment Workshop Agenda

The OKR alignment workshop has two phases: The OKR presentations and publication.

Phase 1: OKR Presentations

During the alignment workshop, OKR's owners present their draft OKRs. They should mention any dependencies they have on others' time or resources.

I like to give OKR reps five minutes each to pitch their OKRs, and then use ±15 minutes for feedback or questions. If you have three team representatives in the room, it'll take about an hour.

I know some companies organize a special OKR marketplace, which looks like an actual market with stands from each country, region, or department, where they bargain over their OKRs. Whatever works for your organization's culture is fine.

Phase 2: Publication

After getting feedback from all of the OKR reps, all team members need to agree on the final OKRs. This can be done during the workshop or afterward, but no more than two days after the workshop.

The OKRs will then be ready for publication via your preferred channel(s), for example, intranet, wiki, and Google Docs.

Remember, in real life, once your OKRs are published, there's no turning back. Next, is your team ready to publicly announce their OKR to the rest of the company?

Over to You

Aligning your OKRs

If your friends/family from the last OKR setting exercise are very patient, you can approach them again:

- Ask them to develop their own OKRs.
- Go through the alignment process described in this chapter.
- As before, you can:
  - Make the process a little less formal and tweak the "workshop" to work for the OKRs you developed.
  - Restrict yourself to two OKR presentations (from a family member or a friend), which makes the session shorter and the feedback discussions more manageable for everyone.

Alternatively, simply develop your own five-minute presentation of the OKRs you've developed while reading this book. Focus on potential dependencies and how they might be overcome.

Reasons for an OKR Kickoff

To work with OKRs successfully, commitment and transparency are vital. If teams create OKRs privately and then upload them into an OKR software tool that makes them available to the rest of the company, most teams are too busy to ever look into the goals from other teams. During the alignment workshop, teams already challenged and learnt about each other's OKRs. However, they haven't yet committed themselves to their OKRs in front of the whole company yet. Putting goals in a software system is a great way to make your goals visible; however, you also need to make sure everybody actually sees them.

The OKR kickoff event (Figure 8.4) is a short event that makes sure everybody in the company will have a common understanding of what each team is up to that quarter. I've created this concept to help teams increase accountability and have implemented it with many clients. I found out that group pressure would help with the achievement of OKRs.

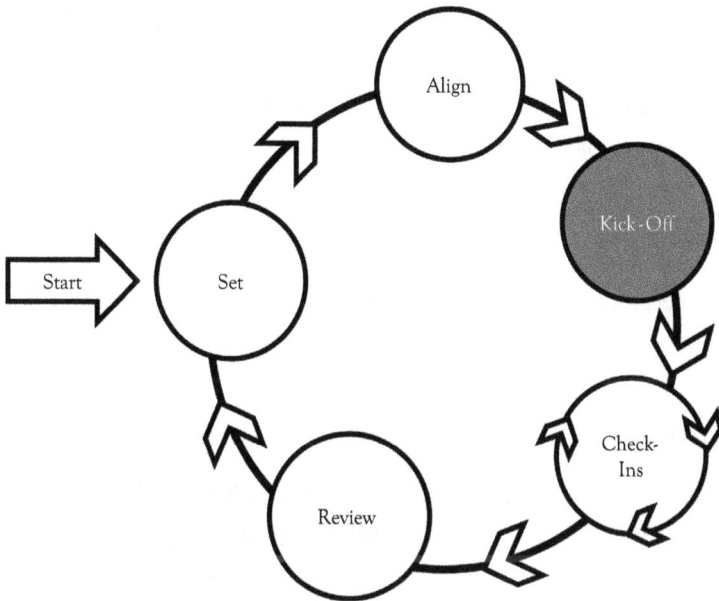

Figure 8.4 The OKR kickoff event

People tend to perform better if they openly commit to a stretched goal, and it helps with the understanding that we are all in it together. At the beginning of each OKR cycle, this event allows the teams to present their OKRs to the rest of the organization. As you will learn in this chapter, the presentation can take many forms.

Trying to achieve OKRs is hard. Publicly committing and making your goals transparent will give you a better chance to fight BAU.

The OKR Kickoff Event

Presentations of your team OKRs during the kickoff can take different forms: from a presentation during a plenary session at an off-site event to something simple such as sending an e-mail with your OKRs to all involved parties. At one company, teams recorded a one-minute video of their OKRs. All the team videos were then collected and professionally edited and presented after the OKR opening speech of the CEO.

Publicly committing to goals is a powerful thing. It acts as a social contract between teams. The OKR kickoff event is also a good moment for leaders to reiterate the company's mission, vision, and strategy. After the presentations, everyone is invited to ask questions on this new set of team OKRs. Depending on the presentation format, these questions can be in person, via chat or e-mail.

When

At the beginning of every OKR cycle, at the opening event for the whole company, business unit, department, or team.

Duration

Depends on the number of team representatives (which is likely to reflect the size of the company and number of teams). Again, a pitching setup can be handy, with a presentation lasting a maximum of five minutes per team.

Who

Everyone in the company/department. If, for logistical reasons, it's impossible for everyone to attend physically or virtually (e.g., they're in different time zones), try to record the meeting.

In most cases, the kickoff is led by the CEO of the company, but in larger organizations, a dedicated host can facilitate and introduce the agenda and speakers. Some companies even like to use a conference setup with guest speakers in-between the team presentations.

Kickoff Agenda

The kickoff agenda has three compulsory stages and one optional stage:

- Recap: Start with a recap of the company's mission, vision, and strategy and optionally the company OKRs.
- Presentations: Team representatives from each team/department present their OKRs.
- Q&As: Anyone can ask questions to clarify the thinking behind the OKRs (in very rare cases, questions can lead to

an OKR being modified, but this is not the time for detailed discussions. By now, the OKRs have already been published).

- Share learning: Teams can share what they have learned from the previous cycle's reflection workshop (explored in Chapter 10), or this cycle's OKR setting or alignment workshops. Sharing this information is optional, but very powerful when you do, especially when leaders share what they have learnt and make themselves vulnerable.

CHAPTER 9

Weekly OKR Check-ins

Chapter Highlights

- The power of progress
- Confidence levels for OKRs
- Daily check-ins (yes, you read that correctly)
- Weekly celebrations
- Reporting out on OKRs

The majority of the time companies bring me in to "fix" their OKRs. they do so because they don't see the results they were hoping for. They express that their OKRs are anything but thriving. My question to them is simple: Do you and your teams have weekly check-ins on your OKRs? Most of the time the answer is no. Sometimes they tell me they've tried and it didn't work, because the check-ins were just an extra burden on the team's already busy schedule.

Achieving OKRs is a team sport. To move the needle, team members need to trust each other, communicate clearly, work together and be accountable. To keep OKRs alive, you need to check-in on them frequently. How frequent? Generally weekly, and in some cases even daily.

I always explain to my clients that regular OKR check-ins are the key to making their OKRs effective. During OKR implementation, I help my clients with installing the weekly OKR check-ins at all levels in the organization. If the executive team created a quarterly OKR, they too need to check-in weekly.

A crucial element of weekly OKR check-ins are the daily or weekly measures in your KRs and they are what will set this kind of activity apart from a regular status meeting. In status meetings, when you huddle with your team, people tend to look at the past (last week we did this and that). Weekly OKR check-ins mostly look at what's coming up (the next 7 days).

Simply put, teams that do perform weekly check-ins perform better than teams that don't. By running OKR check-ins you can reap the advantages many of my clients have experienced, like using collective brainpower (which improves innovation), improved communication, positive peer pressure, accountability and increased motivation. Imagine that all of your teams have weekly discussions and work on OKRs aligned to your (behavior change) strategy. Hence, the power of the weekly OKR check-in.

The Most Essential Event

The OKR check-in (see Figure 9.1) is the most underestimated tool in the OKR tool-suite, forming the most important event of the whole OKR Cycle. Check-ins are the operating system for your OKRs. Without them, OKRs are almost certainly doomed to failure.

OKR check-ins are based on the principle of accountability and improve alignment and motivation. In a study (Phillips 2011) from the American Society of Training and Development (ASTD) on

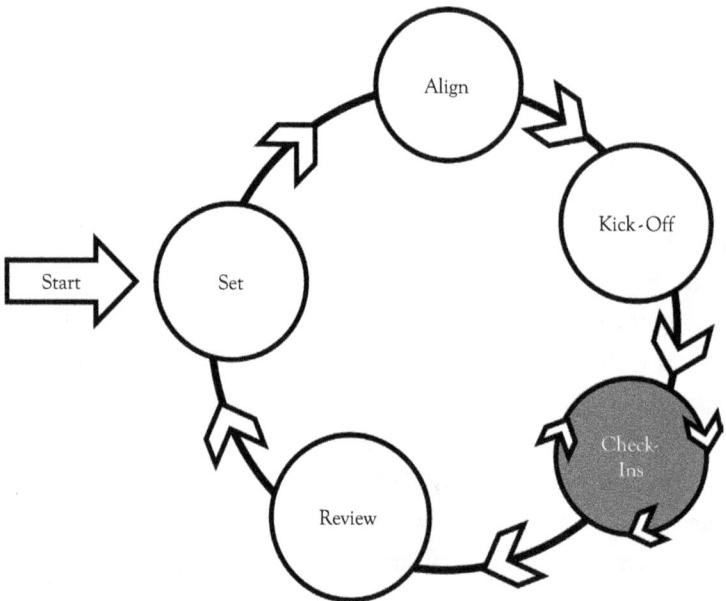

Figure 9.1 The OKR check-ins

accountability, they found that people have a 65 percent chance of completing a goal if they verbally commit to its completion to someone. If they have a regular accountability appointment with the person they've made the commitment to (e.g., a team member), their chance of success increases to 95 percent. This proven method is applied to many other frameworks, like Rockefeller Scale-up (meeting rhythm), Scrum and Toyota Kata. The habit of check-ins gives you exceptional leverage. However, it is one of the most difficult habits to practice since it requires a lot of discipline from leaders and their teams. If you want OKRs to be successful, this is your most important event and you need to integrate it deeply in the DNA of your company.

Some companies understand the concept of meeting rhythm and already have a weekly cadence like a weekly start with an all-hands-on-deck meeting, or a town hall meeting. If this describes your company, then great! You don't need to change much, because you can embed OKR check-ins into your existing weekly meeting rhythm.

The concept behind an OKR check-in is simple. With a regular cadence, you and your teams come together to discuss the progress on your OKRs. Not only will you and your teams report on progress, but you and other team members also personally commit to specific actions to drive the KRs forward.

Cadence

The word cadence is often used in the context of OKRs. It means "from the beat, rate, or measure of any rhythmic movement." Sometimes it is used interchangeably with the word "rhythm." Having cadence means that you build-in the discipline required to make the OKR process repeatable by having a clear structure with check-ins that will result in high accountability and success.

Although a typical OKR check-in cadence is weekly, cadences depend on the type of OKRs level and team maturity. Some teams start fortnightly (every 14 days), while more experienced teams do daily meetings. As a general rule of thumb, you can assume that a higher frequency is better. Weekly is better than fortnightly, daily is better than weekly.

The Power of Progress

The best way to motivate employees to do creative work is to help them take a step forward every day. "The power of progress is fundamental to human nature, but few managers understand it or know how to leverage progress to boost motivation," according to Teresa Amabile and Steven J. Kramer in their Harvard Business Review article titled *The Power of Small Wins* (Steven and Kramer 2011). They continue:

> In fact, work motivation has been a subject of long-standing debate. In a survey asking about the keys to motivating workers, we found that some managers ranked recognition for good work as most important, while others put more stock in tangible incentives. Some focused on the value of interpersonal support, while still others thought clear goals were the answer. Interestingly, very few of our surveyed managers ranked progress first.

Steven and Kramer analyzed diaries of knowledge workers and found out that nothing contributed more to a positive inner work life (the mix of emotions, motivations, and perceptions that is critical to performance) than making progress in meaningful work.

For OKR check-ins, this reflects a very real misconception between the factors managers perceive as being effective, and those that actually satisfy the very real desire in all of us for advancement, development, and growth. In the personal sphere, we feel rewarded when we meet a goal. Similarly, in the business world, we feel rewarded when, likewise through discipline and commitment, we see a project coming to fruition. In our personal lives, popular apps keep track of our fitness progress, our sleep rhythms, and even our time spent meditating. In the business world, we do this through daily, weekly and quarterly check-ins that set the tone and pace based on confidence scores (more on confidence scores coming up).

Dull OKR Check-Ins

Both weekly and daily OKR check-ins can become dull at times, mainly because BAU slowly takes over. It requires discipline to keep the meetings running with motivation and passion. Dull check-ins will demotivate people and eventually people will abandon their new weekly or daily habits, and the status quo will win again.

One of the keys to a successful OKR check-in are good measures (as explored in *Chapter 4*—Measures and Metrics). Good metrics in your KRs will track progress on a daily or weekly basis toward your objective. Without seeing the effects of your experiments and actions on these measures, your check-ins will be tedious and tiresome. Try to avoid vanity metrics like NPS or MRR as the numbers will not be updated on a weekly or daily basis. Also, avoid metrics that aren't influenced by the team; including them anyway will demotivate people. Remember, it's the lead measures that operational teams can influence. Finding the perfect metrics truly is an art and developing them requires patience and often the assistance of a skilled OKR coach or trainer to help get the ball rolling in the right direction.

How to Run a Weekly OKR Check-In

If facilitating consistent progress is the key to good performance, then why is it that most managers don't set a constructive progress loop in motion? Even when they are aware of the power of progress, most companies lack a method for tracking this progress toward meaningful goals. The KPI system, by now adopted by most organization, is not enough. However OKRs can fulfil this need fully. A second problem is that a constructive progress loop requires a significant shift in behavior. OKRs can achieve this shift and central to this is its short term cyclical structure with even shorter accountability cycles, generally designed as weekly OKR check-ins on multiple levels.

What

A short team or group meeting (between 15 to 30 minutes).

OKR check-ins happen on multiple levels within your organization:

- The company or department level check-in. You can choose to only run check-ins with the executive team or do an all-hands-on-deck check-in. The latter can be extremely powerful since it offers complete companywide transparency. At the same time, it asks leaders to be authentic and vulnerable.

- The team level check-in. Team level check-ins are with the team only, of course. Optionally, the team's leader could be invited as well, to answer questions related to the company OKR and goals, but also to act as an accountability touchpoint.

When

OKR check-ins are your "sanity check," because for successful OKRs, consistency and discipline are vital.

Team OKR check-ins are usually held at the beginning of each week (Monday morning is a great time). If the check-in falls on a public holiday, postpone it by a day, but it still needs to happen. From now on, this is each team's most important meeting, and you (and other leaders) need to be there to help the teams take action. If you work with different shifts or time zones, you will need to run the check-in twice on the same day.

Try running the company check-in before the team check-ins so that teams have an updated version of the KR values they will be contributing to.

Who

The participants of the weekly check-in are typically all members of the (executive) team or department. Everybody in the team or department needs to attend—no exceptions, no skipping. If your department has 120 people, find a place where everybody can see, hear and chime in. For virtual teams, Google Meet, Microsoft Teams or Zoom can work. Recording the check-in might be an alternative if you have large time zone differences or working in different shifts.

Agenda

So, how does it work? Typically, an OKR check-in agenda has seven stages:

1. Prepare

- Pre-meeting: All participants should refresh themselves on the status of the tasks and initiatives from the end of the last quarterly cycle.
- Immediately before the meeting starts, the KR owners should write the latest values of their KRs on the OKR dashboard. It is not unusual that for the first few OKR Cycles, the KR owner(s) need to collect data manually. My experience is that the most interesting measures require a significant investment in time to automate. You too should need to make a trade-off between automation and investment.

2. Report

- Participants report on previous results that contributed to the goals. Celebrate good news, for example: "...last week's measure improved by five percent. Great job everybody!"
- Optionally, each team member reports on the commitments they've made in the previous OKR check-in. Be open and honest about commitments that fell prey to the BAU.
- Try to keep the updates short and don't go into too much detail.

3. Review
Review the OKRs and set "confidence scores" (see Figure 9.2). In the next section, we will explore how to use confidence scores, but for now, here is how they are applied in the weekly check-in.

- Per KR, the team members set a confidence score on a 1 to 10 scale (or if it's a fairly simple KR, a 1-3 scale).
- At the first check-in of the OKR Cycle, the confidence score starts at 5 (which is 50 percent).
- Try removing the 7 from the 1 to 10, or the 2 from the 1 to 10 scale to avoid people from picking an average score.
- Discuss any questions and remarks. The whole idea with discussing the confidence score is to trigger a discussion about the obstacles (see stage 5).

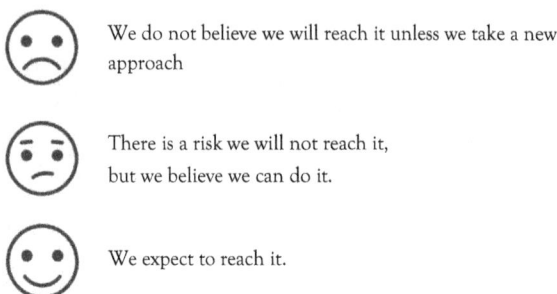

We do not believe we will reach it unless we take a new approach

There is a risk we will not reach it, but we believe we can do it.

We expect to reach it.

Figure 9.2 Confidence scoring

Tip: To spice up your check-ins, try using different symbols for indicating confidence. Use whatever the teams like, for example, smileys, hand gestures, action hero's, fruits or other avatars.

4. Health check

As you are pushing hard to achieve goals, keep an eye on the things that are important to your company/team: revenue, costs, happiness, the state of your codebase, and so on. Since health metrics aren't updated often, it's okay to skip this stage occasionally.

5. Obstacles

If your OKRs are truly stretched, there will be something blocking you from moving the needle. Discuss any obstacles to achieve your OKRs (see *Chapter 11*). Use root cause analysis techniques (like the five whys technique from *Chapter 3*) on low confidence scores to discover new obstacles. Select the biggest obstacle first. If you don't have any obstacles, you can skip this stage and go to stage six. In Part 3, we will explore in detail when and how you can use obstacles to your advantage.

6. Plan/Do/Check/Act

Do you have an obstacle that prevents the team from moving the needle? Set up new bets or experiments that will help you remove the obstacles and have a high probability of moving the KRs forward over the coming week. In larger groups, the group/team leads will give a brief update on the experiments. In *Chapter 12*—Experiments, we will dive deeper into how to run experiments. If the team members know exactly how to remove the obstacle (by simply creating a list of initiatives or tasks), then chances are that the OKRs weren't that much of a stretch. That is fine for now, but discuss this during the OKR review workshop.

An Alternative: High Impact Commitments

An alternative for teams that don't have experience with running experiments is to ask team members to make commitments to each other for the coming week. Only commit to things you can really do this week. Each team member needs to answer: "What are the one or two most important things I can do this week to impact the team's performance on the dashboard?" Each team member needs to be very specific about what their personal responsibilities will be for the coming week. Avoid making vague commitments like "this week I'll reach out to new prospects". Much better would be to make a specific commitment like "I will complete face-to-face meetings with ten executives that have just downloaded our whitepaper." Be careful that team members don't overcommit (danger zone), but certainly be keen on challenging commitments that will push people (learning zone).

7. Close

Close the check-in. Ask everybody to sum up the meeting with a word or phrase. It helps to formally close the meeting and makes sure everybody has had a chance to say something. Follow up on issues or conflicts people might have.

How Confident Are You?

Are you feeling confident in achieving your OKRs? As mentioned briefly in the agenda section, that is the main question you will need to answer in every OKR check-in.

Confidence Scores

A confidence score is an indicator of whether a team or individual contributor believes a KR is achievable. The score can be a number between 1 to 10, 1 to 5 a color coding (red, amber, green) system such as in the

Andon System (Everett 1991), or any scale to set the level of confidence that you have in a KR. Traffic lights, mascots, smiley's or something the team has invented to represent the confident score will all do fine.

At the beginning of each OKR Cycle (typically quarterly), all KRs start at amber (50 percent). Then on a weekly basis, the (executive) team rates the confidence they have in each KR.

Using the color coding system, teams can use the following indicators:

- Green indicates: we are sure we are going to make it because the current metrics look good. The needle is moving steadily.
- Amber signifies: there is a 50/50 chance we are going to make it. The current metrics are behind. The needle is moving slowly.
- Red means: we are way off the mark. The needle hasn't moved an inch. We need to take serious actions or revisit our tactics.

With that said, sometimes all the confidence in the world won't be an automatic success indicator of a KR being achieved. Sometimes things happen that couldn't have been predicted or avoided. Checking in on a weekly basis (as well as quarterly) can be one of the best uses of your time, not only in terms of accountability, but as a way to forecast for the future, especially when something didn't go as planned or wasn't accomplished or fell by the wayside. For a team, with each team member weighing in and giving input, lessons can also be gleaned from these measurable experiences and the team can refocus. Why did we think we were on track and where did it go wrong? How can we prepare for something like this again in the future? What were the important considerations that we missed?

Why Should You Care?

If you score your level of confidence in your KRs on a weekly basis, you can be certain that you will get a lot more feedback from the system (executive colleagues, business partners and team members) regarding small adjustments, pivoting and learning, than you would have with only grading OKRs at the end of the quarter. Weekly scoring of your confidence of your KRs helps you and your team make better and quicker decisions.

It will reflect a plan with milestones and regular check-ins that will not only instill confidence in the progress of KRs, but also put meaning to the "business as usual" work of your team.

You can track your data from week to week tracking the history of your metrics in your KRs, seeing numbers go up or down, seeing graphs, but in the end it's about people. People need to do the work in order to move the needle. Have you ever been in a situation where your intuition is saying something different? You just "feel" something isn't right or working.

The beautiful thing about OKRs is that there is room for people's emotions and feelings. Just like the Objective, part of OKRs is about inspiration, the confidence levels of OKRs are about feelings. Human judgement. The primary reason for providing a confidence score every week is to have conversations around the goals you are trying to achieve. If you or a team isn't feeling confident about a KR, try to use the five whys technique (see *Chapter 3*) to find the root cause of a low confidence score. Then identify the obstacles or impediments and write them down on your dashboard. In *Chapter 13*, I will describe in more detail how you can do this.

When determining the confidence levels of the OKRs, also take into account previous performance. In *Chapter 12*, you will learn more how to use historical data to understand performance of your measures, which can spark conversation about confidence.

How to Measure Team Confidence?

Measuring confidence in a group is difficult. The first thing is to identify who is accountable for the KR. If that is the manager of the team, then only the manager should set a confidence level for the OKRs. He or she can do this during the OKR check-in. A short narrative of why you gave this score will help the team to identify obstacles and possible solutions (see *Chapter 11*).

If the team is responsible for the KR, then you can try the 1:2:4 of the Liberating Structures (Lipmanowicz and McCandless 2014). The structure goes as follows:

- First everybody in the team individually writes down their confidence score of the OKRs together with some keywords that reflect their feelings.

- Then everybody should pair up with somebody else and share their score and their keyword. Then the pair should consolidate the score and the keywords.
- Depending on the size of the team, each pair will find another pair and repeat the previous exercise.
- Finally all groups will share their consolidated score and keywords. The team leader or a skilled facilitator can help to consolidate the final score and update the confident score on the scoreboard.

Daily OKR Check-Ins

Are you crazy? Daily check-ins? The most successful teams I know like to do a daily 10-minute check-in in addition to the weekly check-ins. Maybe you are familiar with the daily huddle or daily stand-up from Scrum. The concept of a daily meeting is used in all sorts of industries. A recent case study at the Rotterdam Eye Hospital in the Netherlands, revealed improved patient safety by having a 10-minute team meeting every day. The goal of a daily check-in is to craft a plan for the day.

A crucial element of daily OKR check-ins is the daily metrics and they are what will set this kind of activity apart from a status meeting. In status meetings, when you huddle with your team, people tend to look at the past (yesterday I did this or that). OKR check-ins mostly look at the upcoming 24 hours. Defining daily team metrics is an art but so critical for any high-performing team and organization. If you can track progress on a daily basis toward your KRs, the Objectives seemingly fall into place, and you can enjoy the added benefit of increased performance and enhanced inner work life. In case your KRs contain lead measures that measure team behavior on a daily basis (e.g. time spent on working together on a user story), this is the time to communicate a specific plan to achieve that target today.

Daily Check-In Agenda

Should you decide to pursue a daily OKR check-in alongside the weekly check-in, then make it happen at a fixed time every day. This will ensure the meeting becomes habitual. The agenda of a daily OKR check-in can look like this:

- Goals for the day. What is it you want to achieve by the end of the day? What is the #1 priority? For example, if you are a team of seven people and the target is to work together for four hours straight on a user story, you may want to organize everybody's agenda for that day.
- The KRs for today. Can we give a confidence score for each? Can we move the needle on the KRs today? If you use daily metrics in your KRs, what do you need today to reach those numbers?
- Hurdles. Are you blocked by anything or anybody? Can someone help you to remove this challenge? If someone has a day off tomorrow, who can help you make the numbers?
- As with the daily huddle, the daily OKR check-in needs to be a stand-up meeting because it increases the productivity of the group and ensures that it doesn't drag on. An ideal time limit for a daily OKR check-in is 10 minutes.

The OKR Dashboard

When you check-in on your OKRs, you need to have a place to keep track of your results. Therefore, most teams create an OKR dashboard. Creating dashboards is not difficult, but creating an effective OKR dashboard needs some more explanation; that's why there is a whole chapter devoted to this topic (see *Chapter 13*).

Long-Running Initiatives

If your team is working on larger initiatives spanning several weeks (e.g. a long marketing campaign or a big product feature), but with a high probability of contributing to a KR, there's a danger that the weekly check-in will become inadequate as there won't be anything to report on.

One solution is to get progress indicators on any larger initiative, for example, the number of customers who've migrated to the new platform, stages completed in the project, and so forth. However, as you will learn in *Chapter 12*—Experiments, trying to slice your bigger projects into smaller "experiments" might be more beneficial.

Run small experiments

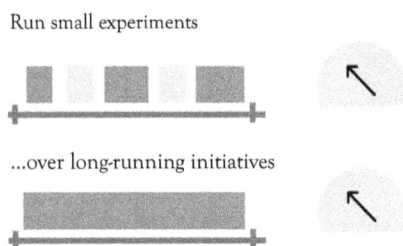

...over long-running initiatives

Figure 9.3 Run small experiments over long-running initiatives

You can be creative here as well, but it is important to track and report on the progress of these longer-term initiatives at each weekly check-in.

Integration With existing meetings

Other existing meetings in your company can be enriched by the OKR check-in. For example, if you already use Agile or Lean ceremonies like a daily Scrum, blend the OKR check-in into the daily Scrum event. Since the daily Scrum is about making a plan for the day, it's easy to add in elements from the OKR check-in. Also, I know that a lot of Agile teams struggle to decide what to present in their "demo." Showing the progress on their OKRs is a great way to demonstrate progress to stakeholders.

The check-in only takes 10 to 15 minutes, so it's easy to add on to existing meetings. Another big benefit is that OKR check-ins will make your existing meetings far more data-driven. No more highest paid person's opinion (HiPPO) discussions, but true data-driven conversations!

Celebrations

OKR celebrations are optional, but highly recommended. Some teams celebrate their failures and their successes at the end of the week. Some combine this in the weekly Monday morning meeting. What do teams celebrate? You can organise a small party if the team managed to move the needle on one of their KRs. Celebration of the succeeded and failed experiments is also common.

Not everything needs to have gone perfectly as planned in order for teams to celebrate. On December 9th 2020, SpaceX launched a shiny silver vehicle called SN8. It's made of stainless steel and is about 50 meters tall. On a 12.5 km test flight from the company's South Texas facility, it did several astonishing maneuvers, one being a belly flop. Most of these maneuvers were considered impossible before. This prototype was able to land where SpaceX wanted, but came in too hard and crashed. Nonetheless, the team celebrated.

Report Out on OKRs

Some teams like to keep other stakeholders informed about the progress they are making. Reporting status outside the team requires a lot of psychological safety and trust within the organization, so be careful here. Reporting these statuses can be as simple as sending a weekly e-mail with your team's OKRs, your obstacles and running experiments. The status e-mail can be sent to any stakeholder that opts-in. Some teams use a newsletter format to not only report on the status of their OKRs, but also report on things that are happening within the team.

Alternatively, if your teams are using an Agile methodology like Scrum, you can use the product demonstration meeting to show progress on your OKRs. Reporting on your OKRs via e-mail or during a product demonstration can replace the necessity for buying expensive OKR software. More on OKR software in *Chapter 13*.

Over to You

Diaries, everyone!

You can't really plan or run a check-in now. But you can think about these questions:

- Where would be the best place to have your check-ins?
- How long would they need to be for your group?
- When would you hold them? Does Monday morning work for your team? What's the ideal time? 9am or later? It may depend on factors like company culture and time zones.
- Could you integrate them with other meetings to save time and data-enrich the meetings?

CHAPTER 10

Reviewing Your OKRs

Chapter Highlights

- The OKR retrospective
- Public OKR reviews
- End of cycle celebrations
- Closing the cycle

Keeping your company up and running, making sure your employees can pay their mortgages at the end of the month, dealing with your competitors, answering questions from your clients…You are too exposed to the whirlwind of BAU. Your teams face similar challenges, so how do you keep learning, keep innovating as a company?

Having the time to reflect back on your goals, your strategy, generating new insights about the business, it's achievement and failures, and then using these insights to improve is one of the top wishes of many leaders.

I can remember one OKR review workshop where the leadership team joined this workshop for the first time ever, after the teams had already ran three OKR cycles solo. During the reflection workshop, we looked at why the none of their past OKRs hadn't made any impact on their strategic initiative to reduce customer churn. Thirty minutes into the workshop, the chief financial officer stood up and said: "I see now. We were running in the wrong direction for several months without any of us realising it." At that moment, the whole team realized their strategy to reduce customer churn wasn't working. They needed to pivot, but never took the time to closely analyze why it wasn't working.

You must use the OKR review workshop to reflect back, to think and to adjust your measures and your OKR processes. To truly embed OKRs into the DNA of your company, you need to make them a part of your company culture. The OKR review is a great vehicle to do so (Figure 10.1).

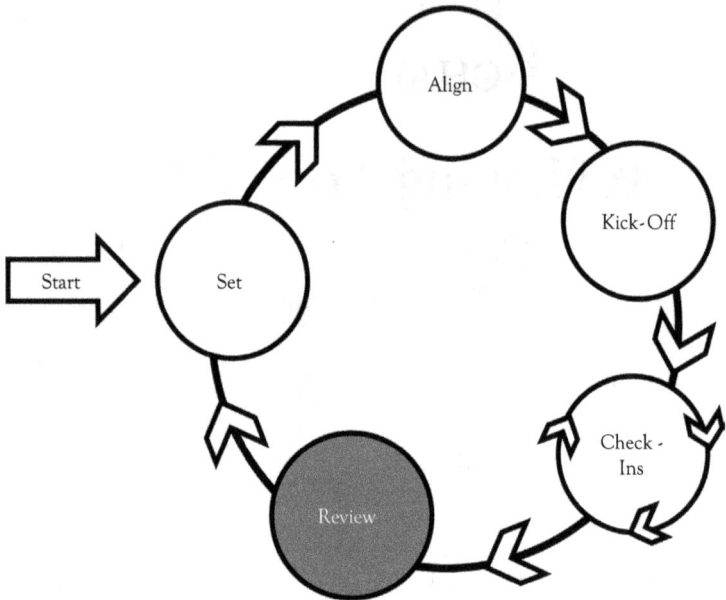

Figure 10.1 The OKR review workshop

Combining Two Review Settings

After running weekly check-ins throughout the entire quarter, the OKR cycle is complete and it's time to reflect. The review workshop is a built-in feedback moment to reflect on, adjust and pivot the OKRs to your organization's needs and processes. It is a great opportunity to look at the lessons learned regarding the goals that make your organization more flexible and adaptable. It also gives you an opportunity to change course if, for example, your competitor makes a bold move, or you see a certain strategy or tactic isn't working. Above all, the review is the moment where the organization and teams will learn from their mistakes.

As most OKR cycles are quarterly, the review workshop is normally held at the end of the 90-day cycle, but before the OKR setting workshop for the next quarterly OKR Cycle. The OKR review workshop looks back for improvements or pivot opportunities. This is different from OKR check-ins where the team is looking forward to make an impact on the KRs. Therefore, it might be useful to also organize the OKR review workshop mid-quarter. If you host them less frequently (e.g. twice a year), then you lose the chance to react and pivot. If you continue running initiatives that do not move any needles, it is a waste of time, energy, and motivation. Reviews prevent this.

To be effective, the OKR review is sometimes separated into two different phases: the retrospective and the review. The difference is that the retrospective always is a private event (only team members can join), whereas the review could also be held publicly and is therefore very powerful.

In my approach, I prefer to first do a team retrospective in which only the team members review their own OKRs first, and tap into the power of a review in public afterward:

1. In a private team setup: retrospect on your OKRs and the OKR process.
2. In a public setting: present what you have learnt in front of the entire organization or department, or for your boss or another accountability partner.

Both meetings are internal and stay within the company.

The OKR Retrospective Meeting

The goal of the OKR retrospective is to gather data about the OKR process, the achievement of your OKRs to generate new insights and to decide what to do next based on them. The action items as a result of this workshop can vary from changing your strategic plan to simply moving the timeslots of your OKR setting workshops.

When

Just before the OKR setting workshop for the next quarter, as you may want to share what you have learnt here with everybody in the company or group.

Duration

One to four hours. Some retrospectives go fast, especially if your OKR process runs smooth and you have a clear indication that your overall strategy is working. However, in the first few OKR cycles, things probably won't run that nicely. This is fine, everybody needs to adjust to this new way of working. Therefore, schedule more time to reflect back.

Who

Only the team is responsible for that specific team OKR. No external people are allowed. The psychological safety needs to be very high as people will share their mistakes, failures and what they have learnt with their team.

Agenda

The OKR retrospective has five stages and if you're familiar with *Agile Retrospectives* (Derby and Larsen 2006), you'll probably recognize the layout. The "gathering data" stage will be used to internally review the achievement of your OKRs by assigning a grade to your KRs.

1. Set the Stage
Set the goal: Give people time to arrive and get in the right mood.

2. Gather Data
Help everyone remember: Create a shared pool of information. During this stage, you should find answers to the following questions:

- What worked well?
- What didn't?
- What are we going to try to do differently?

Never blame people if OKRs aren't achieved. Instead, try to foster a learning culture where OKRs and the process are things you discuss and learn from. Sometimes it can be hard to recall from memory what happened, let's say, 60 days ago. It might be a good idea to capture data (e.g., by using the above questions) throughout the OKR cycle. Then you can bring that information into the review.

Grading Your OKRs

To gather data, your teams often provide a grade to each KR. Grading OKRs is slightly different than providing a confidence score to each KR each week. You can give a final "grade" to your KRs based on to what extent you have achieved it. When you use grading, you can use either the Andon-style (red, amber, green), smileys, or the 0.3, 0.7, and 1.0 type of grading. The Google reWork guide provides some more information about grading your OKRs (Google reWork n.d.). However, if you've followed my approach, you have already used confidence scoring during the OKR check-ins, and spending time on scoring OKRs at this stage is probably be less useful. I suggest to experiment with grading OKRs and see if they generate any new insights for the team. If they do, keep them, but don't be afraid to discard this process if they don't provide you with new insights anymore.

3. Generate Insight

Why did things happen the way they did? Identify patterns. See the big picture:

If we achieved the goal, what did we learn that we can use in the next OKR cycle?

If we didn't achieve the goal, what was the root cause? Too ambitious, vague, easy? (Remember: learning, not blaming.)

4. Decide What to Do

Pick a few issues to work on and create concrete action plans for how you'll address them. For example: "Let's schedule the OKR workshops at least three weeks in advance so that everybody has time to free up their schedule. Jane, can you run with that?" Or: "John will gather data from our data analytics team to create better baseline measures for our KRs".

5. Close the Retrospective

- How could the retrospective be improved?
- Clarify follow-up. Make sure the action items are assigned to individuals and make sure they will report back. Otherwise, your action items won't survive and will die amidst the BAU work.
- Thank people.
- Provide a clear end to the workshop.

Tips to Avoid Boring Retrospectives

To create inspiring reviews and retrospectives, you can use a tool called *Retromat*. It will generate a random retrospectives format to avoid repetitive and boring workshops. Check it out here: https://retromat.org/

Over to You

Time to Reflect

You can't really run a reflection workshop without having been through the OKR Cycle, so instead, let's take the opportunity to reflect on your experience of OKRs as you have been reading this book.

Ask yourself honestly: Am I excited about OKRs? Am I excited enough to be an ambassador for them within my organization?

If yes, you next need to consider why:

- What makes OKRs better than or complementary to the systems that already exist in your organization?
- What, in a nutshell, could be the added value of OKRs to your executive or pilot team?

It's also worth reflecting on where your organization actually is now. Here are a few typical scenarios to get you thinking: My organization—or my part of it—is:

- Desperately in need of OKRs: this could be the motivational booster.
- Ripe for this: we're treading water a bit, or are not as agile as we could be. OKRs could be the answer.
- Considering OKRs: OKRs seem to make sense on paper. We should test drive them and run a pilot.
- Change-averse: Which is, of course, exactly why we need OKRs. But I've no idea how I might successfully introduce them.

The Public Review: Presenting Your OKR Insights

After each team privately reflects on their OKRs and the OKR process, they may decide to share what they have learnt with the rest of the company internally. This is done in a separate public workshop or can be integrated into the OKR kick-off event.

A typical public OKR review meeting agenda:

- The company reviews the results. Duration: ±10 minutes.
- The team/department reviews the results. Duration: ±5 minutes per team.
- Celebrate failures and successes. Duration: ±5 minutes per team.
- Close.

Try to be honest and noble in this meeting. Everybody makes mistakes, and that includes leaders. A review in which the executive team publicly admits their failures is very powerful, but will scare off many leaders. Research has shown that authenticity and being vulnerable deepens human connections and relationships with employees (Seppälä 2014). Don't blame each other for the fact that you didn't achieve your OKRs this quarter or that the process is not working. Instead, focus on what can be learnt and the successes. Celebrate them!

Celebrations

Some companies prefer to set a fun theme around the company's OKR and celebrate successes—which is, of course, *not* tied to any compensation scheme. Don't announce the celebrations upfront, but rather build some excitement around them to create an element of surprise. You could even make a game out of it, for example, roll a double with two dice and only then, announce the celebration. This has the added benefit that people don't assume that there will be a celebration regardless. Depending on the final OKR score at the end of the 90 days, you can have celebrations like:

- 75 percent—Free lunch for a week
- 85 percent—Go out to dine with the whole company
- 85 percent or more: We all go on a ski trip

Of course, the celebrations are optional, but I definitely can recommend to celebrate achievements of your OKRs if you want to make OKRs sustainable. People like to achieve stretch goals, but they also like appreciation (in any format) for all their hard work even more.

Closing the Cycle

After the private and public review meetings, the OKR cycle officially ends. Once per quarter, new company OKRs will be developed, adjusted based on what has been learnt, announced and the whole cycle starts again. Repeat this cycle until the end of the year. In some cases, you might want to use a moving window: Develop four OKR sets every quarter and only pick one. This helps to continuously adjust and evaluate your strategy. The cycle itself may also be adjusted if the results from the review meetings indicate it should be.

It takes time to implement OKRs and fit them into your culture. And they *will change* your culture, which takes time, too. On average, successful OKR adoption takes one to three years, so patience is key!

Recap Part Two

In this part, we've looked into the OKR cycle that will help to adjust and implement the behavior changes into your company culture to help you achieve your most ambitious goals.

We've learnt in detail about the OKR workshops and events, their timelines and how to put them into practice by following the detailed agendas.

By now, you should know that the OKR cycle provides a cadence of accountability at all levels of the organization. What is important is that everybody in the organization holds each other accountable for applying the cycle. Lacking discipline in holding firm to the cycle is often one of the major signals of failing OKR implementation.

Part 2 References

Amabile, T., and S.J. Kramer. May 2011. *The Power of Small Wins*. Boston: Harvard Business Review. From the Magazine.

Castro, F. n.d. "Creating Alignment." https://felipecastro.com/en/okr/creating-alignment/ (accessed February 20, 2021).

Clear, J. 2018. *Atomic Habits*. New York, NY: Avery.

Derby, E., and D. Larsen. 2006. *Agile Retrospectives: Making Good Teams Great*. Pragmatic Bookshelf.

Doerr, J., June 27, 2018. "Conversation with John Doerr and Donald Sull." *MIT Sloan Management Review*. YouTube https://youtu.be/HiQ3Ofcmo50

Everett, R.J., and A.S. Sohal. 1991. "Individual Involvement and Intervention in Quality Improvement Programmes: Using the Andon System." *International Journal of Quality & Reliability Management* 8, no. 2. doi:10.1108/EUM0000000001635

Google ReWork. n.d. "Tool: Grade OKRs." https://rework.withgoogle.com/guides/set-goals-with-okrs/steps/grade-OKRs/(accessed February 20, 2021).

Janlén, J. March 12, 2019. "Make OKRs and Forecasts Come Alive!" https://blog.crisp.se/2019/12/03/jimmyjanlen/make-okrs-and-forecasts-come-alive (accessed February 20, 2021).

Lipmanowicz, H., and K. McCandless. April 1, 2014. *The Surprising Power of Liberating Structures: Simple Rules to Unleash A Culture of Innovation*. Seattle WA: Liberating Structures Press.

Niven, P., and B. Lamorte. 2016. *Objectives and Key Results: Driving Focus, Alignment, and Engagement with OKRs*. 1st ed. New Jersey, NJ: Wiley.

Phillips, P.P. 2011. *The ASTD Handbook for Measuring and Evaluating Training*. Alexandria: ASTD Press.

Seppälä, E. 2014. *What Bosses Gain by Being Vulnerable*. Boston: Harvard Business Review. https://hbr.org/2014/12/what-bosses-gain-by-being-vulnerable

Thomas, G. April 30, 2020. "Turning the Ship Around, A CEO Takes Responsibility for Troubles Caused by "bad" OKRs." www.whatmatters.com/articles/beam-dental-okr-ceo-transparency/ (accessed February 20, 2021).

Wilson, P.F., L.D. Dell, and G.F. Anderson. 1993. *Root Cause Analysis: A Tool for Total Quality Management*, 1st ed. Milwaukee: American Society for Quality.

Womack, J.P., and D.T. Jones. 2003. *Lean Thinking: Banish Waste and Create Wealth in Your Corporation*, 37–49. London: Simon and Schuster.

Facilitation Techniques

Adzic, G. 2012. *Impact Mapping: Making a Big Impact with Software Products and Projects*. UK, Woking: Provoking Thoughts Limited.

Clegg, D., and R. Barker. 1994. *Case Method Fast-Track: A RAD Approach*. Boston: Addison-Wesley.

Dettmer, H.W. 1997. *Goldratt's Theory of Constraints: A Systems Approach to Continuous Improvement*, 62–119. ASQC Quality Press.

Earl, S., F. Carden, and T. Smutylo. 2001. *Outcome Mapping*, 1. CA, Ottowa: International Development Research Centre.

Kano, N., N. Seraku, F. Takahashi, and S. Tsuji. 1984. "Attractive Quality and must-be Quality." *Journal of the Japanese Society for Quality Control* (in Japanese).

Liberating Structures: Lipmanowicz, H., and K. McCandless. April 01, 2014. *The Surprising Power of Liberating Structures: Simple Rules to Unleash a Culture of Innovation*. Seattle WA: Liberating Structures Press.

Martin, K., and M. Osterling. 2013. *Value Stream Mapping: How to Visualize Work and Align Leadership for Organizational Transformation*. New York, NY: McGraw-Hill Education.

PART III

How to Move the Needle

CHAPTER 11

How to Move the Needle?

*We live in a society exquisitely dependent on science and technology,
in which hardly anyone knows anything about science and technology.*
— Carl Sagan

Chapter Highlights

- A model to determine a response strategy
- Achieving OKRs in a complex world
- Scientific thinking 101
- Current and target conditions
- Using micro OKRs
- Identifying obstacles

Defining good OKRs and following the OKR cycle is challenging for
most organizations. It's a big leap and it requires a big cultural change,
too. However, as with any other skill that is learnt, practice makes better, and the more you and your teams cycle through OKRs, the better
you will all become. Your teams will be increasingly focused and aligned
with your overall company strategy. The OKR Cycle makes sure that your
goals are not set and forgotten, rather that they are kept alive throughout
the quarter.

After the executive team has defined the single quarterly OKRs for
the company, the operational teams connect and align their OKRs to
the company KRs. Your teams are ready to start the first week of OKR
check-ins. Immediately the following question arises: How do we move
the needle?

The Cynefin Framework

Every organization and situation is unique, there isn't a cookie-cutter approach to achieving OKRs and therefore the honest answer is "it depends." Sometimes a team knows exactly how it can move the needle. For example, to increase product quality of a software product, software engineers could apply best practice code design techniques and consistently show this behavior throughout the day or week. There can also be moments where teams have no idea on how to move the needle. What is the best way to approach this?

Luckily, Dave Snowden has created the *Cynefin framework* to help us make decisions on how to best make sense of your own and other people's behavior (Snowden 2007). It's a sense-making framework (not to be confused with a categorization model) to help leaders and teams make sense of a certain situation, in our case to decide how to move the needle. For many years I've successfully applied the Cynefin model to OKRs to help teams make decisions about which approach is best to get that needle moving for them.

The Cynefin Framework (see Figure 11.1), when uniquely applied to OKRs, is a way for you and your teams to understand and respond to

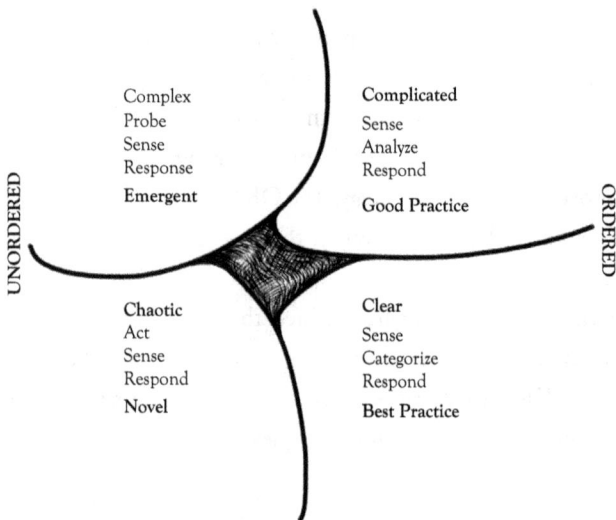

Figure 11.1 The Cynefin framework

your current state, which is especially relevant when you make progress attempts.

In the previous figure, you can see two larger domains (ordered and unordered), which are both divided into two subdomains. The four domains describe a particular state and its associated with steps toward a response. Becoming aware of the status quo and then using the framework as a tool to make sense of appropriate responses that will move their needle, a team can arm itself with the most effective means of problem solving to fit their situation. Let's take a look at the domains that make up the Cynefin framework:

Clear Domain

Where the problem lies and how to act to solve it is clear. This is likely because this isn't the first time your team or company has been in this position. So, while it may not be easy, there are still well-understood best practice guidelines to follow. In *Chapter 4*, you've learnt about leverage behavior measures. For example, if your Objective is to "fit into your wedding outfit," the lag measure is body weight and the lead measure might be your caloric intake per day. Cause and effect are well known here. If you consume less calories, you lose weight. If you then consume less calories over the course of 90 days, you just might achieve your Objective.

In the clear domain, you will find key results that focus on consistent human behavior or weekly outcomes the team needs to achieve. You can check daily or weekly if team members actually showed the desired behavior the day or week before. If not, teams respond by creating a list of possible actions to counter for the undesired effect, behavior and prioritize them and then make commitments to each other to follow up on those actions in the day or week ahead. These actions are different from the horrible action list we discussed in *Chapter 2*, because they will only focus on small actions or commitments for *this* week. This puts teams in direct control of adjusting their own behaviors, giving them autonomy (and therefore is a display of trust), rather than having them follow orders and fostering resentment.

Complicated Domain

The heart of the matter is relatively clear to your team or company and there is a mutually agreed upon outcome. However, the method for getting from point A to point B is not obvious. In this domain, there are many possible paths to take, and you, as a leader, can expect that there will be a lot of (technical) learning going on as team members evolve and adjust to get closer to a workable solution. They will need a lot of feedback in order to adjust swiftly.

Teams first need to understand the current performance of the "system" (more on measuring performance in *Chapter 12*) before they can respond. Then teams can use root cause analysis tools, for example by using the "five whys" technique we discussed in *Chapter 3* or the fishbone diagram from *Chapter 4*, to determine their next course of action. For example, when customers don't come back to your website because your site was lagging, a software team could then define an Objective to boost the website performance, with a KR that would measure website response times. The solution wouldn't be as obvious, so they first need to measure the current website performance and do a root cause analysis before they can proceed. The team could then build prototypes and iteratively find a solution that will move the needle of their KRs.

In the beginning of the OKR cycle, the weekly check-ins will be about learning more about the problem. External help from outside the team is often required. In case of the website performance example, the team could consult a website performance specialist. Based on these lessons, good practices and prototype iterations can be applied and monitored throughout the rest of the quarter.

Complex Domain

This is the domain of competing hypotheses. In the complex domain, you cannot plan activities in order to move the needle. You can only plan for experimentation. The relationship between the problem and the solution is foggy at best and your team or company will need to test different environments in order to crack the code and uncover the actual underlying problem. First, the team needs to make the challenge less hard by envisioning a future state only two to four weeks in the future. Then, on a weekly basis, the team should list obstacles, and hypotheses and run "safe to fail" experiments to remove these obstacles. Sometimes there aren't any obstacles to identify and the only thing you can do is to experiment.

Safe to fail experiments are meant to approach the issue from several angles in a small and safe way, in order to allow possibilities for solutions to emerge. They should occur swiftly and at as low a cost as possible. Prepare your team to run experiments and deal with the results, according to the framework outlined in *Chapter 12*. In this process, teams discover new ways of working, new practices of how to deal with emerging problems, or how existing technologies can be combined smartly to solve problems.

Chaotic Domain

You can accidently enter this domain because of crisis. Both you and your team or company have no clear vision about what can be done to address the problem and any solutions will not be apparent until they eventually emerge. Think of this domain like firefighting: Doing nothing isn't an option; you know you have to do something, but what will stop the fire from burning the whole building down might not be evident until much later in the investigation. You try to firefight to stabilize the system and move the problem back to one of the other domains. As you have no idea how to put out the fire, any crazy idea that you or your teams have is a good one. It is in this domain where true innovation happens.

The Connection to Agile

People new to OKRs often make the same mistake, especially those working in an Agile environment. Software teams in particular are known for their short iterations in order to reduce uncertainty and learn faster. Agile, Scrum, Extreme Programming (XP) and even OKRs were invented in these highly uncertain and complex environments for a reason. The natural tendency of Agile teams is to break down the "OKR work" into initiatives, epics, features or other units of work. After the breakdown, these units of work are then planned, again in short iterations. Hopefully, reading about the aforementioned Cynefin framework, you understand that finding solutions to move the needle isn't always something you can predict or plan. If you can break the activities down that you need to do into work items, it means the work is in the "clear" or "complicated" domain.

Of course, it is fine to use the Agile and Lean mindsets and best practices to overcome obstacles to OKRs but be careful not to mix the regular "Agile" work of the team with the strategy of finding solutions to complex problems described here, which is running experiments to learn more about the problem.

When companies and teams start with OKRs, their goals aren't that much of a stretch yet, because their first priority is to make OKRs work in their organization. Therefore, the solution to move the needle can often be found in the more ordered, safe, and predictable domains (clear or complicated).

If companies run OKRs for a few cycles, the OKRs can really become stretched. If you have defined real stretch goals, all of your work fall into one of the unordered domains (complex or chaotic).

Solutions in the clear domain are relatively straightforward. To dive deeper in the chaotic domain would deserve a whole new book, so I suggest you study chaos theory and complexity theory if you would like to know more about this domain. In the remainder of this chapter, I will describe in detail how to achieve results in the complicated and complex domains. We encounter these domains most often, and they produce increasingly difficult problems the more we stretch our goals, because uncertainty is high, solutions aren't obvious and some degree of failure is inevitable.

Our Complex World

The problem with achieving ambitious results is that we live in a complex, unpredictable world. Perhaps you can recall the Cone of Uncertainty in *Chapter 5*. To be more specific, we are part of a complex adaptive system

(CAS). This is a system that is made up of multiple interacting parts within a closed system, with the capacity to change and learn from experiences. Within this dynamic network of interactions, we can never predict the results of our actions. So what *can* we do then?

Let's start with what prevents us from achieving our results: obstacles. In the book *Lean Enterprise* it says "The purpose of setting aggressive target conditions is to reveal obstacles so we can overcome them through further improvement work" (Humble et al. 2015, 124). Thus, stretched goals, which are a signature of the Lean OKR approach, will also help you to reveal constraints in your organization.

What's in a name?

In management literature, the words "barriers," "obstacles," "roadblocks," "rocks," and "impediments" are often used interchangeably. In this book, I prefer to call them *obstacles*, but feel free to use your own lingo here.

Whether you are trying to climb K2, win the World Cup, go to Mars, make strides in decreasing our carbon footprint or become the market leader in your space, eventually, you will face obstacles, big and small. The problem is that you don't know which obstacles you will encounter. Going for stretch goals—moonshot goals in particular—means you enter into unknown territory. That is a scary thought for most people. As mentioned before, people hate uncertainty. Not knowing how to achieve a goal is a good recipe for demotivation and anxiety.

Thus it may happen that, after the first week of your first OKR cycle, you check in on your OKRs for the first time and find that there is a problem with the team's confidence levels. Pursuing OKRs is hard because you venture out into unknown territory, you experiment, and you take risks. Navigating this unknown territory requires a different way of thinking.

Scientific Thinking at Toyota

The solution is called *scientific thinking*. There are two kinds of thinking we call "scientific." If you engage and reason about scientific content, such as force, mass, gravity or quantum physics, then you are thinking about science, which is rather obvious. The second kind of scientific thinking includes "the set of reasoning processes that permeate the field of science" (Dunbar and Klahr 2013, 701). These processes include, but are not limited to, induction, deduction, experimental design, causal reasoning, concept formation and hypothesis testing. In this and the following chapters, we will look into this second kind of scientific thinking that is required to achieve your OKRs.

Scientific thinking is the skill you need to adapt to an ever changing world. Researcher and author Mike Rother writes the following about scientific thinking: "[S]cientific thinking may be the best way we have of navigating through unpredictable territory to achieve challenging goals" (Rother 2018, 1). For many years, Rother and his colleagues researched the underlying managerial routines and thinking processes that resulted in Toyota's success with continuous improvement. During their research, they identified patterns, behaviors and practices that showed a strong relation with scientific thinking. Rother created a four-step behavioral model that he called the "improvement kata" which helps people to get closer to accomplishing a challenging goal. He also defined a routine that managers can use to help teach their employees how to use scientific thinking. He calls this the "coaching kata" (Rother 2009). Finally, he identified a third practice to help people get started with scientific thinking and named this the "starter kata" (Rother 2018).

Kata is a Japanese word that means "form" and is a pattern of martial arts movements that one should deliberately practice on a daily basis. With regular practice, you may improve until you master a new task. Deliberate practice focuses on tasks beyond your current level of competence and comfort (Ericsson 2007). Similar to deliberately practicing martial arts movements, people need to deliberately practice scientific thinking, preferably daily. This happens in the Toyota car factory, where everybody is practicing this way of thinking. Imagine what this could do to your company.

Although these routines and behaviors have been proven many times in an industrial context, applying these behavior and thinking patterns in the context of achieving OKRs is not only new, but can be groundbreaking for many organizations. Let's look how the improvement kata and the coaching kata can be applied to OKRs.

Over to You

Deliberate practice refers to a special type of practice that is purposeful and systematic. While regular practice might include mindless repetitions, deliberate practice requires focused attention and is conducted with the specific goal of improving performance (Clear n.d.). Deliberate practice can be used to try to interrupt your automated practices and habits. That means changing your methods and introducing discomfort to your routine practices. Well known examples to apply this in daily life can be to brush your teeth with the other hand or to pat yourself dry with a towel from the toes up instead of from your head down. At work, you could practice something daily that you've never tried before, learn a new (computer) language or interact with customers.

To explain deliberate practice, I've got an exercise for you. First, with your left hand's index finger, draw a circle in the air. Now with you right hand's index finger draw a triangle. How this this feel? Probably awkward, weird, slow, unnatural, stiff, uncomfortable, or difficult. It feels wrong and you had to really concentrate. These words are also used when people experience change. This is totally normal and it's supposed that you feel this way when working to moving the needle.

The Improvement Kata

The improvement kata can be used by teams on a daily basis to get closer to their OKRs. An improvement kata is a daily deliberate practicing routine that people at Toyota use to continuously improve processes and create innovations by learning how to apply principles from scientific thinking into their habits and routines. The improvement kata is especially suitable for, but not limited to, changing processes, and I am sure you have found that most of your OKRs are related to changing processes, as well. Think about it for a moment. You want to increase your sales? You need to look at your sales process (sometimes called a funnel). Marketing? The same thing: You need to look at your marketing process. Customer on-boarding and customer journey? They are both processes.

There are four steps in the improvement kata that help you move the needle. You always start with (1) understanding the direction you want to go. Then you need to (2) understand your current condition and (3) understand your target condition. Subsequently you (4) observe the problems and any obstacles you are facing, and conduct a series of experiments that will remove the obstacles (Figure 11.2). Following the steps of Plan, Do, Check, Act (PDCA) will guide you through a rapid loop of discovery that gets you to your target.

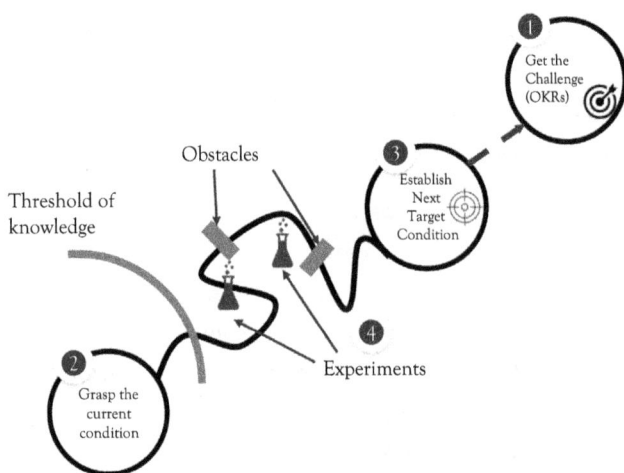

Figure 11.2 The four elements to reaching an OKR

So, how can we apply these steps to achieving your OKRs? Let's look at each step:

1. Establish an understanding of the direction in which you're going. That's your company or team OKRs.
2. Grasp the current condition. Where are you now? Teams working on an OKR need to understand the current condition (or the baseline) before they can define their target. Remember the *FROM X to Y* formula from *Chapter 3*? It described how to set good KRs. The "X" is the current condition here. In the OKR setting workshop, the team is responsible for grasping the current condition, based

on measures. Thus, you should already have this embedded in your KRs. To understand the current condition even better, you can use the statistics techniques from the next chapter as well.

3. Establish a new target condition, which brings the team just a little bit closer to moving the needle of your KRs. It's important to note that a target condition is *not* the same as your target, the "Y," inside your KRs. A target condition is the condition the team wants to achieve one or four weeks from now. It's a subgoal in order to break down the big 90-day challenge into easier to digest pieces. It's not always required, but it can be a great tool to use. Later in this chapter, we will explore target conditions in more detail.

4. Use the OKR experimentation loop which is based on the PDCA: First, you define the most important obstacle that is preventing the team from achieving their target condition, then you develop an experiment to remove it. Therefore, you need to employ the OKR experiment steps to get closer to the target condition. In the complicated domain, you can identify obstacles first, however, it isn't always possible to define obstacles when you find yourself deeply in the complex domain. Then you only can run experiments. The whole of *Chapter 12* is devoted to running experiments with the OKR experiment loop.

The Coaching Kata

The coaching kata is the routine used by Toyota's managers to *teach* their teams how to use the scientific thinking to reach their goals. When using OKRs, your leaders and managers also need to teach their teams how to get better at achieving results. Without a learning practice in place, it will become very hard to scale this systematic and scientific way of thinking. This includes not only teaching people how to apply scientific thinking, but also teaching them techniques to deliberately practice new skills. If you want to win Olympic gold on the 200m butterfly or if you want to become the best piano player in the world, you need to use deliberate practice a lot. For some reason, in the business world this isn't very usual.

By default, teams are not familiar with working with OKR inspired challenges and behavior changes. They tend to gravitate toward the stuff they are familiar with (e.g. building features, and using Scrum or Kanban). There is a tendency then to see each OKR as a project, leading them back to the whirlwind, or the BAU. It's a leader's or manager's job to teach and coach teams on how to get a step closer to KRs: to help them wire their brain differently. As the authors of *Lean Enterprise* put it: You need "to design, evolve, and operate a system in which the people doing the work have the necessary skills and resources to run their own experiments, thus learning individually and collectively, developing and growing their knowledge" (Humble et al. 2015, 59).

Teaching scientific thinking is thus spurring employee empowerment. If you teach people this way of thinking, they will be able to handle more difficult challenges. At Toyota, they are able to generate and utilise an entrepreneurial mindset and accompanying behavior in their people (Rother 2019). Teaching and practicing scientific thinking is critical to embed into your organizational culture in order to beat your competition and innovate at scale.

Case Study: Making Customer On-Boarding a Seamless Experience

You should check in on your OKRs on a regular basis to see if they are going in the right direction, but how do you get closer to your OKRs? Let's use an example to show how the improvement kata can work in practice.

Let's say you are working in a product development team. Recently, your company has announced a very ambitious company OKR for the quarter. Now it is up to your team to see how they can impact the company's KRs. During the OKR setting workshop, your team decides to set the following OKR (step 1. Direction): "Customer on-boarding is a seamless experience" to contribute to the company's ambition for this quarter. By using the measure guidelines from *Chapter 4*, the team defined measures for their success. "Average drop-off rate during on-boarding" could be a good indicator to put into one of the KRs, for example.

The team already tracked the customer drop-off performance for some time and noticed that the average drop-off rate is currently 12 percent per week (step 2. Current condition). Now your team is about to set a target for this quarter. Eleven percent is easy, while 0 percent is impossible. As you learnt in *Chapter 3* on how to write good OKRs, you should start with a 50 percent chance of achieving the target. The team decides to set the target at 5 percent. By using the formula *FROM X to Y*, they define the following OKR:

Objective: Customer on-boarding is a seamless experience

KR 1: Decrease the customer on-boarding drop-off rate from 12 to 5 percent per week

Great. Now What?

So your product development team has a clear baseline and a target for the next 90 days. It's a very big challenge for the team. They have never tried to reduce the drop-off rate of customers so dramatically, so they should try to respond to this situation according to the complex domain. But where do they begin? Where do they start with achieving their ambitious goals? What should the team do in the first week they are going to work on their OKR? They should develop a target condition.

Target Condition

A target condition (step 3) is a state one to four weeks into the future. Using an American football analogy, you can think of the OKR as "scoring a touchdown." A target condition can be similarly thought of as "getting a first down." With a target condition, your team is clear on the direction in which they must move the ball and even more clear on the positioning needed in order to land that touchdown. What's not clear are the steps that your team needs to take to get there, as the required steps are largely dependent on external factors your team can't control, such as the other team's offensive and defensive plays. For that, your team needs to figure it out as they go. The same is true for moving their needle.

A target condition can answer questions like:

- How should this process operate?
- What is the intended normalized pattern?
- What situation do we want to have in place at a specific point in the future?
- In which direction do we want to be moving next?

After the team develops a target condition, they use confidence scores to rate their confidence in achieving their KRs. In case of a low confidence, the team can identify obstacles that prevent them to get closer to the target condition. Subsequently, they select one obstacle, for example, "why do our customers drop off early?" When the team has identified their obstacle, they can design safe to fail experiments to learn more about their obstacle and eventually use that knowledge to remove it.

You will learn how to define and select obstacles later in this chapter, and in the next chapter we will look at how to use and create experiments. Here, we first continue to look at how to define target conditions by exploring a technique I developed, based on the OKR rationale.

Micro OKRs as the Next Target Condition

Traditionally, target conditions are described by process steps, process characteristics, process metrics and outcome metrics. To simplify this, you can also use the OKR format to describe the next target condition. This results in what I refer to as "micro OKRs," which help you to get a small step closer to your regular OKR.

Just like target conditions, micro OKRs are small challenges to get you closer to your longer-term challenge step by step (your summit, see Figure 11.3). What is important is that you only define one set of micro OKRs at a time (similar to the annual and quarterly technique discussed in *Chapter 5*, with one Objective and the accompanying key results).

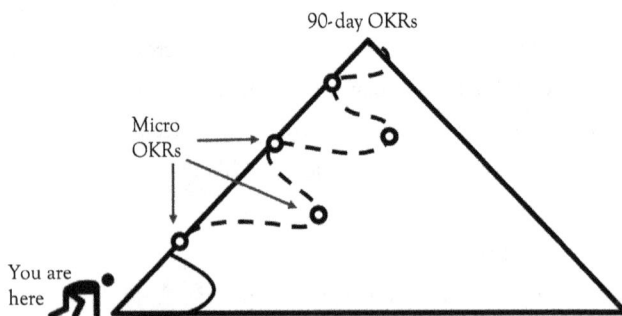

Figure 11.3 Micro OKRs as the steps toward the regular 90-day OKRs

By using a series of these micro OKRs, teams can focus on small wins and learnings, which also helps to have more celebrations, progress and improve motivation. Some companies that have more experience with OKRs, only use team-level micro OKRs, instead of running the default quarterly OKR cycle s. This comes with an important note: Your teams should never lose sight of their larger challenge.

Ideally, the lifespan of micro OKRs sits between one and four weeks. In practice, this might vary, so use common sense here and try out what works best for you. As a leader or coach, you need to ask the team working on the micro OKR which variable needs to change in order to get closer to the target condition. Working with micro OKRs ensures the team has only one subfocus for the coming period, and forces people to think only about a limited future state.

Like regular OKRs, micro OKRs also use an OKR cycle. Because the cycle is short, following all of the workshops would be too taxing and confusing. Instead, try to be pragmatic. Give your micro OKRs a good amount of thought (a maximum of four hours) and give them a go. You can skip the alignment workshop and the kick-off can be done during the regular weekly OKR check-in. The reflection at the end of the short micro OKR Cycle gives you a nice learning moment. The opportunity to experiment and quickly receive feedback makes micro OKRs a great way to practice OKRs within the larger 90-day cycle. I will explain in *Chapter 13* how you can include micro OKRs in the updates of your OKR dashboard.

Methods Toward Developing Micro OKRs

Micro OKRs are the next target condition a team needs to focus on. You can develop micro OKRs at the start of the OKR cycle, but you will also need to develop new ones throughout the main OKR cycle. There are two approaches to develop the next target condition with micro OKRs:

1. Stabilize the current condition. After the team has understood their current performance, you might want to Stabilize the system first before you modify it. You develop smaller OKRs with that stable Objective in mind. For example, if new customers come in

unpredictably, you might want to use micro OKRs to streamline the inflow of new customers first, before you can improve the process of acquiring new customers. In the next chapter, you will learn more about understanding performance.

2. Future state. Based on the current condition, the team develops smaller OKRs that will contribute to one of the main KRs, but only describes a future state one to four weeks from now. For example, if your main set of OKRs contains a KR to "increase your daily products usage by 25 percent," a micro Objective could be to increase daily product usage by 10 percent for the next four weeks.

Which approach you should take depends on the stability of the measures you use inside your KRs. If the measures do highly fluctuate, you need to stabilize them first. Otherwise use the baseline of your measures and set a target one to four weeks from now.

Micro OKRs With Lead Measures

Do you recall the wedding example from *Chapter 4*? The larger Objective was to reduce body mass and waist size to get us in our wedding outfit in six months' time. The KRs were thus focused on a slightly abstract, long-term goal. After looking at your current condition, you noticed that both body mass and waist size are stable measures, so you can break these main OKRs into smaller ones. One set of micro OKRs could be to cut the number of calories in the next four weeks, which can be done by a KR that decreases consumption and a KR that increases what we burn. These micro OKRs are less abstract, and can be measured daily. Moreover, it's efficiency lies in the predictive lead measures toward change in our body mass and waist size.

Removing Obstacles to Achieve Extraordinary Results

Obstacles don't have to stop you. If you run into a wall, don't turn around and give up. Figure out how to climb it, go through it, or work around it.

—Michael Jordan

Whether you decide to work with micro OKRs or only with regular OKRs, identifying and dealing with obstacles (step 4) is a major activity when moving ahead in the complicated and complex domains. In 2017, I was part of an OKR workforce team for a medium size software company located on the coast of the Netherlands. The executive team had a very ambitious goal to reduce its software product defects while increasing the speed of innovation in order to build a superior product than it's competitors. The company started its quarter with the following product department OKR:

Objective: Boost product quality
KR: Diminish our weekly product defect rate from 20 to 0
KR: Decrease customer complaints on feature XYZ by 70 percent
KR: Increase mean time between failure from 2 days to 10 minutes

To start working on these OKRs, we needed to find out what the number one bottleneck was to product quality.

I joined their product department to help them find the constraint that prevented them from achieving higher product quality and speed of deployment. Instead of focusing on solutions, I helped the product teams brainstorm their obstacles. In this process, we selected the number one obstacle for them: knowledge on building quality software.

When we identified their main obstacle, we could define several experiments to begin addressing it. By thinking in obstacles first, we avoided jumping to a conclusion too soon, and we took the first steps in boosting their product quality. Do you know the obstacles that prevent you from achieving your OKRs?

How to Approach Obstacles

What are the main obstacles to problem solving? Firstly, we tend to drastically overestimate the number of problems that stand in the way of our goals (Kahneman 2013). A good way of dealing with this is to ask: Do you need to resolve all of them? Often, if you overcome one obstacle, other obstacles seem to melt away. By focusing on obstacles one at the time, the team has a directive to break them down. In the next chapter, you will learn how exactly to overcome obstacles, but first you need to be able to identify what "real obstacles" are, which we will look into in the next section.

Secondly, when problem solving, we too often frame obstacles in a negative way, as complaints, instead of formulating them observantly (Boeg 2019). "Customers don't like our user interface" is not a valid obstacle. The real obstacle might be "We don't know if customers can navigate easily through our on-boarding process." This is both more specific in terms of what the problem might be, as well as more realistic in terms of information that is actually available, being careful not to make unfounded assumptions. The bottom line is to pay attention to your assumptions and observations when distinguishing symptoms from the real problems. The fact that customers are dropping off during on-boarding is not the real problem. It's a symptom of something else. Of course, the final outcome is that you want your customers to not drop off. Similarly, "the sales team is always too late calling back hot leads" is not a valid obstacle. The real obstacle in this case could be "we don't know how call back time influences new sales."

Identifying Your OKR Obstacles

After you have set and aligned your (micro) OKRs, teams go into the weekly rhythm of OKR check-ins. During the first OKR check-in, the whole team provides confidence scores in relation to the KRs. In case there is a low confidence score, the team members look at one or more of your KRs and list all of the obstacles they can think of in a sort of brainstorming session. Most people are good at listing problem areas. Framing your obstacles as questions can help. For example:

- How can we …?
- Which [customer segment] is doing X?
- When are we/customers …?
- Where are we/customers…?
- How might we improve…?
- What is now preventing us from achieving the target condition?

Be careful with obstacles such as time and resources. "How can we get more time or budget to improve our customer on-boarding process?"

is not a good question to ask, because time, budget and the number of people on the team can never be a valid obstacle. You will always have to deal with the constraints of the system.

Using the concept of free listing, affinity mapping and dot-voting from *Chapter 7* let each team member write down their obstacle on a (digital) sticky note. Next, group all related obstacles together. Use dot voting to select the most important one. This winning obstacle will now become the focus point for the team in the coming weeks (Figure 11.4).

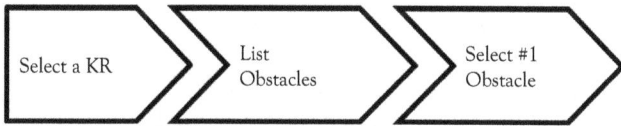

Figure 11.4 The obstacle selection process

An example: With the aforementioned technique, a product development team identified three obstacles to achieving their "5 percent customer on-boarding drop-off rate per week":

- #1 Why do customers drop off early?
- #2 Which customers are dropping off?
- #3 When do customers drop off during the on-boarding process?

They have selected 3 as the most important obstacle. This became their number one focus point.

In case the team uses micro OKRs, note that some people might want to write down an obstacle that relates to the main OKR. Design a separate space on your dashboard (see *Chapter 13*) for this. It's good to have these obstacles listed.

Brainstorm Obstacles

When you want to move your KRs in a positive direction, you should try to focus on one obstacle at the time. A good technique to isolate obstacles is to use the following template. Try to come up with at least three or four obstacles and fill in the following template:

We cannot achieve our KR, because ....

Obstacle 1:............

Obstacle 2:............

Obstacle 3:............

Obstacle 4:............

Obstacle 5:............

Pick the #1 Obstacle

The next step is to pick one obstacle that has the most impact on getting closer to your KRs. Pick only one! The 20/80 rule applies here, which obstacle (20 percent), when removed, will most likely move the needle of your KR substantially (80 percent). If you have trouble selecting one, pick the easiest one, especially if a team is new to this way of working.

Chapter Recap

In this chapter, we've explored the Cynefin sense-making framework as a tool to determine how to respond to OKRs. We've explored scientific thinking and Toyota's Katas as a way to instill a change of approach that will encourage genuine shifts in behavior and habits at team level, and we've looked at how this can work in practice.

We've learnt about target conditions as a key part of this change to establish a new, ideal view of how processes should look in the future, and we've seen how micro OKRs can link to target conditions as measurable steps toward that future.

We've established the importance of identifying obstacles as part of achieving OKRs and explored strategies for doing so. We've identified ways of ranking obstacles to identify the number one obstacle that needs to be overcome.

At this point, you should have a much clearer vision of the future you want to realize and a stronger understanding of the small, measurable steps you can take toward achieving genuine, tangible change in your organization. You should have a stronger awareness of how to identify, manage and overcome the most unpredictable and extensive obstacles that accompany the most ambitious OKRs.

Chapter References

Appelo, J. 2010. *Management 3.0: Leading Agile Developers, Developing Agile Leaders.* Boston: Addison-Wesley Professional.

Bland, D.J., and A. Osterwalder. 2019. *Testing Business Ideas: A Field Guide for Rapid Experimentation.* New Jersey, NJ: Wiley.

Boeg, J. 2019. *Level Up Agile with Toyota Kata: Beyond Method Wars, Establishing Core Lean/Agile Capabilities Through Systematic Improvement.* Independently published.

Clear, J. n.d. "The Beginner's Guide to Deliberate Practice." https://jamesclear.com/beginners-guide-deliberate-practice (accessed February 23, 2021).

Dunbar, K., and D. Klahr. 2013. *The Oxford Handbook of Thinking and Reasoning, Scientific Thinking and Reasoning.* Oxford: Oxford University Press.

Ericsson, K.A., M.J. Prietula, and E.T. Cokely. July-August 2007. *The Making of an Expert.* Boston: Harvard Business Review. Magazine.

Gothelf, J., and J. Seiden. 2016. *Lean UX: Designing Great Products with Agile Teams*, 2nd ed. Sebastopol: O'Reilly Media.

Humble, J., J. Molesky, and B. O'Reilly. 2015. *Lean Enterprise: How High Performance Organizations Innovate at Scale*, 1st ed. Sebastopol: O'Reilly Media.

Kahneman, D. 2013. *Thinking, Fast and Slow.* New York, NY: Farrar, Straus and Giroux.

Leybourn, E., and S. Hastie. 2018. "#noprojects." C4Media, publisher of InfoQ.com

Rother, M. 2009. *Toyota Kata: Managing People for Improvement, Adaptiveness and Superior Results*, 1st ed, 30. New York, NY: McGraw-Hill Education.

Rother, M. February 18, 2019. "Introduction to Toyota Kata." YouTube. Captured at the 5th annual North American KataCon conference in Savannah, GA on https://youtu.be/1l68cFskC7Y

Snowden, D.J., and M.E. Boone. 2007. *A Leader's Framework for Decision Making*, 68–76. Boston: Harvard Business Review.

CHAPTER 12

Experiments: Navigating Through Unknown Territory

It doesn't matter how beautiful your theory is, it doesn't matter how smart you are; if it doesn't agree with experiments, it's wrong.
—Richard Feynman, American Theoretical Physicist

Chapter Highlights

- Learning fast about your obstacles
- The importance of experimentation
- The OKR experiment loop
- Six practical steps to running your experiment
- Understanding performance
- People overreact to outliers
- Systemic or real change

We sometimes feel awkward when learning something new. It turns out that as adults, we are not very good at learning. We need to practice things that we don't know, also called deliberate learning. We like to stay in our comfort zone. In his famous TED talk, Tom Wujec (2010) showed that the best learners are kindergarten graduates. Why? In one of his design workshops, he challenged people to build a structure out of tape and spaghetti and put one marshmallow on the top. Many teams failed to succeed, from business students to Fortune 500 CTOs. However, the kids built the highest and the most wonderful structures. That is because they built many more prototypes of their structures, helping them to learn faster than the average adult.

The majority of my work is with tech companies where I work intensively with (software) engineering departments. Engineers love to build solutions straight away, so experimenting doesn't come natural to them. One engineering team had very stretched OKRs to increase their software delivery speed. The team wanted to go from a monthly release cycle to deploying software in production on a daily basis. All team members had good ideas on how to remove the obstacles they were facing. However, finding consensus in the group about what approach would work best was harder. So I asked them: "What would you like to learn about the obstacle?" They wrote down a list of learning points, and based on this list, we created hypotheses and ran experiments with the intention to learn more. In just a few weeks, they learnt so much about their obstacle that within four months, they were able to deploy their software 20 or more times per day to production, without customers even knowing it.

How Can We Learn More About Our Obstacles?

In the previous chapter, you learnt about the Cynefin model and how to apply scientific thinking with the help of the improvement kata to move the needle of your OKRs in the complicated or complex domain. With the four-step behavioral model of the improvement kata, you focused on the challenge (OKRs), the current condition (where you are right now) and the target condition (micro OKRs).

Through a focus on addressing obstacles, the problem to move the needle was broken up even further. You also selected one obstacle that you and your team are going to work on. Now you need to ask a critical question: How can we learn more about our obstacle? Meet experiments. The purpose of an experiment is to learn about the problem, expand your knowledge and finally remove the obstacle. The current condition line in Figure 12.1 will move to the right every time you learn more about the obstacle, thus expanding your knowledge and reducing uncertainty.

Deep in the complex domain, there might not be any identifiable obstacles, because the environment is highly uncertain and trying to find true obstacles is hard. However, you can still use experiments to probe if you are heading in the right direction.

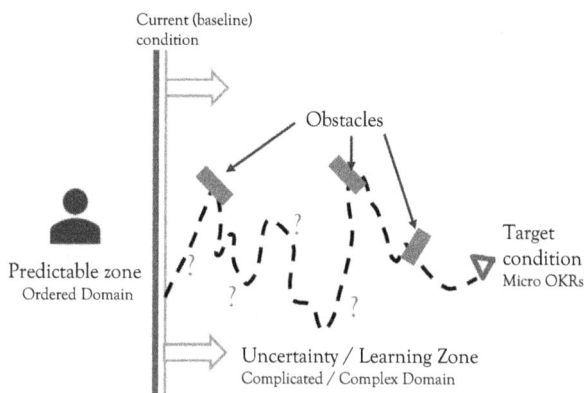

Figure 12.1 The predictable zone vs. the learning zone

The Importance of Experimenting

A lot of digital companies have embraced experimentation. Experiments have, for instance, helped Microsoft's Bing unit to make dozens of monthly improvements, which collectively have boosted revenue per search by 10 to 25 percent a year (Thomke 2020). As companies scale up their (online) experimentation capacity, they often find that their obstacles are not in the realms of tools or technology. Generally, the real obstacles for organizations are shared behaviors, beliefs, and values. This is why OKRs are valuable, as through them behavior changes can be achieved. In one study, the authors declare that of all experiments that software giant Microsoft conducted, one third failed (Kohavi and Thomke 2017). Most people don't like failure, but it is of utmost importance that you and your teams learn how to deal with and respond to failures. Experimentation is important when you are using OKRs and therefore you must invest in these necessary skills.

Types of Experiments

In the context of OKRs, there are two types of experiments:

1. Hypothesis testing. Ideally, a single-factor experiment with a prediction of what you expect to happen. This type of experimentation works best in the complicated domain.

2. Exploratory: Introduce a controlled change to learn more about the effect. For example, run a special online advertisement and see how customers respond, conducting a customer interview to learning more about their problem or pain or a feature stub to see if customers click on the feature you think they want. This type of experimentation works best in the complex domain where you want to probe the system, but don't yet understand cause and effect, only in retrospect.

The book *Testing Business Ideas* (Bland and Osterwalder 2020) is a great resource if you want to know more about these specific experiments. Hypothesis testing is about testing fast and getting rapid feedback in order to discover new things. You don't want to run an experiment to see if it works if you already know that it won't. The real question is *why* it doesn't work. The idea behind running an experiment is that you want to learn what it takes to make it work.

In a highly competitive and changing market (especially in IT), we sometimes don't have the luxury to wait a couple of weeks. We need to act now. Running experiments doesn't mean you need to run a few tests every now and then; it often means you need to engage in a lot of experimenting within the 90 days that you have to reach your OKRs. Think of smartphones. When Apple and Samsung were aggressively competing for market share, the products released to the market were good-enough, but not perfect. Perfect isn't even expected because year after year, new phone models are released to grow and expand market share. There's a reason why your phone requires regular updates to the operating system and to repair bugs: market leaders need to act fast so they have run calculated experiments to get an edge on their competitor but left enough room for adjustments.

Designing Experiments

When you run an experiment, you interfere with the system (organization, software) and expect a certain outcome to occur (if X then Y). However, that is not enough evidence that your experiment was successful. There might be other reasons or variables that could have influenced outcome. To really show there is a causal relationship, you also have to prove that if you don't interfere with the system, the outcome does not occur.

There are so many different experiment design possibilities in relation to goal achievement that many books are written about this subject alone. One easy to use technique is called "two-group" experimental design. Let me show you how this works by using an example.

Experimentation in software product development often involves running multiple different versions of a product feature over a short period of time and testing which version customers like most. This can be as simple as running two versions of a "Buy now" button on an e-commerce website, for example the original "red" one and a new "blue version," and observe which button will be used more. With a special randomized algorithm, 50 percent of the customers will see the original button and the other 50 percent will see the blue button. We also call this type of experiment an "A/B tests." If you run more versions, for example red, blue, purple and yellow, we call this "multivariate testing." After a couple of days of running this experiment, the team can analyze which version of the button worked best, and make a decision which color the button should have in the final product.

The OKR Experiment Loop

The OKR experiment loop, which is based on PDCA, can be applied to remove the obstacle that is preventing you from achieving your OKRs. Let's see how you can use this technique in practice. We will use the OKR experiment canvas (see Figure 12.2) to keep track of our running OKR experiments.

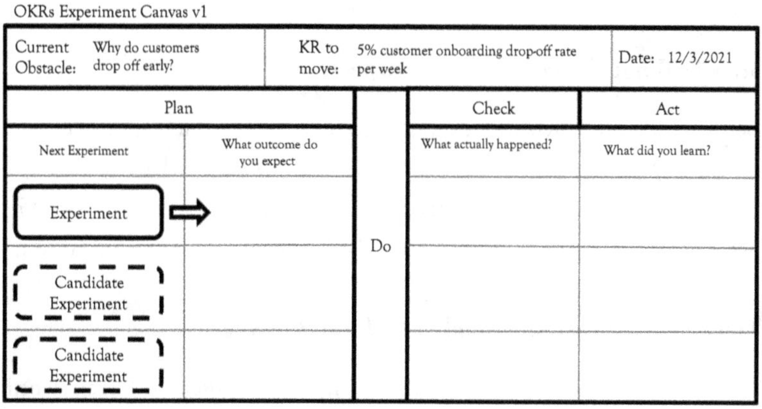

OKRs Experiment Canvas v1

Current Obstacle: Why do customers drop off early?	KR to move: 5% customer onboarding drop-off rate per week	Date: 12/3/2021

Plan		Check	Act
Next Experiment	What outcome do you expect	What actually happened?	What did you learn?
Experiment ⇒			
Candidate Experiment	Do		
Candidate Experiment			

Figure 12.2 The OKR experiment canvas1

Remember to run one experiment at the time to avoid mixed results. Doing so can have negative effects on other experiments. Also, you want to exclude any side-effects from other active experiments.

First, write down the obstacle that is preventing the team from achieving its Objective. Also write down the KR that will be impacted if you remove the obstacle or if your experiment is successful.

To illustrate how you can create experiments, let's use the KR and obstacles from the previous chapter. We've identified three obstacles for the "5 percent customer on-boarding drop-off rate per week":

- #1 Why do customers drop off early during on-boarding?
- #2 Which customers are dropping off?
- #3 When do customers drop off during the on-boarding process?

For now, we will focus on the first obstacle: Why do customers drop off early? So how do you create an experiment?

For every experiment you run, you need to use the following six steps:

1. What outcome do you expect?
2. Define your experiment.
3. Ask five powerful questions.
4. Do, run or try out the experiment.
5. Check what happened?
6. What did you learn?

Let's dive into each step in more detail.

Step 1: What Outcome Do You Expect?

Before you write down your experiment, first think about what you expect to learn. What outcome would you like to achieve, or what are you trying to accomplish? This statement often starts with "To learn..." or "We believe that...." Write that down. This is the hypothesis you want to test.

Meet Your New Best Friend: The Hypothesis

The English word hypothesis comes from the ancient Greek word "hupothesis," meaning "to put under" or "to suppose." Some refer to a hypothesis as an "educated guess." What do you and your teammates suppose would remove the obstacle you identified earlier? *Suppose that we do [INSERT PROPOSAL] to remove our obstacle.* OKRs are themselves also a hypothesis on at the company level. In fact, in the process of doing experiments, we try to break down the big 90-day hypothesis into smaller ones by the defining the obstacles that prevent moving the needle in your KRs.

One of the best techniques to overcome obstacles is to use the scientific approach. For a hypothesis to be a scientific hypothesis, the scientific method requires that one can test it.

To write a good hypothesis, you can use the following template:

To learn/We believe that _____.

We believe that *customers will drop-off during on-boarding if they need to provide credit card information (too) early in the process.*

You might want to define multiple hypotheses with your team, but only turn the one which is most important and doesn't have any evidence yet, into an experiment. Ideally, you want to associate customer behavior with your hypotheses, just like in the prior example.

Step 2: Define Your Experiment

"Experiments are the means to reduce the risk and uncertainty of your business idea" (Bland and Osterwalder 2020, 44). When preparing your experiments, consider these questions:

- For whom are you doing the experiment?
- Where will you do the experiment?
- What are you going to do?
- What activity must you plan to achieve the outcome from step 1?
- What measures or metrics (beyond your KRs) will you measure?
- What success criteria can you define?
- Which experiment can be cheap and fast to learn quickly?

Good experiments can be replicated and create data that can be usable and comparable. In the next section, I will explore several techniques that will help you to look at and understand the data.

To define an experiment you can use the following template:

We believe that [hypothesis]
To verify that, we will [experiment]
And measure [the data you will look at].
We are right if [the needle moves in our KRs].

For our example, the software development team created the following experiment. They created two versions of the on-boarding process where new customers need to leave their credit card information. One version is just the original process and with the new process, they moved the form with credit card information to the last step. They then randomly routed 50 percent of their new on-boarding customers to the new and 50 percent to the old version of the on-boarding process. The team used the following template to define their experiment:

We believe that customers drop-off during on-boarding because they need to provide credit card information too early in the process.
To verify that, we will put the credit card form as the last step in the process.
We then measure the drop-off rate during the on-boarding process.
We are right if we find a decrease of 5% in the weekly drop-off rate.

Try to define multiple experiments to gather as much evidence as possible in the shortest amount of time. Teams that master OKRs run tens or even hundreds of experiments each OKR cycle.

Step 3: Ask Five Powerful Questions

Before the team moves to running the experiment (the "do" column on the sheet), they need to verify their hypothesis and experiment by having a conversation with their manager or coach. This is not because the manager or coach needs to give permissions or approval, but to have a healthy conversation to avoid confirmation bias from the team. The team may also have an internal conversation to this purpose, but from experience I know it helps if a manager or coach brings a fresh perspective to the table. This is because we are often blind to our own presuppositions.

This conversation can be streamlined by asking the following five powerful questions (Rother 2009, 155):

1. What is our target condition or micro OKR?
2. What is our actual condition now?
3. What obstacles are now preventing us from reaching the target condition and which one are we addressing now?
4. What is our next step?
5. When can we see what we have learnt from taking that step?

After having such a conversation, the team can feel confident in running the experiment.

Bias and Preconceptions

Bias and assumptions can be a real problem. The team that is designing experiments can introduce errors in the recording of the data or, simply by virtue of having certain expectations of the outcome, create designs that are in line with the outcome they have in mind. This is a case of self-fulfilling prophecy. Your customers or employees can alter their behavior to accommodate the expectations of the people running the experiment. Such possible biases need to be taken into account when you design the experiments. Using the five whys exercise can help to weed out blind spots but above all else, those running the experiments need to have an open mind. While they are likely to be extremely intelligent people, it is important to set aside stereotypes of customer or employee behavior and for them to let the evidence be their guide. This works best in an environment where there is some time set aside for failure, otherwise you risk encouraging bias to speed up the process.

Step 4: Run the Experiment

Test your hypothesis and observe closely. It works best if the team observes the data themselves. For example, team members could take part in the user tests, observe customers in a lab setup or observe the internal process they are trying to improve. These days, it's relatively easy to use out of the box analytics software to analyze the result of your experiments, but make sure your teams have the right skills to interpret the results.

In our example, the team decided to use their built-in analytics software to analyze the drop-off rate results of their experiments.

Step 5: What Actually Happened?

What actually happened? What did you observe? What is the actual outcome of the experiment compared to the expected outcome? What evidence do you have? Write it down. I recommend you employ the following tools to determine statistical significance, in order to separate noise and chance from your actual results.

The team that measured the drop-off rate could now observe that the original process had a drop-off rate of 30 percent, while the new process had a drop-off rate of 7 percent.

Step 6: What Did You Learn?

What new insights have you obtained? Standardize and stabilize what works. If your experiment had positive effects on your KRs, then define the appropriate action to take. Otherwise, repeat the experiment loop.

Our development team also collected some very useful insights. Moving the credit card form to the end of the customer on-boarding process resulted in a large decrease in customers dropping off too early. They decided to improve the on-boarding process, based on this new insight.

Over to You

Now have a look at one of your obstacles to achieving your OKRs. Try to brainstorm some possible experiments, then fill in the experiment template from the OKR experiment loop section. It's fine to write down multiple experiments, but you should only work on one at the time.

Understanding Performance

I have been struck again and again by how important measurement is to improving the human condition.

—Bill Gates

When you want to grasp the current condition to determine the targets for your KRs, when you want to know if the experiments you have conducted actually worked, or if you simply want to know if your company or team is healthy, then you need to understand the performance of your measures. What is performance and how do you understand and track performance? When do you react? When do you look at variation or chaos? Let's dive into these questions in more detail.

As we learnt in *Chapter 2*, setting and forgetting your OKRs is a common reason for failure. With the help of lead measures (see *Chapter 4*) and your weekly check-ins, you can actually see regular progress and keep OKRs active in your mind. But how do you know that the experiments you have conducted to remove your obstacles have had the desired effects? How do you know you have actually achieved the strategic result you wanted with your OKRs? If your measures haven't significantly improved, or have not brought sustained improvement, something is wrong. To make a sustainable impact on business results, we don't want our OKRs to make an uptick in performance just once. You want to make changes to the system that have statistical significance. "Statistical significance helps quantify whether a result is likely due to chance or to some factor of interest" (Gallo 2016) writes Amy Gallo after a talk on statistical significance with Tom Redman, author of the book *Data Driven: Profiting from Your Most Important Business Asset.* You don't need to be a data scientist to determine the significance of your measures. In this section I'll provide you with practical tools you can use on a daily basis to help you analyze the results of your experiments, your current conditions, but also to better interpret your KPIs.

To see progress and track performance on a weekly, or even daily basis, you need to compare sustained results. To achieve statistical significance, you need to acquire at least eight data points over time. A mistake that many leaders and teams make is that they compare their latest measures or KPIs with those of the day, week, or month before to track performance and progress, thus observing only two data points.

Two data points cannot prove significance

In many business review reports I see "year to year" (Y2Y), "month to month" (M2M) and "week to week" (W2W) measures. The argument for these types of measures is often seasonality. If you are an ice cream seller, you might believe you should compare the number of ice creams sold from June 2021 to June 2020. However, these give you a false sense of performance. Two data points can never provide significance. Read on to understand what you should do instead.

Simply comparing last week's (or last year's) results to today's score might give you a clouded view. To really understand whether you are hitting your target, or whether your experiment has had a positive effect, or whether your OKRs have had the desired outcome on your business strategy, you need to compare your current performance to something more.

When you look at the following chart (Figure 12.3) on your dashboard, how can you possibly know whether your obstacle has been removed or whether your previous experiments were successful? Do you have enough feedback to make new and better decisions? Two data points cannot yet be called a trend; we need more data to identify a positive trend.

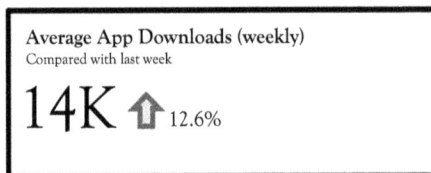

Average App Downloads (weekly)
Compared with last week

14K ⬆ 12.6%

Figure 12.3 App downloads performance

Good visual indicators must always try to answer the following three questions (Graban 2018):

- Are we achieving our target or goal? Are we doing so occasionally? Are we doing so consistently?
- Are we improving? Can we predict future performance?

- How do we improve? When do we react? When do we step back and improve the system? How can we prove we've improved?

To answer these questions, we need more data points, but simply reporting on all these data points in your monthly business review in a graph or chart doesn't give a clear overview that helps answering the previous questions.

Look at the following KPI in Figure 12.4. Can you use it to answer any of the aforementioned questions?

Summary: ✓ 6 ▲ 2

KPI	Status	Trend	Jan	Feb	Mar	Target
Sales from new customer as percentage of total	✓	⬆	22.4	22.0	23.1	30.0
Average Purchase Frequency	✓	▬	7	7	7	5
MRR (USD) (Mi)	▲	⬇	27.1	26.2	26.4	30.0
Customer Satisfaction	✓	⬆	7.2	7.2	7.3	7.5
Gross Profit Margin (%)	✓	▬	36.2	35.8	36.3	35.0
Employee Engagement	✓	⬇	6.1	6.2	5.9	7.0
Average Lead time for change (days)	✓	⬇	12	13	11	10
# critical incidents	▲	⬆	4	6	7	0

Figure 12.4 KPI summary chart

It turns out that with only this representation, it is very hard to provide answers to these questions. What do these numbers tell us? Are we getting closer to our goal? When should we react? So instead we should present this data in a chart. A chart is always easier to read than a list of numbers.

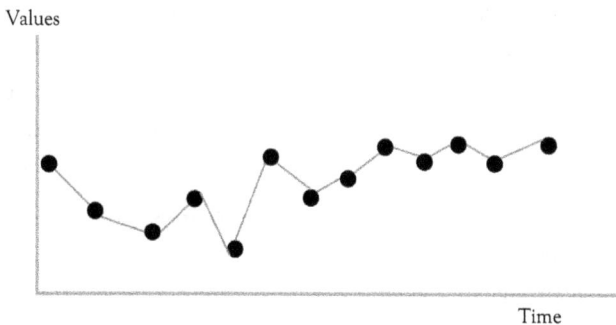

Figure 12.5 A simplified run chart

The above run chart tells us way more about the measure(s) over time, but it doesn't help us to answer all of the prior questions. Most importantly, it doesn't yet tell us how the team can react and improve.

X-Charts to the Rescue

The only proper response to a metric is to investigate.

—*Martin Klubeck*

A principle for understanding data states: "While every data set contains noise, some data sets may contain signals. Therefore, before you can detect a signal within any given data set, you must first filter out the noise." (Wheeler 2000, 30). As I've learnt from Wheeler's work, the tool for filtering out that noise is a control chart that combines individual values (X) and moving ranges (mR), also known as the XmR chart. This chart will tell you if you are looking at a normally performing system, at noise, or if there are signals that prove your experiments and changes are sustainable.

To explain in detail how this chart works is beyond the scope of this book, but I will outline the most important basics as follows. If you want to know more about XmR, I recommend reading *Understanding Variation* by Wheeler (2000). What I can tell you, is that XmR is a great tool for helping leaders and teams separate the noise from real signals in OKRs and KPI performance. Whether you are measuring business, team or individual performance, control charts help you to separate noise from the signals that really matter.

Essentially, the XmR chart combines an individual's chart, called the X-chart, and a moving range (MR) chart. The individual's run chart is used to filter out the noise from the data, while the MR chart is used to measure the variation between successive values, for example month to month or week to week. To understand the basics behind XmR chart reading, we will use the simpler X-chart here, which provides an easier way of interpreting information.

To build an X-chart you need at least six or more historical data points. Then you add an average line and two "natural limit" lines to the normal

Individuals (X) chart

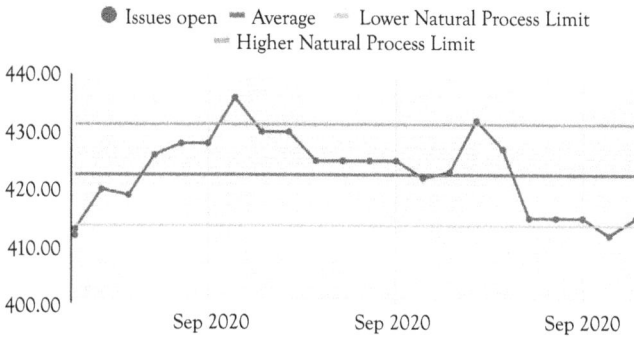

Moving Range (MR) chart

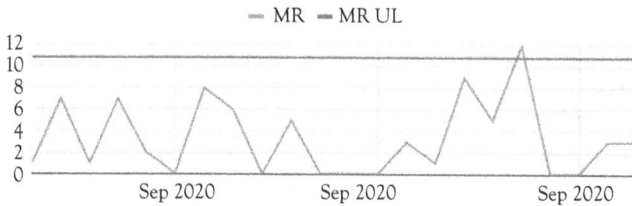

Figure 12.6 The XmR chart combines two control charts: individuals (X) and moving range (mR)

run chart. We call the two natural limits *upper* and *lower* process behavior limits which are automatically calculated based on a statistical algorithm. Read Wheeler's book if you would like to dive into the statistics of how to calculate these. In addition, you can also add your KR target as a separate line. In the *Appendix*, you will find a link to an XmR template, where all the statistic calculations are already done for you. You can use it to create a chart like this:

The natural process limits help you to distinguish noise from actual significant performance improvements. The average line is the actual performance of your measures. In the X-chart from Figure 12.7, you will see that the average line is 21. The weekly values are fluctuating around the average, so you are looking at a stable process. This information will also help you predict future performance, unless there is a something changed.

Number of Bugs per Week

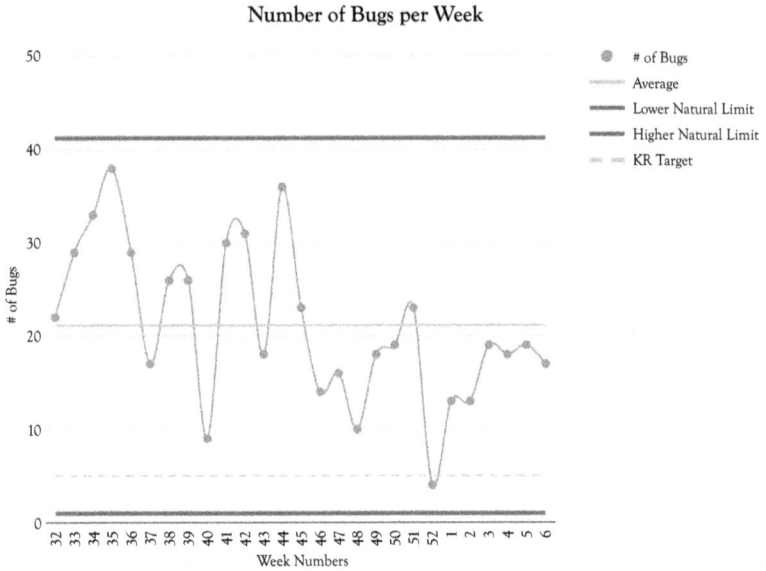

Figure 12.7 An X-chart showing the total number of bugs (defects) per week

Three Signals to Look for

Not everybody has a degree in advanced statistics required to interpret complex charts. Luckily, you don't have to. With the X chart as well as the XmR chart, you only need to look for three signals to detect changes. When any of these signals occur in your data set, you should start asking questions.

Signal 1: Special Change

Any data point that is outside the natural process limits (upper or lower) indicates that something has changed significantly. The team's call to action is to investigate and find its root cause. You don't react to this signal. It's only a glitch. You do, however, need to understand why it happened and then learn from that (Figure 12.8).

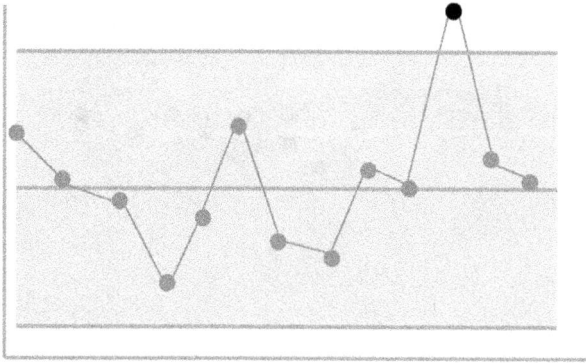

Figure 12.8 *Signal 1, a special change is visible (one data point above the natural process limit)*

Signal 2: Sustained Change

If you want to be sure that your change in performance is significant, you need to have at least eight data points on the same side of the central line (often the average line). There is almost no chance (less than 1 percent) that this has anything to do with natural variation, so you can trust your last OKR experiment had a significant effect on the performance of your KR measure. Or better yet, you OKRs had a significant impact on one of your business KPIs. Make sure you investigate the results anyway to be sure that an unexpected factor hasn't caused it.

If your team is using X-charts to understand performance and they check-in weekly, then using monthly data can take some time to see this signal. Ideally, you would use daily or weekly data when possible. If this is not possible, you can always look for a lead measure that can be measured more frequently. You can use the guidelines and techniques provided in *Chapter 4* to discover lead measures (Figure 12.9).

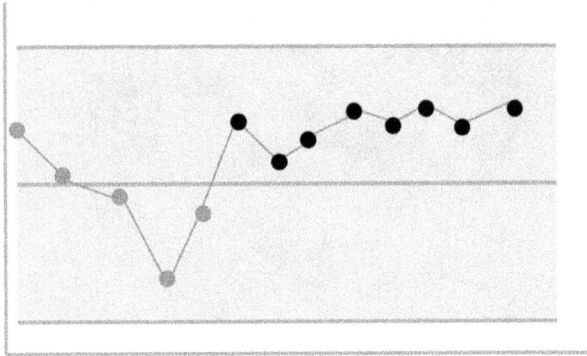

Figure 12.9 Signal 2, a sustained change in the chart is visible (eight points above the natural process limit)

Signal 3: Short-Term Big Change

Sometimes you cannot wait for weeks or months to let the pattern from signal 2 emerge. You can either change the *frequency* of measurement or you could look for big short-term changes. Three out of four consecutive data points that are closer to the same natural limit (upper or lower) than they are to the central line is a signal that you should pay attention to. Again, your first response should be to investigate, not react. Ideally, these big changes will get you closer to the Objective, faster, but don't only hone in on these big changes. Sometimes an incremental approach, with a series of signal 2 changes, is more telling with regard to significant change (Figure 12.10).

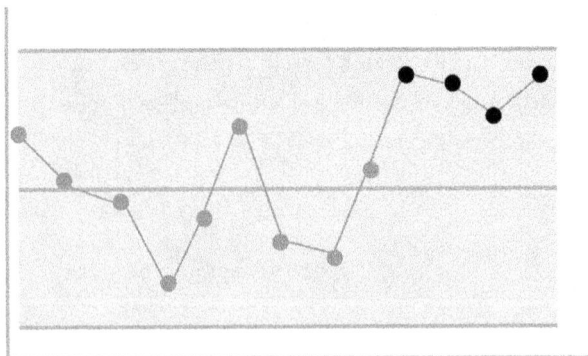

Figure 12.10 Signal 3, three out of four consecutive data points that are closer to the same natural limit

Each of the aforementioned signals tells you something about the true performance of your company or team OKRs and the impact that your OKR experiments have had. Many leaders and teams only look at changes from week to week. However, in the long term, only significant changes will make a true transformation of your business possible.

What to Do About Chaos

Sometimes measures are chaotic. They are not stable. When you plot them on a time axis, you will get something like Figure 12.11. The fluctuations are changing dramatically over time. A measure that is inconsistent and fluctuates unpredictably over time is what defines chaos. If we have a measure that acts chaotically, it will be very hard to set targets and thus OKRs for them. Find the root cause of the chaos and stabilize it. Once you have a stable and predictable system (variation is fine here), you can set targets and OKRs for it.

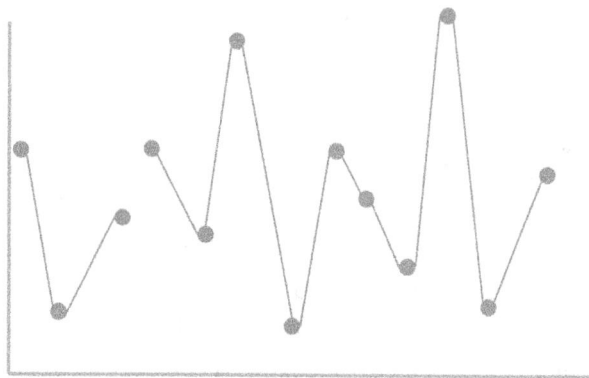

Figure 12.11 A chaotic measure

Over to You

Collect at least five to 20 data points for the measure you want to include in your KR before you start with the OKR Cycle. In the *Appendix*, you will find a link to an Excel spreadsheet you can use to build your own XmR chart to check whether any of your experiments have had an impact on your KR's performance. For each measurement in your KR set, you might want to have a separate XmR chart.

X-Charts for OKRs and Health Metrics

The X-chart helps not only to determine the statistical significance of your experiments, but also to analyze the results of your measure inside your KRs and your KPIs. Most teams using OKRs want to keep track of historical data. There are some nice software systems that can collect data points and represent them in a histogram. Unfortunately, most of those tools (as well as dedicated OKR software tools), don't have the features to plot your measures onto X-charts. I strongly recommend you download the digital X-chart template from the website (see the link in the *Appendix*) and plot the weekly or daily results of your KR measures or KPIs in it.

For Executive Teams

In addition, I recommend you to use X-charts to visualize your company KPIs. Plotting the weekly results of the measure of your BHAG, for example. Or what if you plot your MRR or NPS in X-charts? Is your company really achieving sustainable revenue or profit?

For Teams

For operational teams that try to influence the company KRs, it can be helpful to also plot the company KR measures into a X-chart. In doing so, teams can see if their efforts have had an impact on the overall OKRs. In addition, operation teams can also plot their health metrics into X-charts, to understand if they are looking at noise, or at signals. In case the data shows signals, it's time for the team to take appropriate actions.

Chapter Recap

We've learnt how experiments can be used to remove obstacles and help us navigate through uncertainty. We've established that their purpose is to expand our knowledge, to help us learn about our problem and to remove obstacles. Importantly, we've recognized that we need to have the right mindset to experiment successfully, and that we need to learn to deal with and respond to failures. We've explored how we can measure whether the experiments we've conducted to remove obstacles have had the desired effects and whether using OKRs is actually helping us achieve the sustained improvement we targeted.

We've looked at the OKR experiment loop and then delved deeper into hypothesis testing as a means of overcoming our most challenging obstacles. We've established that to see progress and track performance, we need to compare results, and we've identified X-charts as an easy way of interpreting information. We've looked at how at a simplified version can be used and established to make the complex more straightforward.

At this point, you should have a stronger working knowledge of your obstacles and the experiments you can use to overcome them. You should also have a stronger understanding of how signals in data can be recognized and used to identify actual significant performance improvements and significant changes that require investigation.

Chapter References and Notes

Thomke, S. March-April 2020. *Building a Culture of Experimentation*. Boston: Harvard Business Review.

Kohavi, R., and S. Thomke. September-October 2017. *The Surprising Power of Online Experiments*. Boston: Harvard Business Review.

Gallo, A. February 16, 2016. *A Refresher on Statistical Significance*. Boston: Harvard Business Review.

Wujec, T. February 2010. "Building a Tower." *Talk recorded at Palm Springs*, TED www.ted.com/talks/tom_wujec_build_a_tower_build_a_team

Bland, D.J., and A. Osterwalder. 2020. *Testing Business Ideas: A Field Guide for Rapid Experimentation*. New Jersey, NJ: Wiley.

Rother, M. 2009. *Toyota Kata: Managing People for Improvement, Adaptiveness and Superior Results*, 1st ed. New York, NY: McGraw-Hill Education.

Graban, M. 2018. *Measures of Success: React Less, Lead Better, Improve More*. Constancy, Inc.

Wheeler, D.J. 2000. *Understanding Variation: The Key to Managing Chaos*, 2nd ed. Knoxville: SPC Press.

Notes for further investigation

Hilborn, R., and M. Mangel. 1997. *The Ecological Detective: Confronting Models with Data*. New Jersey, NJ: Princeton University Press.

Trochim, W.M. 2021. "The Research Methods Knowledge Base." Available at https://conjointly.com/kb/ (accessed February 23, 2021).

Gothelf, J., and J. Seiden. 2016. *Lean UX: Designing Great Products with Agile Teams*, 2nd ed. Sebastopol: O'Reilly Media.

Ries, E. 2017. *The Startup Way: How Modern Companies Use Entrepreneurial Management to Transform Culture and Drive Long-Term Growth*. Redfern: Currency.

CHAPTER 13

OKR Check-in Dashboards

However beautiful the strategy, you should occasionally look at the results.

—Winston Churchill

Chapter Highlights

- Elements of the OKR dashboard
- Where to put the dashboards
- The OKR room
- Building engaging dashboards
- Adding gamification elements
- Dashboard software and OKR software

Achieving OKRs is a team sport and every team likes to keep score. "People play differently when they are keeping score" (McChesney, et al. 2014, 12). It doesn't matter if you are in a basketball, cricket, football, or water polo team. For a long time, I was a volleyball coach. If you are in the game and the stakes are high, you look at the scoreboard constantly. You get instant feedback if you made a wrong decision (in my case, selecting the wrong player or the wrong offensive technique). The players' scoreboard is simple and provides only critical information: *are we winning the game or not?*

Within a nonsporting context, you also want to know if you are winning "the game." You want to know in an instant. The game of business is easy: Are you getting any closer toward your Objective? Therefore, creating a simple dashboard for your OKRs is critical. To design a simple dashboard, it is important to understand in which Cynefin domain your OKRs approach is in (see *Chapter 11*). In this chapter, you will learn that each domain requires different elements on the dashboard.

Figure 13.1 Players' dashboard
Source: University of the Fraser Valley, November 7, 2014

I hear you thinking, yet another dashboard. I agree. Dashboards are overrated. You see them everywhere. Google Analytics, Salesforce, AdWords, LinkedIn Ads, bug and work tracking dashboards (like Trello, ServiceNow, Jira and Asana), IT analytics, customer service dashboards, and so on. Our world is surrounded by a tremendous amount of data, all presented on dashboards. The problem with most dashboards is that they don't really invite teams to engage with them on a frequent basis. So how can you create engaging dashboards?

Progress takes priority

In a 1968 issue of Harvard Business Review, Frederick Herzberg published a now-classic article titled *One More Time: How Do You Motivate Employees?* (Herzberg 2003). The findings of today, more than 50 years later, are consistent with his message: People are most satisfied with their jobs (and therefore most motivated) when those jobs give them the opportunity to experience achievement.

Researchers reviewed diary entries of more than 230 employees from seven different companies, pouring over more than 12,000 diary entries of workday highs and lows. What they uncovered is an underlying mechanism of a sense of achievement, which takes priority over recognition for good work, incentives, and interpersonal support. By now, their conclusion should come as no surprise to you. The *progress principle*, which is the more frequently people experience a sense of progress, the more likely they are to be creatively productive in the long run. The researchers wrote "Whether they [people] are trying to solve a major scientific mystery or simply produce a high-quality product or service, everyday progress—even a small win—can make all the difference in how they feel and perform." (Amabile and Kramer 2011). You can apply the progress principle by having OKRs with lead measures and showing progress on a dashboard designed by the team itself.

Elements of the OKR Dashboard

What should you put on an OKR dashboard? The most important elements of the OKR dashboard are, of course, your (micro-) Objective and the KRs. They deserve a prime spot. In Part 2, we covered all of the important elements of the OKR check-in. Each of these core elements also need to find a space on the OKR dashboard:

- The team's OKRs
- Confidence scores
- Health metrics

OKRs

Obviously, your OKRs need to be there. Give the Objective a prominent place on the dashboard. For example, make it the title of the dashboard itself. Then visualize progress for each measure in your KRs. Trendlines (preferably visualized with the use of X-charts from *Chapter 12*) are mostly used to display lag measures.

With lead measures, the team can get more creative. Here all sorts of graphical representations can be used, such as gauges, thermometers, Andon charts, bar charts, and flow charts. Sometimes teams use also maps like value stream maps, world maps, knowledge maps or heatmaps to visualize trends. Bear in mind that these representations are less suitable to read and understand trends, but can be useful to track lead measures such as behavior shown throughout the day or week.

Make sure you keep the progress indicators simple, and everybody needs to be able to read and understand them. Graphs can be digital, printed and put on a wall or even drawn on a whiteboard.

In case you also use micro OKRs, put both the micro and main OKRs on the dashboard. For both, you visualize their progress.

Confidence Scores

Confidence scores on you current (micro-) Objective and KRs (in *Chapter 9* you will find more information) need to be on the dashboard as well. Put the confidence score close the OKRs.

Health Metrics

Your team or company health metrics (as explored in *Chapters 1* and *5*) need to go on the dashboard as well, because you want to keep an eye on them while the team is working hard on achieving their stretched goal. Visualize your health metrics with the same visualization techniques as discussed with the measure inside your KRs.

Be careful not to add too many health metrics or KPIs to the dashboard. For operational teams, I recommend to keep them between two to five to keep the dashboard simple. There are a million things you can track, but that that doesn't mean you should.

For company or department dashboards, I recommend you pick one or two key measures from the each of following perspectives: people, process, product, and business. That doesn't mean you shouldn't track and monitor other important measures, but only put the ones on the dashboard that are key for your current operation. Must measures aren't that exciting anyway, once you use XmR-charts to monitor performance, you will notice that most measures only fluctuate around the average line. I've helped companies to leverage business intelligence software to automatically track noncritical measures and receive e-mail alerts when a measure exceeds a certain threshold (you can use the natural processing limits here from the previous chapter). When you receive an alert, you can do root cause analysis and put the measure on the dashboard to keep an eye on it. This technique will help you to only focus on the operational measures that matter. In the next sections, we discuss software to use for dashboards in more detail.

Domain Specific Elements

The following elements also need to have a space on the dashboard, but depend on the sense-making domain you're in (see *Chapter 11*, the Cynefin framework):

- Micro OKRs: If you are in the complicated or complex domain you want to use a micro OKRs as the next target condition and display them on the dashboard.
- Obstacles your team faces: Always display the current obstacle you are facing. This dashboard element is applicable if you are in the complicated or complex domain.
- OKR experiment canvas: The currently running experiment(s) should be displayed on the dashboard. Showing experiments is only helpful if you are in the complicated or complex domain. Use the experiment canvas from the previous chapter and put it on (or close) to the OKR dashboard.
- Top three tasks or commitments: When you are in the clear or complicated domain, you won't have obstacles and running experiments won't be needed. You can replace the experiments list with the top three tasks or commitments that help to move the needle on your KRs.

The easiest way to put these elements on a dashboard is to make a square (see Figure 13.2), which is also known as the OKRs Commitment Square (Wodtke 2014). Other forms are also possible, but I found the following one giving the most convenient overview.

Sometimes, companies already have KPI dashboards that could be enriched with OKRs, obstacles and experiments. Ideally, these dashboards are digital, but sometimes a physical (paper or whiteboard) version

Experiments

OKRs and confidence score

Obstacles

Team health

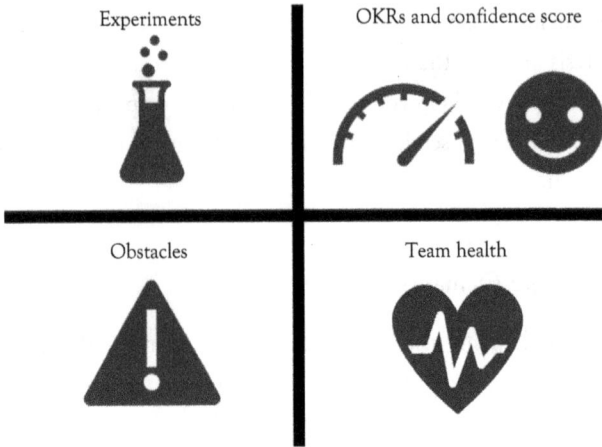

Figure 13.2 A simplified version of an OKR dashboard

provides some advantages. A physical dashboard is easier to swarm around physically with colleagues, and use as a focal point for real life interactive discussions. However, when some team members are working remotely, then you need to use digital versions. If everybody is working remotely, then you should stick to a digital dashboard only.

Where to Put the Dashboard?

I've walked the floors of many office spaces. Sometimes there's nothing on the walls, no scores, no measures, nothing. Yes, they might be in digital systems, but who is looking at that all the time? Thanks to open office spaces, teams don't even have their own wall anymore—open office spaces are a terrible idea anyway (Bernstein and Waber 2019). Sometimes I do see dashboards displayed on walls or large screens, but in many cases, nobody is really looking at them. There are no measures and metrics and only if you are lucky will you spot a vague goal—acting mainly as decoration. No wonder you lose track of your goals. To create an engaging dashboard, you need to put it where people can see it, where it invites interaction on a day basis.

If possible, hang the dashboard on a wall where it is visible for every team member (or even the whole company). It needs to be present at all times. Remember, a key trait of OKRs is that they are transparent. If

Figure 13.3 A combined digital and paper department dashboard at Harver, the pre-employment assessment platform for hiring at scale

you use a digital dashboard, hang a big screen on the wall. Sometimes, a hybrid version is possible (see Figure 13.3).

When you work in a 100 percent remote company (a trending development), you need to make sure the dashboard is always available and that it pops up regularly. Putting it on an intranet page, Wiki page or shared drive is possible. Your team OKR check-ins will make sure the team is engaging with the dashboard at least weekly. Make sure people *want* to look at it. Using good OKRs definitely helps with this (see *Chapter 3*). Furthermore, show the dashboard during weekly all-hands-on-deck department or company check-ins (which I recommend you explore), during weekly "leadership" videos, and during one on one meetings with your direct reports. Try to use as many contact moments as possible to share it. Repetition is your friend here.

The OKR Room: Going Large With Dashboards

Sometimes, you might need a whole room to put everything together. I once worked for a bank that used one wall for each element (OKRs, health metrics, KPIs, obstacles and initiatives) (Figure 13.4). This concept is not new; in fact Toyota was using the "Obeya" (Japanese for *big room*) concept back in the 1990s (Warner 2012), while they were building the Prius. Later, the Obeya concept was added to the Lean tool suite. In the Obeya, you focus on operations (BAU). By adding in OKRs, you add a very powerful component to your weekly check-ins. In fact, OKRs deserve their own wall and should (see Figure 13.5), of course, be discussed first during a check-in. On a weekly basis, all business units or department managers visit this room and discuss OKRs, health metrics, projects, improvement initiatives, customers, obstacles and running experiments. By having all managers in one big room, you improve on commination and reduce silo thinking.

Figure 13.4 A physical OKR dashboard with running experiments/ projects at ING Bank Netherlands (photo is deliberately obfuscated for compliancy reasons)

Figure 13.5 Obeya room

Developing Dashboards

Just as teams should define their own quarterly team OKRs, they should always design their own dashboards. Sometimes a seasoned (OKRs) dashboard designer might assist. Try to develop these dashboards incrementally. A dashboard is an instrument that can always be perfected. I know of companies that have new dashboard designs every month to reflect their new reporting insights. Less is more on these dashboards, so don't post everything up on these walls just because you can. Try out different formats to see what works and what doesn't work. I prefer to use simple masking tape and some sticky notes to develop the initial dashboard. Every dashboard is custom made, because every company and every team needs different information. Using the core elements (OKRs, health metrics, obstacles and experiments) will give you a head start.

Creating Engaging Dashboards

Maybe you've been part of weekly town hall meetings or Scrum "stand-ups." If so, you'll recognize this: half of the people are staring at their toes while the other half are checking their phones. If you want to make sure that your teams are motivated to engage with the OKR dashboard during a weekly check-in, you need to ensure that:

1. The information is up-to-date and accurate.
2. The information is worth looking at (engaging).

With the help of weekly OKR check-ins, you can make sure that the OKR dashboard is part of a regular routine (see *Chapter 9*). Highly engaged teams use these dashboards on a weekly or even daily basis. Make sure the information on the dashboard is accurate and up-to-date *before* the OKR check-in starts. If you use a digital dashboard, it's easy. If you use an analog version, make sure the KR owners update the information on the dashboard on time.

The second part is a bit more tricky. How do you make sure the information on your dashboard is relevant and motivational for your team? Have good lead measures (see *Chapter 4*) defined for your KRs plays an important part here. Lead measures can be tracked on a weekly or even daily basis and are directly influenceable by the team, which makes them perfect candidates for improved engagement. If you have lag measures on the dashboard that can only be updated on a monthly basis, the information won't be that attractive to look at. Only good measures are only part of the solution to create high engagement. To keep people engaged with the dashboard on a weekly or daily basis, something more is needed. Meet gamification.

Game Design Elements on the OKR Dashboard

Based on research (Sailer, et. al. 2017), embedding game design elements into a nongaming context increases motivation (Table 13.1). "Among these typical game design elements [...] are points, badges, leaderboards, performance graphs, meaningful stories, avatars and teammates." (Sailer et al. 2017, 371–380). Teams that use these elements in their OKR check-in dashboard are more likely to be engaged in their OKRs.

Employees of a younger generation are used to being exposed to real-time dashboards, like the ones embedded in popular online games (e.g.

Table 13.1 Game design elements

Game elements	Description
Points	Reward system for achievements can represent progress and provide feedback
Badges	Symbol of merit, level, or achievement can denote membership in a group and provide feedback
Leaderboards	Visual ranking of participants can indicate success and/or progress compared to other participants
Performance graphs	Performance graphs (which are often used in simulation or strategy games) can provide information about the players' performance compared to their preceding performance during a game (Sailer et al. 2013)
Meaningful stories	Meaningful stories can help to contextualize the customer or the outcome you are trying to solve with OKRs. The narrative context in which a gamified application can be embedded, contextualizes activities and characters in the game, and gives them meaning beyond the mere quest for points and achievements (Kapp 2012)
Avatars	Avatars can increase the feeling of belonging. Avatars are visual representations of players within the game or gamification environment (Werbach and Hunter 2012). Usually, they are chosen or even created by the players themselves (Kapp 2012)
Team mates	Formation of a group or team can foster cooperation, competition, and avenues to prevent or solve conflict
Themes	A historical or fantastical setting. The team can choose a theme for this quarter. Maybe, it's a movie theme, super hero theme, or even a 80s theme

World of Warcraft). These dashboards are similar to OKRs, with short feedback cycles.

I challenge you to think creatively about how each of these game design elements could increase engagement during an OKR check-in. As explored in *Chapter 9*, you can use smiley emojis to indicate your confidence in the current results. Adding magnets with a photo of each team member can act like an avatar for your KR owners. Using charts is a tool I recommend that all teams use. You want to see and track historical data and plot it in a diagram, chart or any visual representation that will help to tell the story of the progress made with your measures and metrics.

Software to Use With a Dashboard

Manually updating dashboards daily or weekly can be a cumbersome task. Luckily, there is a rapidly growing list of software products on the market that can help you track and collect customer, product, process, and employee data and display it in a chart on a single dashboard. The trick, of course, is to aggregate all data from different sources into meaningful charts, displaying your metrics and measures to build a near real-time dashboard. Most software as a service companies have developed their own tools, but with the help of Business Intelligence (BI), there are tools that let you develop your own OKR and KPI graphs and reports with data sources from within your organization. There are some great cloud-based BI tools available. I suggest you select one you can easily operate yourself or find (data) engineers that can build one for you. At the time of writing, these professions are scarce resources, so maybe educating BI engineers in-house is a better option.

Be aware that data for lead measures are difficult to collect. Most metric software systems are only built to collect lag measures. My advice is to collect the data manually for some time. Find out if each measure is useful and only then find a way to automate (part of) the collection process.

A Word About OKR Software

I'm not a big fan of using dedicated OKR software. Here are the most common reasons you might think you need OKR software, and why these reasons are flawed.

Tracking and Managing OKRs

There is no need to *manage* your OKRs from top to bottom. Why do you want to have this kind of control? Be aware that OKRs are not a tool for micro-managing your teams, or to do project management. OKRs are about trust. If you don't trust your teams, don't use OKRs. What you want is transparency of your goals and to see if you can help out others. If you need a status report, ask teams to send a weekly e-mail on Friday (Wodtke 2014, 141) containing their latest updates of their OKRs, confidence scores, obstacles and running experiments.

Dealing with OKR Complexity

Having too many OKRs can require software to *manage* them. As explored in *Chapter 5*, you only need a single OKR. Even if your company is a very large corporation, writing down a handful of OKRs can be done on a Wiki or be recorded in a one-minute video. You think this is impossible? A very well known bank with 20,000+ employees in the Netherlands only uses a Word document stored in Microsoft SharePoint. They don't need anything more.

Viewing Historic Data

As explored in the previous section, it's indeed not ideal to manually update all of the data. However, there is a great variety of quality software available to automate and update your numbers and display trends over time. I've yet to see OKR software that is capable of collecting, aggregating and delivering your historical reports from multiple sources within your organization. I strongly recommend you consider buying software that helps you providing insights into the actual performance of your measures. For example, software that can provide XmR-charts as we discussed in the previous chapter.

Engagement

As discussed earlier in this chapter, teams need to create their own dashboards, embed game design elements and make sure the information is worth looking at. Most OKR software only shows standard reports, have limited to no capabilities for customization and are often boring to look at. Maybe this will change in the future, but I haven't seen this in practice.

With the methods and techniques described in this book, I hope to consider the effectiveness on future iterations of OKR software options and capabilities. The most successful companies that use OKRs have never needed OKR software. What you really need is accurate and (near) real-time insights into your key business metrics (see previous section) and better managers rather than OKR software. Lean OKRs can educate your managers to set fewer and better goals.

What About BAU Dashboards?

I've worked a lot with product and software development teams. In this context, people love to work with Scrum or Kanban boards to manage and track their work. You would think that these boards would help you get closer to your goals. Unfortunately, this is not really true. While they help you to see the completion of projects, tasks or features, what they don't tell you is if you are getting closer to the desired outcome. In practice, they help you to track your BAU, not your OKRs. Blending them together is, in my opinion, not advisable. Having two separate dashboards might seem overkill, but it keeps your BAU work separate from the strategic work you need to do to achieve your OKRs.

Food for thought: Using OKRs to update others

Whether you need to report progress to your manager, stakeholders or shareholders, OKRs are a great way to show progress on business outcomes. It turns out OKRs are also a great way to report progress during a Scrum demo, product demo, strategy update, status update meeting or weekly status e-mail update. By using the dashboard (or elements of it), you have a versatile tool in your hands. Have you ever had discussions about "showing business value" during demos and meetings? Now you have the tool to respond accurately. If a team can show that they actually moved the needle on one of their KRs, then this becomes a powerful way to demonstrate to stakeholders that the initiatives or experiments worked.

A Safe Dashboard Environment

During his talk at the Agile 2018 conference in San Diego, Troy Magennis pointed out a call to action to all executives and leaders that blindly put data on dashboards (e.g., bug counts) in public places (Magennis 2018). It does not only upset people, but also leads to unreliable data (people just manipulate the numbers to make them look good). We need to collect better data so that people don't feel unsafe and get demotivated. Make sure people and teams feel safe to speak about "bad" data that can appear on dashboards. Only then will it help to increase the quality of the data you do use.

Over to You

Design your own dashboard

Based on the information in this chapter, you should have a better awareness of everything that needs to be on your OKR dashboard. (Remember: the dashboard should be crafted by the team, but your attempt to create one as well, in advance, will help you to guide them if needed. I'm interested in your creative powers, so if you can, it would be great if you would share your design with me and I promise to provide you with my feedback (see About the author for my contact details). To give you a head start, download a copy of the OKR dashboard by following the link provided in the *Appendix*.

Chapter Recap

In this chapter, we've explored the importance of dashboards in keeping teams aware of real-time progress toward their goal. We've learnt that dashboards are often reviled by teams as out of date and irrelevant, because they are not used correctly.

We've established the key elements that need to be present for OKR dashboards to function successfully, where to place them and the importance of all the information appearing on them being up to date, accurate and engaging. We've seen that providing effective, motivational OKR dashboards takes work, but that highly engaged teams use these dashboards on a weekly or even daily basis. We've recognized that there is software out there that can make the task of using and updating OKR dashboards more manageable.

By now, you should understand the importance of OKR dashboards and how effective they can be in engaging and motivating in order to create highly effective teams. You should have a good understanding of what needs to be on your dashboard and how creative and novel approaches like gamification can keep dashboards engaging and relevant.

Chapter References

Amabile, T., and S.J. Kramer. May 2011. *The Power of Small Wins*. Boston: Harvard Business Review.

Bernstein, E., and B. Waber. November–December 2019. *The Truth About Open Offices*. Boston: Harvard Business Review Magazine.

Herzberg, F. January 2003. *One More Time: How Do You Motivate Employees?* Boston: Harvard Business Review.

Kapp, K.M. 2012. *The Gamification of Learning and Instruction: Game-Based Methods and Strategies for Training and Education*. San Francisco: Pfeiffer.

Magennis, T. 2018. "What's the Story about Agile Data." Video. Filmed August 2019 at Agile 2018 in San Diego. 16:35. www.agilealliance.org/resources/videos/whats-the-story-about-agile-data/

McChesney, C., S. Covey, and J. Huling. 2012. *The 4 Disciplines of Execution: Achieving Your Wildly Important Goals*, 1st ed. New York, NY: Free Press.

Sailer, M., J.U. Hense, S.K. Mayr, and H. Mandl. 2017. "How Gamification Motivates: An Experimental Study of the Effects of Specific Game Design Elements on Psychological Need Satisfaction." *Elsevier. Computers in Human Behavior* 69, pp. 371–380.

Warner, F. October 22, 2012. *In a Word, Toyota Drives for Innovation*. Fast Company. www.fastcompany.com/45195/word-toyota-drives-innovation

Werbach, K., and D. Hunter. 2012. *For the Win: How Game Thinking can Revolutionize Your Business*. Philadelphia: Wharton Digital Press.

Wodtke, C. February 16, 2014. "Monday Commitments and Friday Wins." https://eleganthack.com/monday-commitments-and-friday-wins/ (accessed February 23, 2021).

Conclusion

I designed Lean OKRs as a thorough but lightweight goal-setting system for contemporary companies. In this book I have explained how they can be used to achieve big hairy audacious goals in a world of increasing uncertainty. Building on insights of the theory of constraints, Lean Thinking and Agile software development, Lean OKRs form an evolved version of the OKR strategy execution tool that has powered the transformational journeys of giants, including Google and Facebook. My method is rooted in applied behavioral science and management techniques, and builds on Toyota Kata, Cynefin, 4DX, game design and the use of integrated dashboards to facilitate critical thinking and reflection. It was tested by a variety of companies, and this book forms a comprehensive guide that makes it available widely.

Lean OKRs are a response to a global trend to create an excess inventory of OKRs throughout the organization. This method is about setting less and more meaningful goals. It teaches you to only use a single OKR on just a few levels of your organization. This focus means making tough choices but brings the transformative potential of OKRs to full fruition by boosting transparency, experimentation and alignment in your organization.

Setting Lean OKRs should be a collaborative process between teams and their leaders. Leaders should provide challenges for teams to solve, rather than dictate which solutions to implement or what features to build. OKRs can only be effective if you are dedicated to empower the skilful people you work with. This is because they require leaders to describe outcomes and then pass the complex problems that arise to be solved by equipped and engaged teams.

This book has described a radical model to use OKRs in your organization that is geared toward moving the needle of your most important business metrics. In a nutshell, the key elements of the Lean OKRs method are as follows:

- Focus on a single OKR.
- Create OKRs that focus on outcomes.
- Establish an OKR cycle with weekly check-ins at its heart.

- Work towards a generative company culture as part of a mission-command organization.
- Empower teams to be in the learning zone.
- Implement and coach your teams on methods to move the needle. This includes running experiments effectively by employing Cynefin and Toyota Kata models, while creating compelling dashboards to measure and display results.

Interweaving OKRs with the right leadership strategies produces the most powerful tool for reaching goals that I have come to know during over a decade of experience as a corporate consultant. Lean OKRs are designed as a comprehensive method that is spear pointed toward addressing the reasons why most organizations fail with OKRs, and I hope this book has guided you to implement them to reach your most ambitious goals.

What to Expect the First 90 Days

In the first couple of cycles through your workshops and weekly OKR check-ins, it is vital to keep expectations in check; there are no overnight miracles. This initiative takes time, so start simple. When starting out, pick just one company OKR (or in exceptional cases two). Focus on something achievable to build confidence. Creating the outcome measures will be tricky enough, so it's better to start out with training wheels.

The Workshops

- Setting and alignment: You won't develop great OKRs overnight. Accept that the first 90 days are for learning purposes only. Coach teams and people as much as you can, but don't try to go for perfect OKRs.
- Logistics: Work out the kinks of planning the workshops. Make sure that there is enough seating, appropriate A/V, and other equipment (screen, whiteboard, etc.).

- Running the workshop: Consider that the initial planned time slots for the workshop might be insufficient. Plan a second workshop if necessary.
- Review: Expect a lot of feedback. This is a great opportunity to see what you missed in the initial implementation. People will provide you with their observations and reactions, and let you know their current emotional state.
- Data: The first 90 days will be messy. You are learning a lot about how to collect data and finding outcome metrics that make sense.
- OKRs: The company OKR is probably more internally focused to change employee behavior as preparation for the big stuff that is coming up. It's common that the first cycle is about improving internal processes.
- Results: Early on, define the difference between activity measures (Did it get done?) and outcome measures (For what benefit?). This helpful idea comes from Dan Montgomery's book *Start Less, Finish More* (Montgomery 2018), which I highly recommend.

The People

- Developing the routine early on will get your team in the habit of meeting weekly. This way, by the fourth quarter, the weekly check-in process will be a well-oiled machine.
- In the first couple of weeks, set an agenda reminder for attendees 15 minutes before the start time to set the tone that being prompt and prepared is expected.
- Getting used to the idea of transparent goals and outcome measures is often a big cultural shock, and this is to be expected at this stage.
- Be prepared for some early adopters and others that will push back or reject the changes. In the early stages of OKRs, not everyone will be open to experimentation and out-of-the-box thinking in order to move the needle.

- Manage expectations: You will need to go through a full-year cycle to see the full effect of this new way of working. One of the root causes of failure when implementing OKRs is giving up too soon.
- I recommend getting coached by a seasoned OKR coach to help get you started and avoid beginner's mistakes.

The Check-Ins

- While it is too early to have much usable information with regard to the KRs, the team can still meet to reaffirm experiments or initiatives, report on any early outcomes, and catch any early obstacles.
- This is the learning phase, so you can most definitely expect some issues. These issues are completely normal, but it is important to deal with them before they become bigger problems that lead to severe drawbacks, like demotivated people.
- To make check-ins function efficiently, make sure:
  - Check-ins are short (no longer than 30 minutes)
  - Check-ins are interesting (report on more than just status)
  - People show up on time
  - The required data are available
  - Progress is seen or felt after a couple of weeks
  - Team member(s) are committed to their task(s)
  - You don't talk in detail about health check metrics during the check-ins
  - You anticipate and avoid tech problems with remote check-ins (i.e. having no sound or screen sharing not working)
  - Data that are shared are relevant and linked to higher-level OKRs
- If you have software development teams in your organization, you will notice that these teams pick up the OKR check-ins more naturally, because they are used to running daily stand-ups. Therefore, starting in these teams often helps to start training your "OKR muscles." Later, these teams can help spread your OKR knowledge throughout the organization.

What to Expect After Six Months...

The Workshops

- The major growing pains are out of the way and your workshops, and check-ins are more structured and time efficient. You're seeing that discussions are focused, resulting in improved metrics.
- If you have remote teams, you've likely figured out a way to run the workshops and check-ins smoothly.
- Now is the time to increase the goal temperature by setting an OKR that is very ambitious compared to the ones from the previous cycles.
- You have collected some historical data from your first quarter, so you will begin to see some significance in your data. With these data points, you can now also plot these data in charts, resulting in rich dashboards.
- Scoring confidence levels is becoming easier with each passing week, with the colors green, yellow or red assigned to KRs, in order to indicate that everything is on track, that there are obstacles that need to be addressed to stay on track, or that there is a need for immediate intervention.
- Encourage flexibility: There isn't a set deadline at the end of a cadence. Sometimes, issues, challenges or opportunities emerge as time passes.

The People

- The introduction of very ambitious OKRs into the mix will lead teams to rethink preconceived notions. They will be challenged and pushed into unfamiliar territory. As a leader, now is the time to step up, be patient, and repeat the overarching Objective. Encourage your teams to be experimental.
- After 25 weeks of check-ins, teams understand that this is the new way of working. People are now used to OKR check-ins and will not easily fall back into old habits. They are accountable, committed and supported by senior leaders, who are modelling the desired behavior.

The Check-Ins

At this stage, it is important that you, as a leader, keep the OKR check-ins alive. Enriching the check-ins with new elements often helps, like discussing process improvements on a weekly basis, introducing new colleagues or combining it with celebrations or Friday wins.

What to Expect After a Year

The Workshops

- Most organizations see the positive return on investment of OKRs after one year.
- The cycle becomes more predictable and teams have now improved their skills to focus on outcomes and learning.
- Perhaps the cadence of the OKR cycles needs to be adjusted from quarterly to something more frequent or less frequent.

The People

- You will observe that other teams will adopt an experimental and agile mindset sooner.
- This is often a huge cultural shift. Management may now decide to increase the "OKR temperature" even further and challenge the whole company with moonshot OKRs.

The Check-Ins

- You will notice a big shift in your OKR check-ins. Instead of focusing on confidence scores and commitments, you will get more focus on experimentation and obstacles. Your OKR system is moving toward maturity!

The Future of OKRs

Only after one or more years will an organization utilise and feel the full potential of OKRs. While some organizations will never reach this level of fluency and will simply be happy with the alignment and focused results that OKRs bring, others will want to push the envelope. Very ambitious organizations will want to go for the bold 10× goals. The words of the ever inspiring Larry Page, cofounder of Google: "OKRs have helped lead us to 10× growth, many times over." (Doerr 2018, xii). Such results require the organization to take a full scientific experimental approach when it comes to OKRs. Some may never reach this stage, but if they do, the results are long-lasting and the effect on the bottom line is felt companywide.

Keep this in mind: OKRs are, at their core, about creating commitments, facing challenges, ongoing dialogue and adaptability. Although the 90-day cadence may suggest otherwise initially, you may have realized by now that this isn't a sprint, it's a marathon.

Whatever the format of goals will be in the future, the 90-day (or shorter) cycle that is so typical of OKRs has been proven to be the biggest game changer over recent decades. However, in order to be effective, it has to be embedded in the larger context of the organization and executed over time. In this book, I have provided you with a comprehensive method to implement OKRs in using a Lean approach to help you integrate structural and leadership approaches in your company's daily work life, whether you are a small company, start-up or an established large organization. I designed this method to fit the needs of contemporary companies that strive to achieve ambitious goals in an increasingly uncertain world.

As the OKR system continues to develop, the stages of the cycle may change, be improved and perhaps be simplified. Maybe OKRs won't be needed at all anymore once we know how to develop truly sustainable leadership skills. Whatever the future will bring, I do trust that the processes, tools and techniques in this book will be a great addition to your entrepreneurial toolbox.

By now, you should feel confident that OKRs can make a significant positive difference in your company. You should feel empowered to get started and know what your next steps look like. You should have a much stronger awareness of all of the processes, tools and techniques that will make your OKR journey a success.

It's time to step out of that comfort zone.

Appendix

Additional Resources

For more information, including the downloadable versions of the dashboard, XmR chart templates, list of weasel words, lists of example OKRs and measures, and blog posts please visit the website: https://leanokrs.com/

About the Author

Bart den Haak is the industry authority on Objectives and Key Results in Europe. He has more than 10 years of experience of applying OKRs and training professionals on their usage. As an international speaker, he inspires people to start using the OKR goal-setting technique that has changed the course of many tech giants like Google, Facebook, and Intel. He helps executive teams all over the world like Nike, ING, BinckBank (part of SaxoBank), Mural, Jampp, Mambu, Backbase, and Bol.com to use OKRs to their advantage. He coaches both executive and operational teams in applying OKRs to their fullest potential.

Bart holds a bachelor degree in IT and Organization Management and master's degree in Software Engineering. He has a strong background (20+ years) in software engineering and Agile Product Development, which makes him the ideal candidate for advising SaaS companies and their leaders on how to change the way in which they operate. Having advised and coached hundreds of leaders and their teams worldwide, Bart decided to use his wealth of knowledge and insight to write a book that goes beyond the basics of OKRs.

Today, as the founder of "Moving the Needle," he helps technology companies to define their most critical Objectives. To move the needle, he works with executives, senior management, and Lean and Agile (software) teams to strengthen their current way of working with this state-of-the-art goal setting methodology. Bart regularly speaks about these topics at public conferences or private in-house events.

LinkedIn profile: www.linkedin.com/in/bartdenhaak/

Twitter handle: https://twitter.com/bartdenhaak

Website: https://movingtheneedle.com/

Index